THE NEW AVENGERS

POWER

Writer: **Brian Michael Bendis**

Secret Invasion: Dark Reign
Artist: **Alex Maleev**
Color Artist: **Dean White**
Letterer: **Chris Eliopoulos**

New Avengers #48-50
Penciler: **Billy Tan**
Inker: **Matt Banning**
Color Artists: **Justin Ponsor (Issue #48 & 50)**
& Paul Mounts (Issue #49)
Guest Artists, *Issue #50*: **Bryan Hitch & Rain Beredo; David Aja &**
Dave Stewart; Michael Gaydos; David López & Álvaro López;
Alex Maleev; Steve McNiven, Dexter Vines & Morry Hollowell;
Leinil Yu, Mark Morales & Dave McCaig; Steve Epting; and Greg Horn
Letterer: **RS & Comicraft's Albert Deschesne**
Cover Art: **Billy Tan, Matt Banning, Jason Keith & Justin Ponsor**
Associate Editor: **Jeanine Schaefer**
Editor: **Tom Brevoort**

Collection Editor: **Jennifer Grünwald**
Editorial Assistant: **Alex Starbuck**
Assistant Editors: **Cory Levine & John Denning**
Editor, Special Projects: **Mark D. Beazley**
Senior Editor, Special Projects: **Jeff Youngquist**
Senior Vice President of Sales: **David Gabriel**
Vice President of Creative: **Tom Marvelli**

Editor in Chief: **Joe Quesada**
Publisher: **Dan Buckley**
Executive Producer: **Alan Fine**

NEW AVENGERS VOL. 10: POWER. Contains material originally published in magazine form as NEW AVENGERS #48-50 and SECRET INVASION: DARK REIGN. First printing 2009. Hardcover ISBN# 978-0-7851-3559-3. Softcover ISBN# 978-0-7851-3560-9. Published by MARVEL PUBLISHING, INC., a subsidiary of MARVEL ENTERTAINMENT, INC. OFFICE OF PUBLICATION: 417 5th Avenue, New York, NY 10016. Copyright © 2008 and 2009 Marvel Characters, Inc. All rights reserved. Hardcover: $19.99 per copy in the U.S. (GST #R127032852). Softcover: $15.99 per copy in the U.S. (GST #R127032852). Canadian Agreement #40668537. All characters featured in this issue and the distinctive names and likenesses thereof, and all related indicia are trademarks of Marvel Characters, Inc. No similarity between any of the names, characters, persons, and/or institutions in this magazine with those of any living or dead person or institution is intended, and any such similarity which may exist is purely coincidental. **Printed in the U.S.A.** ALAN FINE, EVP - Office Of The Chief Executive Marvel Entertainment, Inc. & CMO Marvel Characters B.V.; DAN BUCKLEY, President of Publishing - Print & Digital Media; JIM SOKOLOWSKI, Chief Operating Officer; DAVID GABRIEL, SVP of Publishing Sales & Circulation; DAVID BOGART, SVP of Business Affairs & Talent Management; MICHAEL PASCIULLO, VP Merchandising & Communications; JIM O'KEEFE, VP of Operations & Logistics; DAN CARR, Executive Director of Publishing Technology; JUSTIN F. GABRIE, Director of Publishing & Editorial Operations; SUSAN CRESPI, Editorial Operations Manager; ALEX MORALES, Publishing Operations Manager; STAN LEE, Chairman Emeritus. For information regarding advertising in Marvel Comics or on Marvel.com, please contact Mitch Dane, Advertising Director, at mdane@marvel.com. For Marvel subscription inquiries, please call 800-217-9158.

10 9 8 7 6 5 4 3 2 1

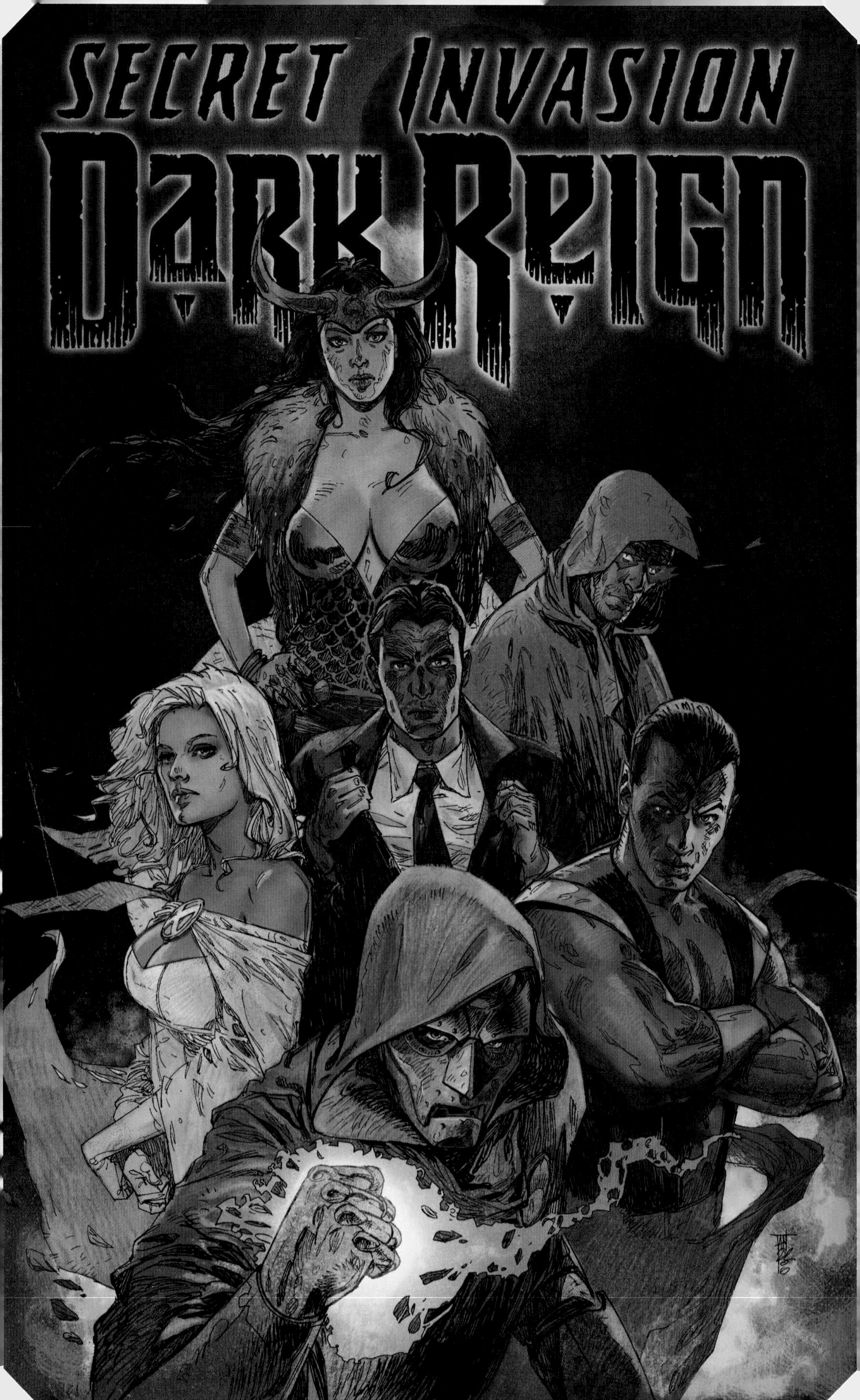
SECRET INVASION
DARK REIGN

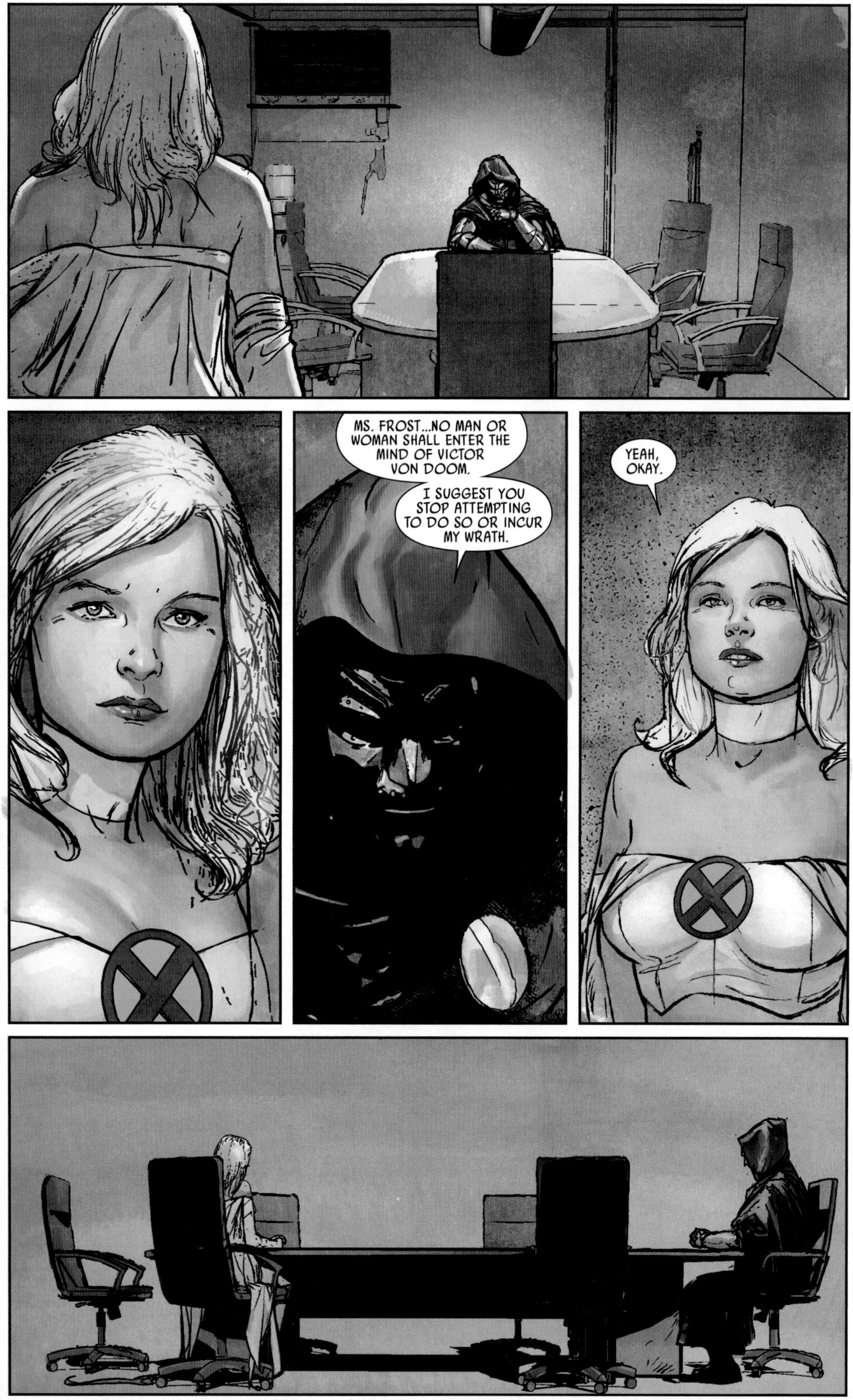
MS. FROST...NO MAN OR WOMAN SHALL ENTER THE MIND OF VICTOR VON DOOM.
I SUGGEST YOU STOP ATTEMPTING TO DO SO OR INCUR MY WRATH.
YEAH, OKAY.

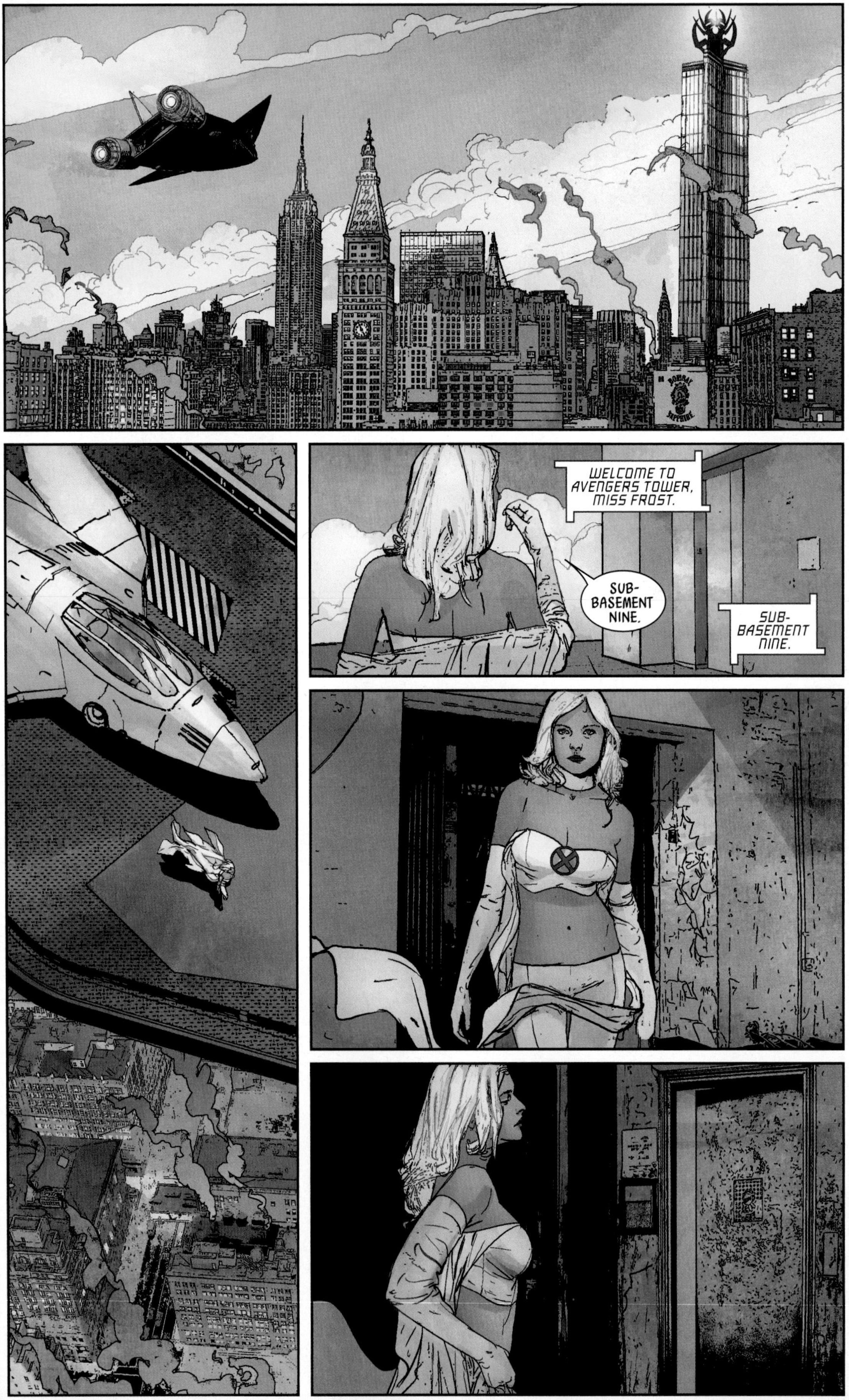

WELCOME TO AVENGERS TOWER, MISS FROST.
SUB-BASEMENT NINE.
SUB-BASEMENT NINE.

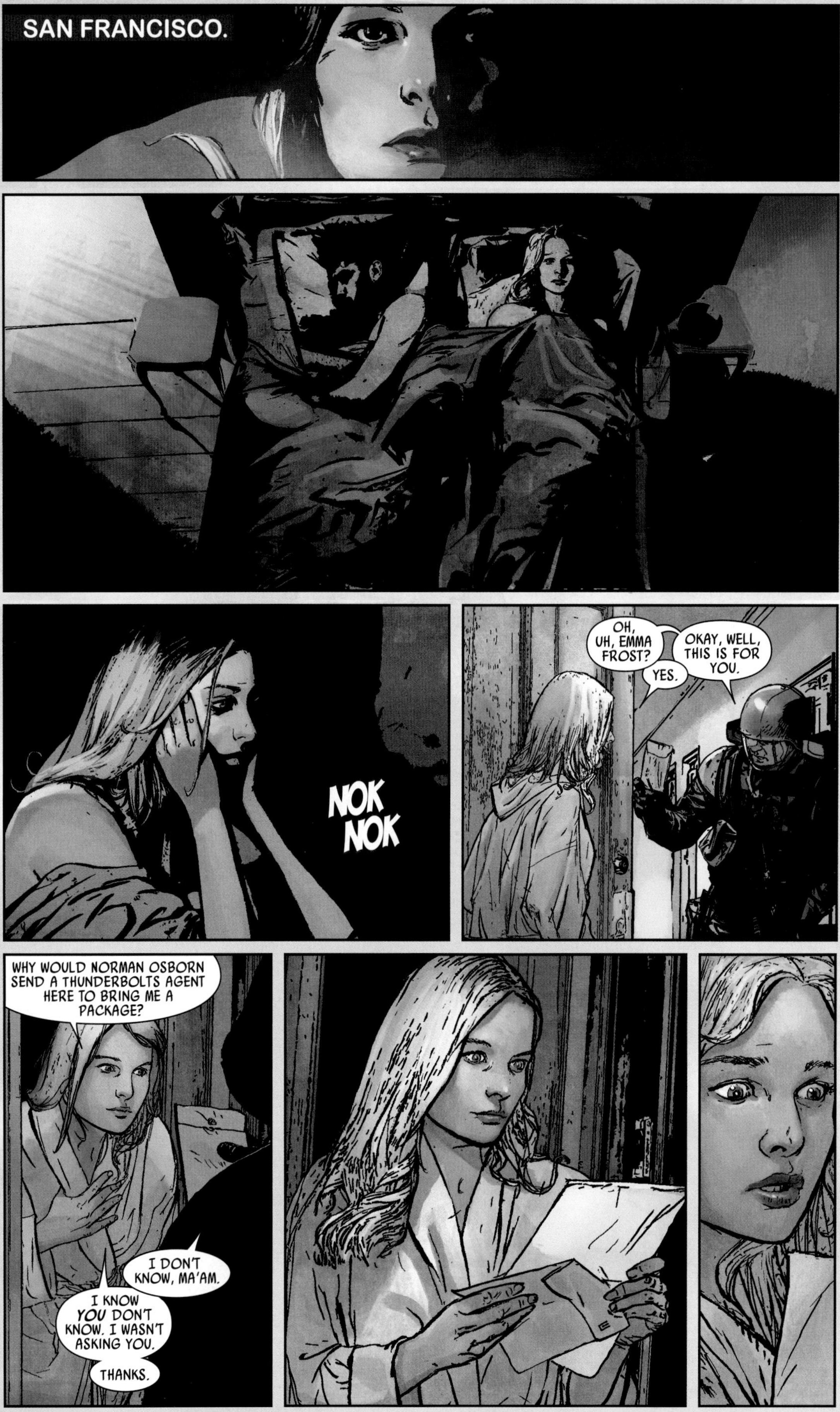
SAN FRANCISCO.
NOK NOK
OH, UH, EMMA FROST?
YES.
OKAY, WELL, THIS IS FOR YOU.
WHY WOULD NORMAN OSBORN SEND A THUNDERBOLTS AGENT HERE TO BRING ME A PACKAGE?
I DON'T KNOW, MA'AM.
I KNOW *YOU* DON'T KNOW. I WASN'T ASKING YOU.
THANKS.

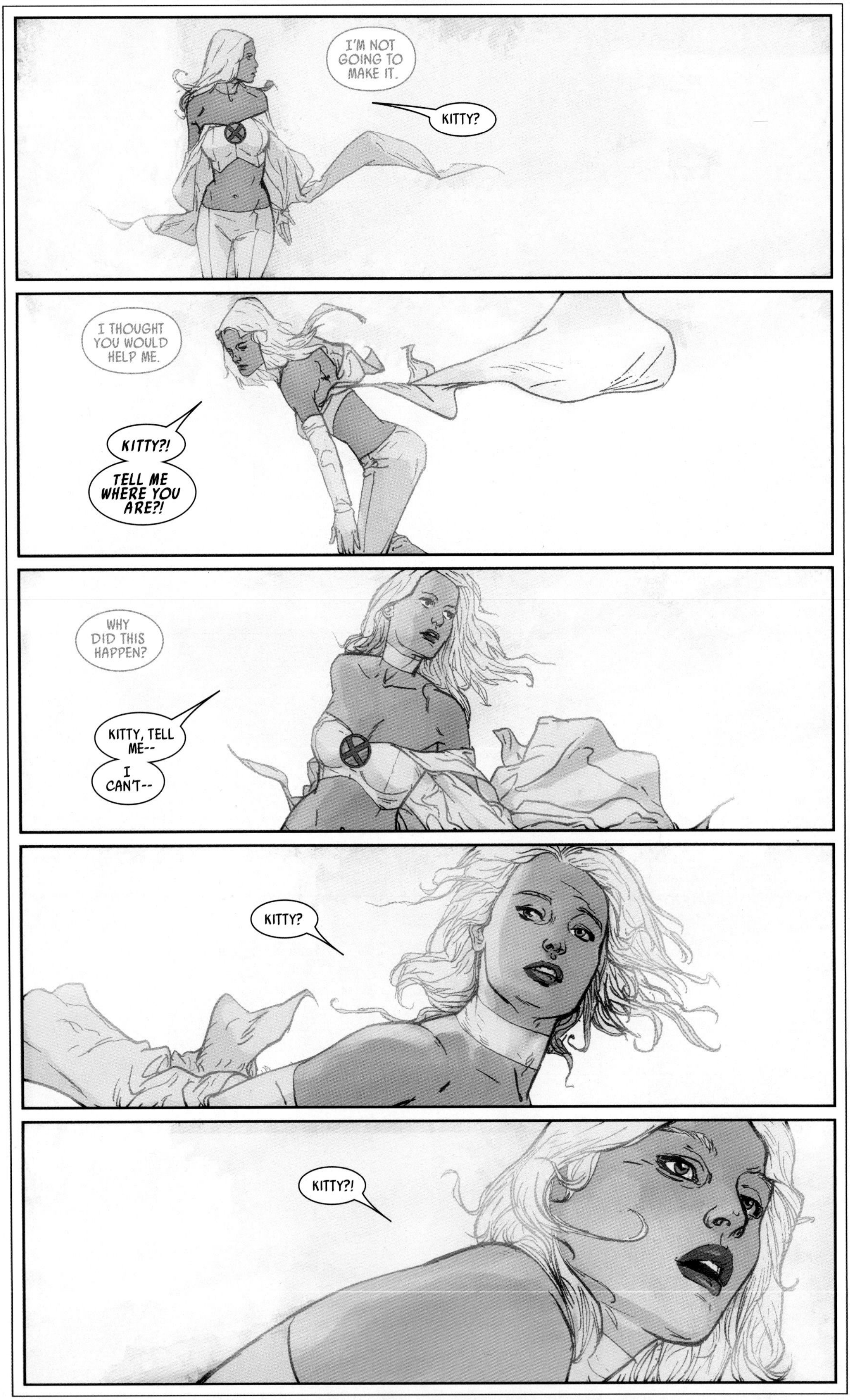
I'M NOT GOING TO MAKE IT.
KITTY?
I THOUGHT YOU WOULD HELP ME.
KITTY?!
TELL ME WHERE YOU ARE?!
WHY DID THIS HAPPEN?
KITTY, TELL ME--
I CAN'T--
KITTY?
KITTY?!

PREVIOUSLY:

THE SHAPE-SHIFTING ALIEN RACE KNOWN AS THE SKRULLS RECENTLY INVADED EARTH THROUGH A WELL-PLANNED SECRET INVASION, USING THEIR SHAPE-SHIFTING ABILITY TO SEED MISTRUST AMONG THE AVENGERS AND OTHER HEROES AROUND THE WORLD.

ALL LOOKED LOST, BUT THE SKRULLS' PLANS QUICKLY UNRAVELED WHEN THE MIGHTY THOR SUMMONED BOTH THE HUMANS AND SKRULLS TO A BATTLE ON THE FIELDS OF CENTRAL PARK: FOR THE FIRST TIME IN YEARS, THE ORIGINAL AVENGERS ARE UNITED AND NICK FURY IS BACK ON THE BATTLEFIELD. AND FOR THE FIRST TIME EVER, WITH THE HELP OF THE SUPER-VILLAIN KINGPIN THE HOOD, HEROES AND VILLAINS FIGHT AS ONE.

THE TURNING POINT COMES WHEN NORMAN OSBORN, ONCE THE VILLAINOUS GREEN GOBLIN AND RECENTLY THE LEADER OF THE THUNDERBOLTS, STEPS UP AND MAKES THE KILL-SHOT THAT TAKES OUT THE SKRULL QUEEN.

THE HUMANS PREVAILED, BARELY, OVER THE ALIEN ARMY.

IN THE AFTERMATH, THE INTERNATIONAL PEACE-KEEPING ORGANIZATION, S.H.I.E.L.D. IS DISMANTLED. ITS DIRECTOR, TONY STARK, TAKES THE FALL FOR THE INVASION AND IS OUSTED FROM HIS POSITION WHILE NORMAN OSBORN COMES OUT A HARD-AS-NAILS MEDIA HERO AND IS PUT IN CHARGE OF THE INITIATIVE AND ALL THAT ENCOMPASSES.

SECRETLY, NORMAN HAS CALLED A MEETING OF CONTROVERSIAL FIGURES: NAMOR, THE KING OF ATLANTIS; X-MEN LEADER EMMA FROST; OUSTED LATVERIAN MONARCH, DOCTOR DOOM; LOKI, THE GOD OF MISCHIEF; AND THE HOOD.

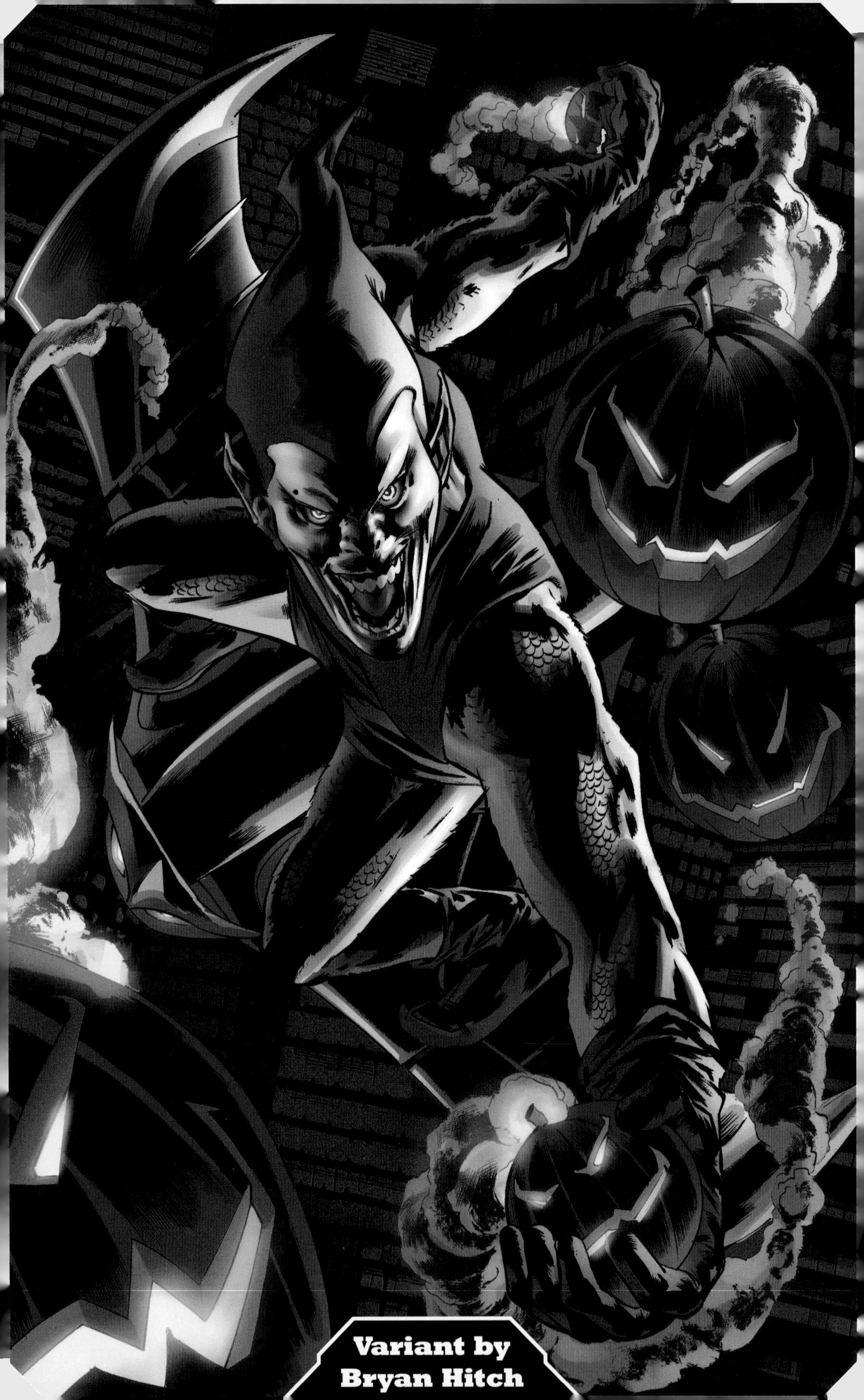
Variant by
Bryan Hitch

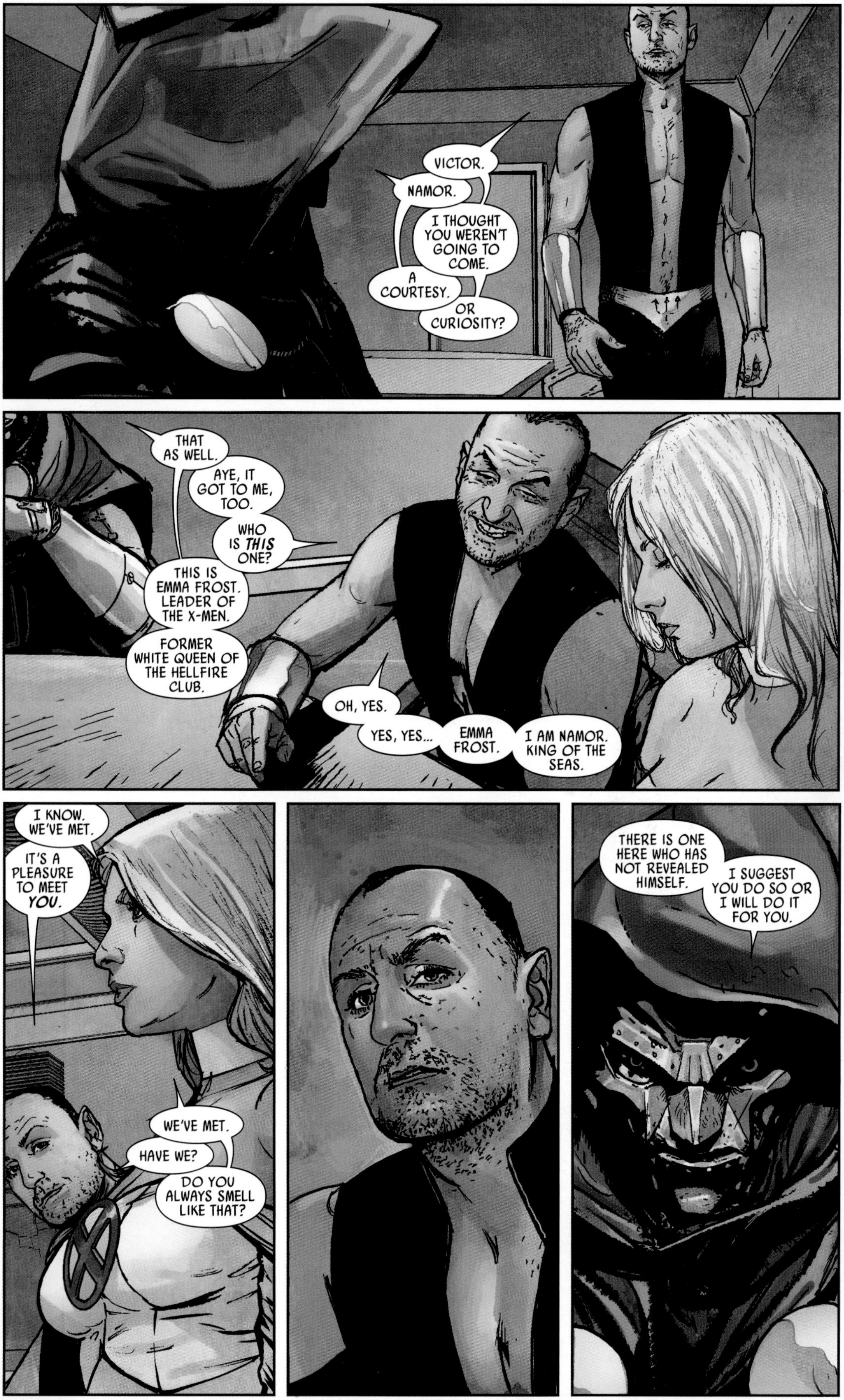
VICTOR.
NAMOR.
I THOUGHT YOU WEREN'T GOING TO COME.
A COURTESY.
OR CURIOSITY?
THAT AS WELL.
AYE, IT GOT TO ME, TOO.
WHO IS *THIS* ONE?
THIS IS EMMA FROST. LEADER OF THE X-MEN.
FORMER WHITE QUEEN OF THE HELLFIRE CLUB.
OH, YES.
YES, YES...
EMMA FROST.
I AM NAMOR. KING OF THE SEAS.
I KNOW. WE'VE MET.
IT'S A PLEASURE TO MEET *YOU*.
WE'VE MET.
HAVE WE?
DO YOU ALWAYS SMELL LIKE THAT?
THERE IS ONE HERE WHO HAS NOT REVEALED HIMSELF.
I SUGGEST YOU DO SO OR I WILL DO IT FOR YOU.

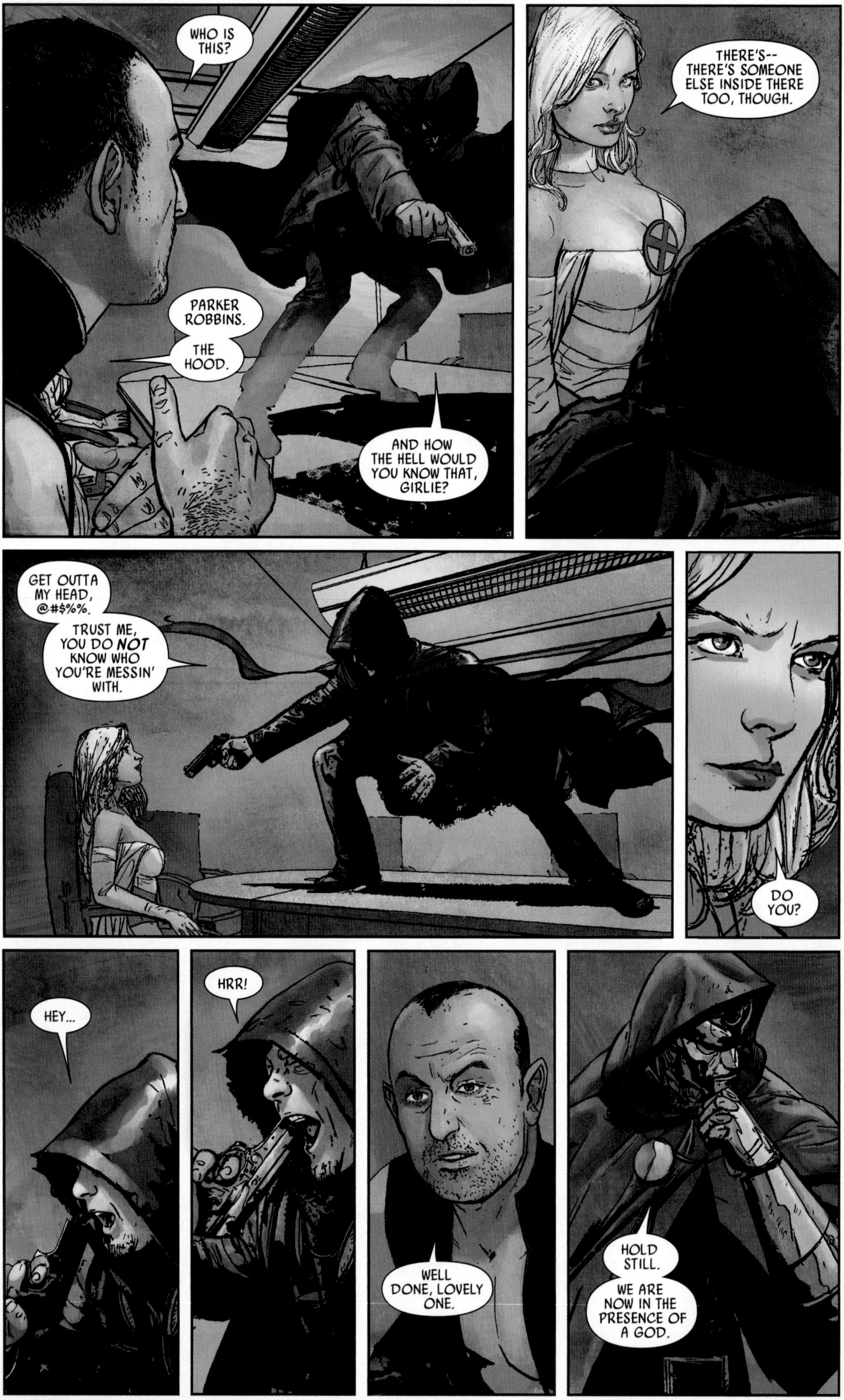
WHO IS THIS?
PARKER ROBBINS.
THE HOOD.
AND HOW THE HELL WOULD YOU KNOW THAT, GIRLIE?
THERE'S-- THERE'S SOMEONE ELSE INSIDE THERE TOO, THOUGH.
GET OUTTA MY HEAD, @#$%%.
TRUST ME, YOU DO **NOT** KNOW WHO YOU'RE MESSIN' WITH.
DO YOU?
HEY...
HRR!
WELL DONE, LOVELY ONE.
HOLD STILL.
WE ARE NOW IN THE PRESENCE OF A GOD.

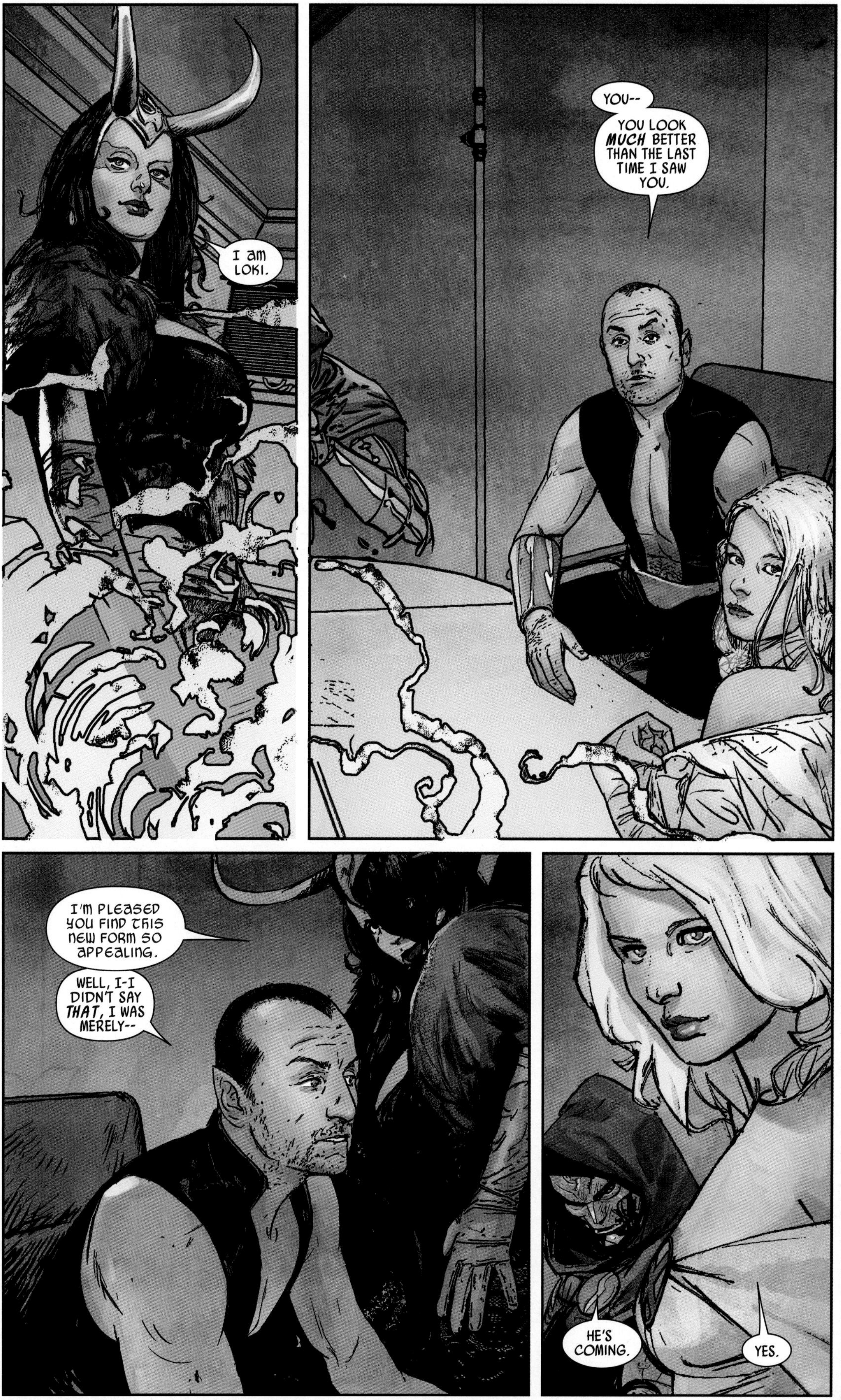
I am LOKI.
YOU--
YOU LOOK MUCH BETTER THAN THE LAST TIME I SAW YOU.
I'M PLEASED YOU FIND THIS NEW FORM SO APPEALING.
WELL, I-I DIDN'T SAY THAT, I WAS MERELY--
HE'S COMING.
YES.

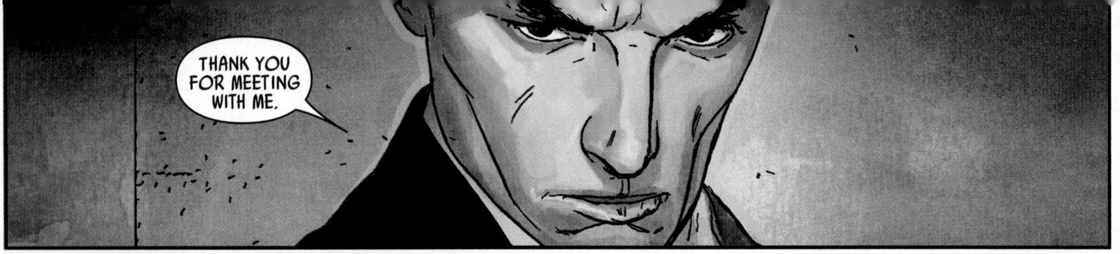
THANK YOU FOR MEETING WITH ME.

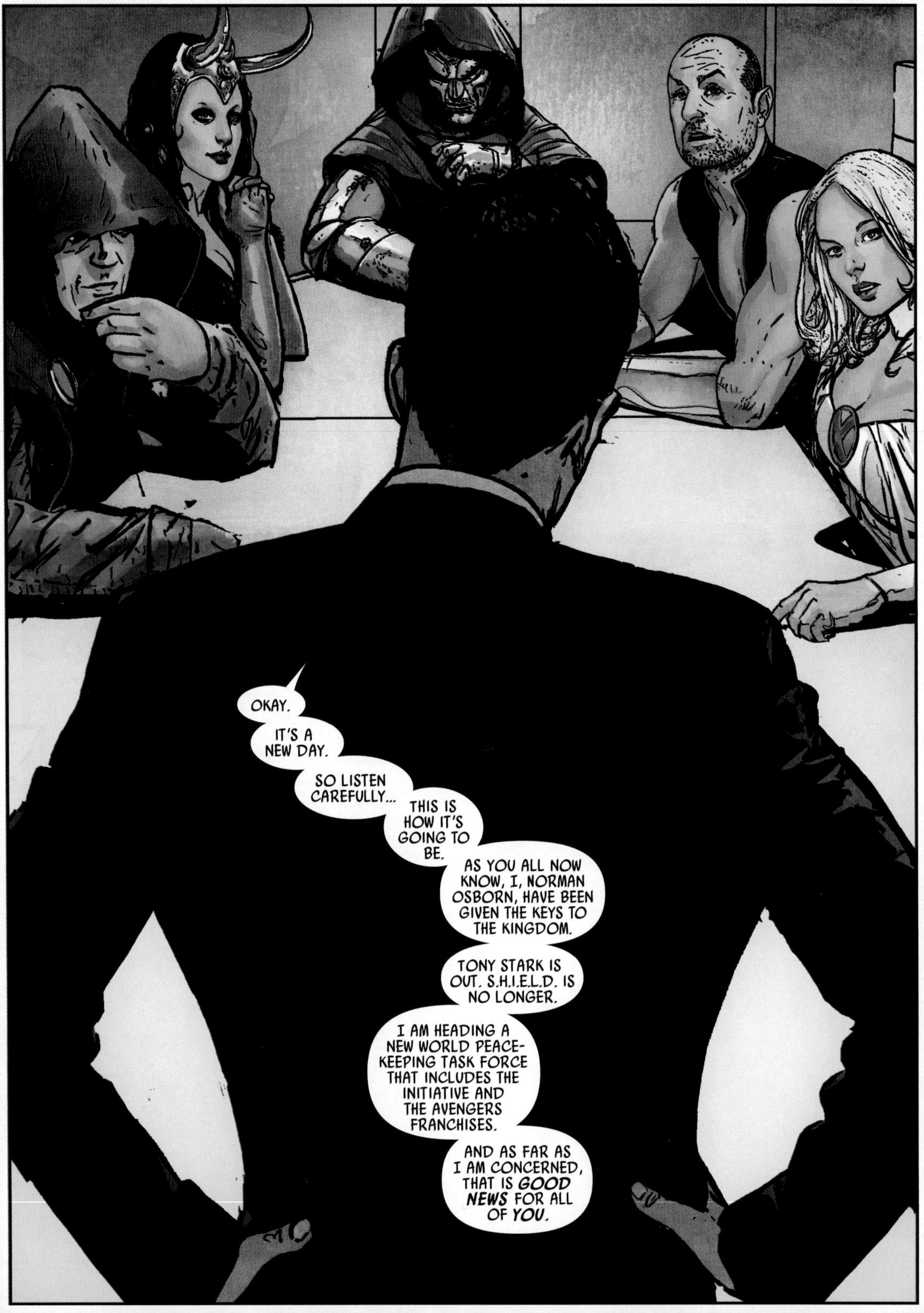
OKAY.
IT'S A NEW DAY.
SO LISTEN CAREFULLY...
THIS IS HOW IT'S GOING TO BE.
AS YOU ALL NOW KNOW, I, NORMAN OSBORN, HAVE BEEN GIVEN THE KEYS TO THE KINGDOM.
TONY STARK IS OUT. S.H.I.E.L.D. IS NO LONGER.
I AM HEADING A NEW WORLD PEACE-KEEPING TASK FORCE THAT INCLUDES THE INITIATIVE AND THE AVENGERS FRANCHISES.
AND AS FAR AS I AM CONCERNED, THAT IS GOOD NEWS FOR ALL OF YOU.

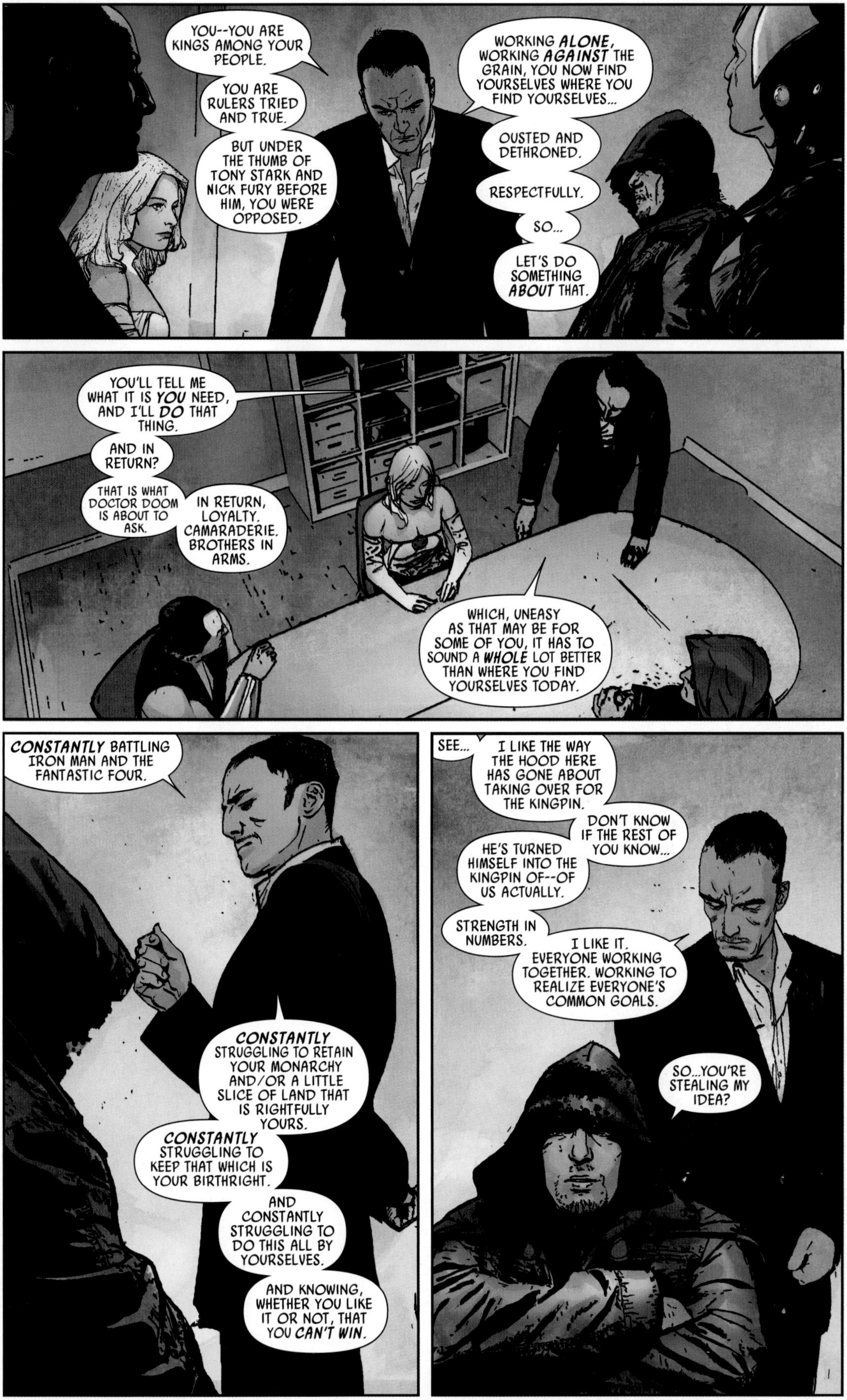
YOU--YOU ARE KINGS AMONG YOUR PEOPLE.
YOU ARE RULERS TRIED AND TRUE.
BUT UNDER THE THUMB OF TONY STARK AND NICK FURY BEFORE HIM, YOU WERE OPPOSED.
WORKING ALONE, WORKING AGAINST THE GRAIN, YOU NOW FIND YOURSELVES WHERE YOU FIND YOURSELVES...
OUSTED AND DETHRONED.
RESPECTFULLY.
SO...
LET'S DO SOMETHING ABOUT THAT.
YOU'LL TELL ME WHAT IT IS YOU NEED, AND I'LL DO THAT THING.
AND IN RETURN?
THAT IS WHAT DOCTOR DOOM IS ABOUT TO ASK.
IN RETURN, LOYALTY. CAMARADERIE. BROTHERS IN ARMS.
WHICH, UNEASY AS THAT MAY BE FOR SOME OF YOU, IT HAS TO SOUND A WHOLE LOT BETTER THAN WHERE YOU FIND YOURSELVES TODAY.
CONSTANTLY BATTLING IRON MAN AND THE FANTASTIC FOUR.
CONSTANTLY STRUGGLING TO RETAIN YOUR MONARCHY AND/OR A LITTLE SLICE OF LAND THAT IS RIGHTFULLY YOURS.
CONSTANTLY STRUGGLING TO KEEP THAT WHICH IS YOUR BIRTHRIGHT.
AND CONSTANTLY STRUGGLING TO DO THIS ALL BY YOURSELVES.
AND KNOWING, WHETHER YOU LIKE IT OR NOT, THAT YOU CAN'T WIN.
SEE...
I LIKE THE WAY THE HOOD HERE HAS GONE ABOUT TAKING OVER FOR THE KINGPIN.
DON'T KNOW IF THE REST OF YOU KNOW...
HE'S TURNED HIMSELF INTO THE KINGPIN OF--OF US ACTUALLY.
STRENGTH IN NUMBERS.
I LIKE IT. EVERYONE WORKING TOGETHER. WORKING TO REALIZE EVERYONE'S COMMON GOALS.
SO...YOU'RE STEALING MY IDEA?

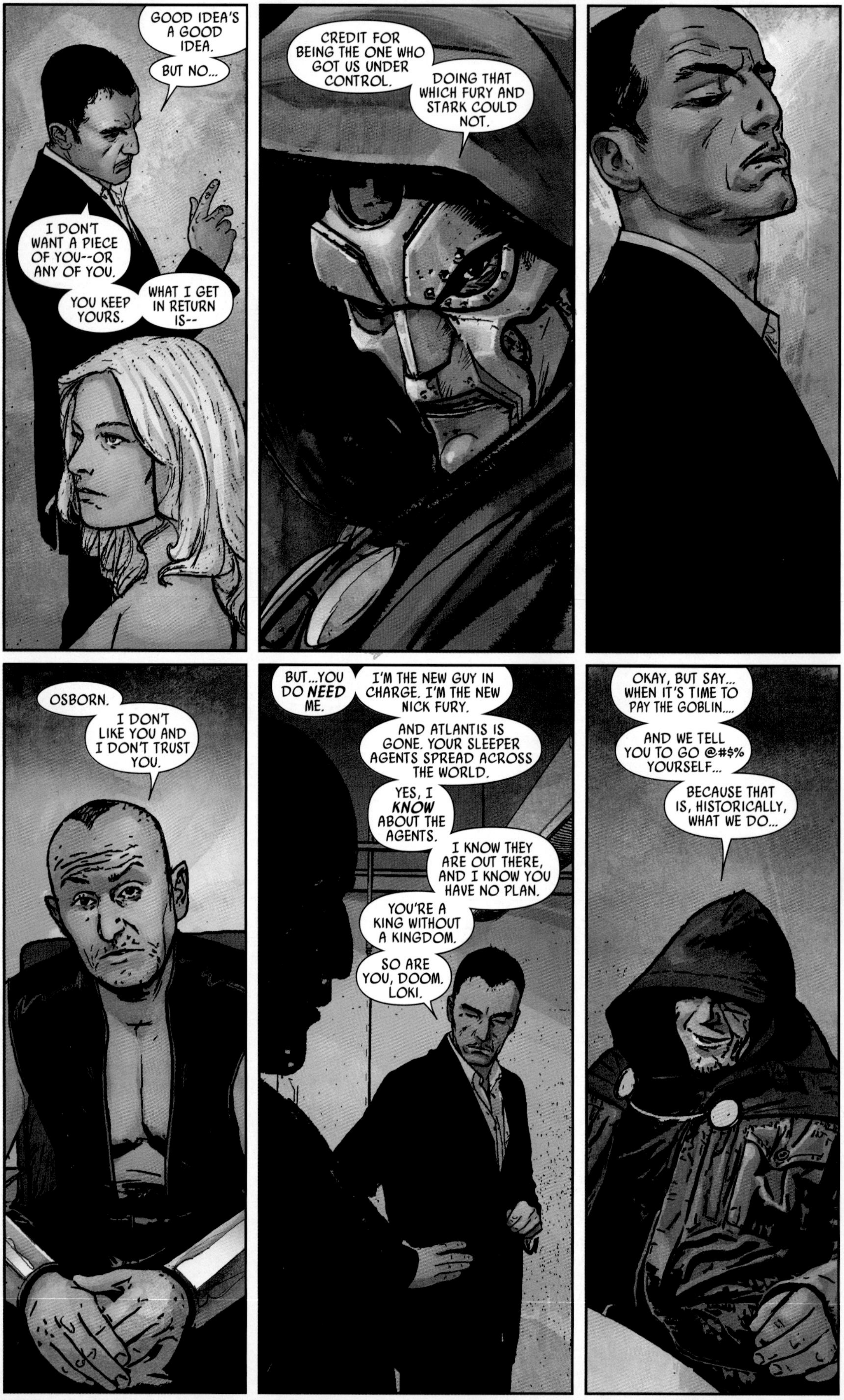
GOOD IDEA'S A GOOD IDEA.
BUT NO...
I DON'T WANT A PIECE OF YOU--OR ANY OF YOU.
YOU KEEP YOURS.
WHAT I GET IN RETURN IS--
CREDIT FOR BEING THE ONE WHO GOT US UNDER CONTROL.
DOING THAT WHICH FURY AND STARK COULD NOT.
OSBORN.
I DON'T LIKE YOU AND I DON'T TRUST YOU.
BUT...YOU DO **NEED** ME.
I'M THE NEW GUY IN CHARGE. I'M THE NEW NICK FURY.
AND ATLANTIS IS GONE. YOUR SLEEPER AGENTS SPREAD ACROSS THE WORLD.
YES, I ***KNOW*** ABOUT THE AGENTS.
I KNOW THEY ARE OUT THERE, AND I KNOW YOU HAVE NO PLAN.
YOU'RE A KING WITHOUT A KINGDOM.
SO ARE YOU, DOOM. LOKI.
OKAY, BUT SAY... WHEN IT'S TIME TO PAY THE GOBLIN....
AND WE TELL YOU TO GO @#$% YOURSELF...
BECAUSE THAT IS, HISTORICALLY, WHAT WE DO...

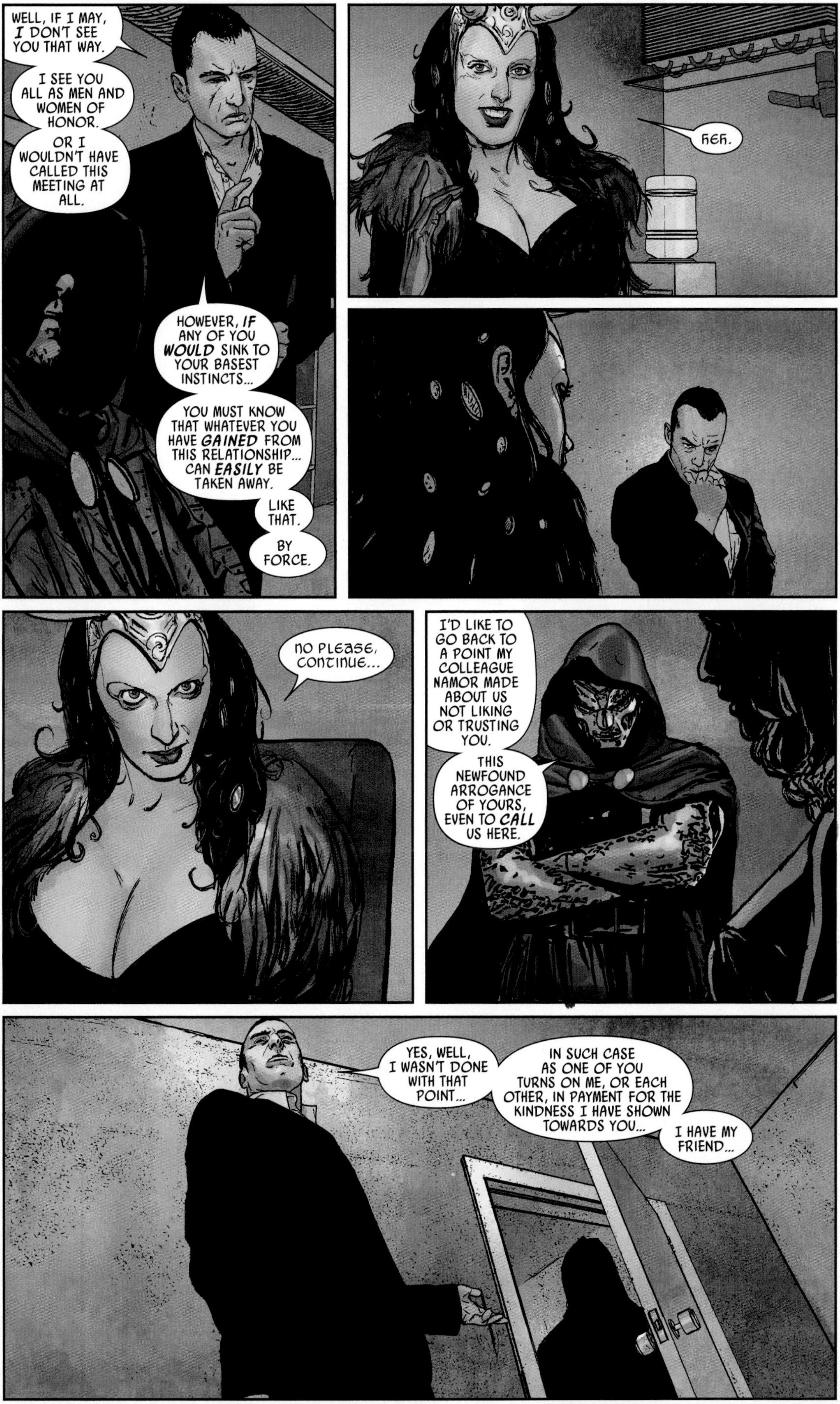
WELL, IF I MAY, I DON'T SEE YOU THAT WAY.
I SEE YOU ALL AS MEN AND WOMEN OF HONOR.
OR I WOULDN'T HAVE CALLED THIS MEETING AT ALL.
HOWEVER, IF ANY OF YOU WOULD SINK TO YOUR BASEST INSTINCTS...
YOU MUST KNOW THAT WHATEVER YOU HAVE GAINED FROM THIS RELATIONSHIP... CAN EASILY BE TAKEN AWAY.
LIKE THAT.
BY FORCE.
HEH.
NO PLEASE, CONTINUE...
I'D LIKE TO GO BACK TO A POINT MY COLLEAGUE NAMOR MADE ABOUT US NOT LIKING OR TRUSTING YOU.
THIS NEWFOUND ARROGANCE OF YOURS, EVEN TO CALL US HERE.
YES, WELL, I WASN'T DONE WITH THAT POINT...
IN SUCH CASE AS ONE OF YOU TURNS ON ME, OR EACH OTHER, IN PAYMENT FOR THE KINDNESS I HAVE SHOWN TOWARDS YOU...
I HAVE MY FRIEND...

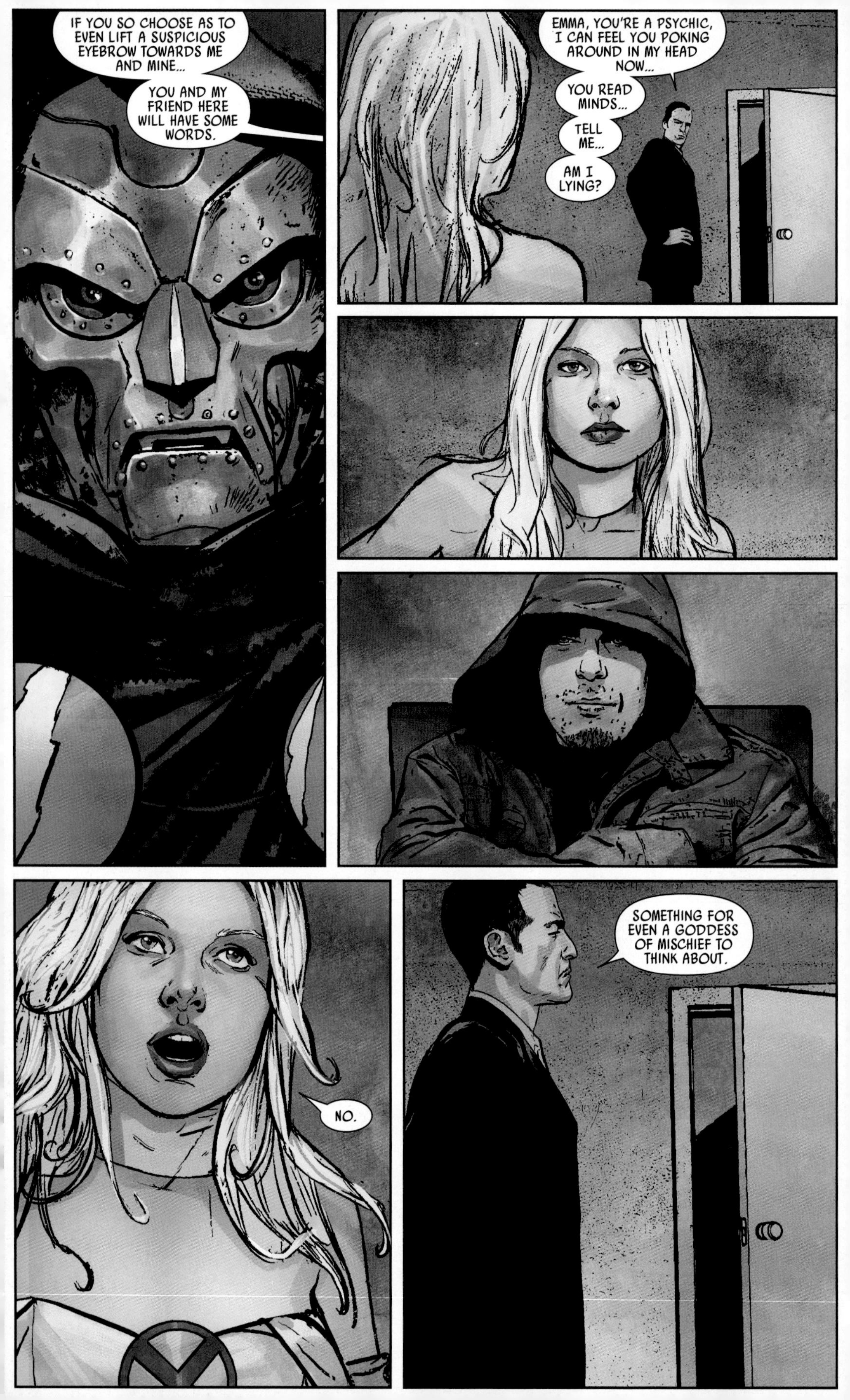
IF YOU SO CHOOSE AS TO EVEN LIFT A SUSPICIOUS EYEBROW TOWARDS ME AND MINE...
YOU AND MY FRIEND HERE WILL HAVE SOME WORDS.
EMMA, YOU'RE A PSYCHIC, I CAN FEEL YOU POKING AROUND IN MY HEAD NOW...
YOU READ MINDS...
TELL ME...
AM I LYING?
NO.
SOMETHING FOR EVEN A GODDESS OF MISCHIEF TO THINK ABOUT.

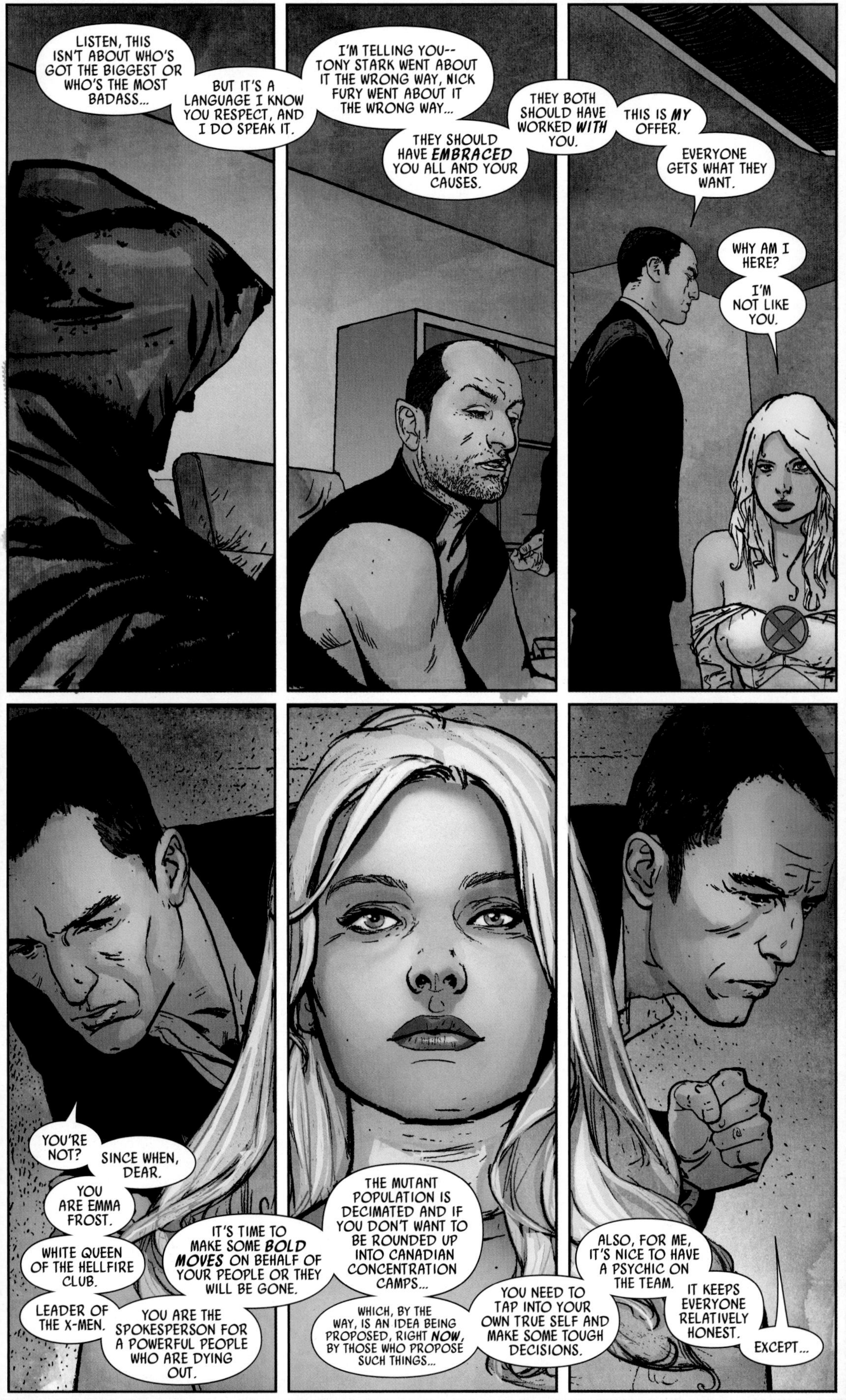
LISTEN, THIS ISN'T ABOUT WHO'S GOT THE BIGGEST OR WHO'S THE MOST BADASS...
BUT IT'S A LANGUAGE I KNOW YOU RESPECT, AND I DO SPEAK IT.
I'M TELLING YOU-- TONY STARK WENT ABOUT IT THE WRONG WAY, NICK FURY WENT ABOUT IT THE WRONG WAY...
THEY SHOULD HAVE EMBRACED YOU ALL AND YOUR CAUSES.
THEY BOTH SHOULD HAVE WORKED WITH YOU.
THIS IS MY OFFER.
EVERYONE GETS WHAT THEY WANT.
WHY AM I HERE?
I'M NOT LIKE YOU.
YOU'RE NOT?
SINCE WHEN, DEAR.
YOU ARE EMMA FROST.
WHITE QUEEN OF THE HELLFIRE CLUB.
LEADER OF THE X-MEN.
YOU ARE THE SPOKESPERSON FOR A POWERFUL PEOPLE WHO ARE DYING OUT.
IT'S TIME TO MAKE SOME BOLD MOVES ON BEHALF OF YOUR PEOPLE OR THEY WILL BE GONE.
THE MUTANT POPULATION IS DECIMATED AND IF YOU DON'T WANT TO BE ROUNDED UP INTO CANADIAN CONCENTRATION CAMPS...
WHICH, BY THE WAY, IS AN IDEA BEING PROPOSED, RIGHT NOW, BY THOSE WHO PROPOSE SUCH THINGS...
YOU NEED TO TAP INTO YOUR OWN TRUE SELF AND MAKE SOME TOUGH DECISIONS.
ALSO, FOR ME, IT'S NICE TO HAVE A PSYCHIC ON THE TEAM.
IT KEEPS EVERYONE RELATIVELY HONEST.
EXCEPT...

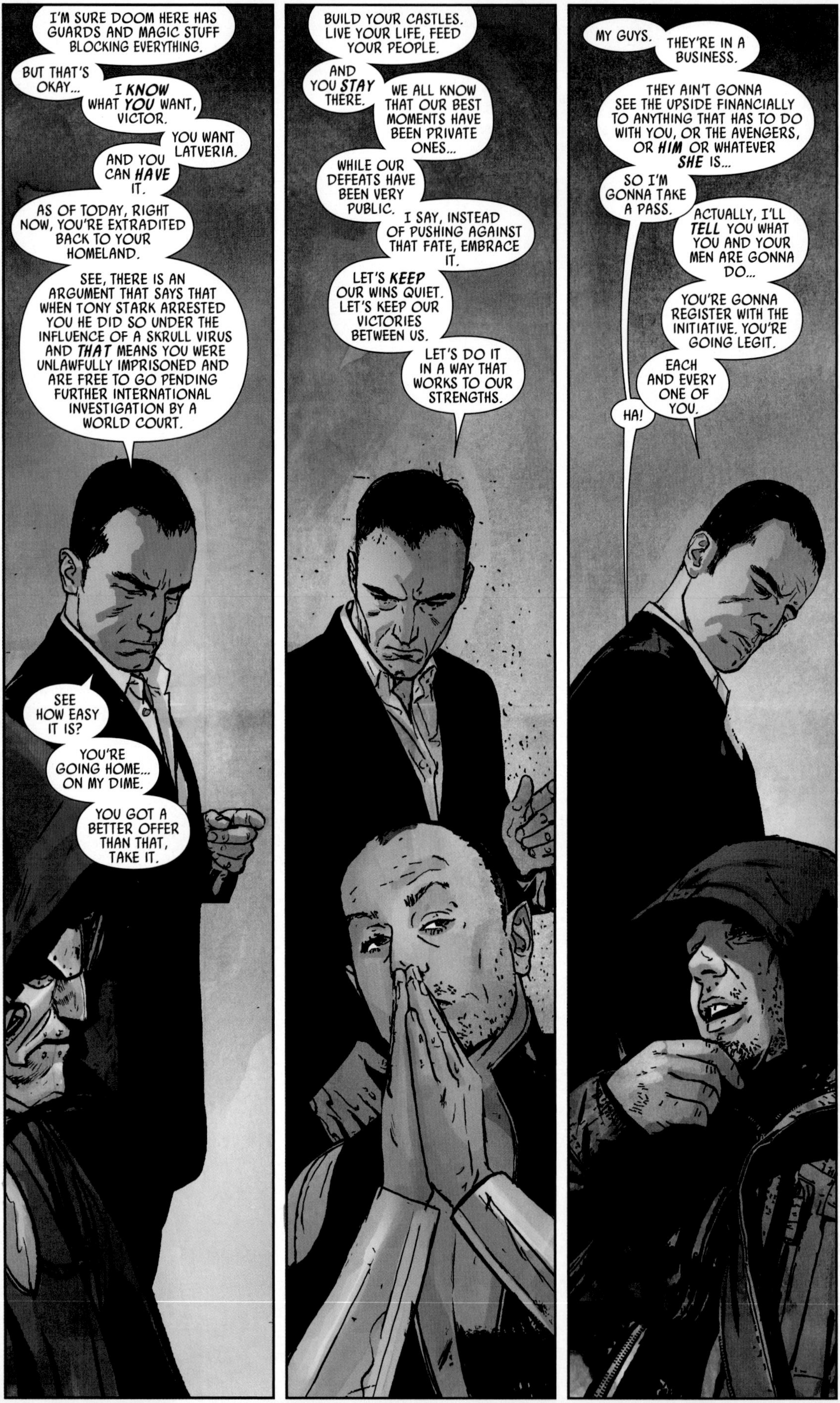
I'M SURE DOOM HERE HAS GUARDS AND MAGIC STUFF BLOCKING EVERYTHING.
BUT THAT'S OKAY...
I KNOW WHAT YOU WANT, VICTOR.
YOU WANT LATVERIA.
AND YOU CAN HAVE IT.
AS OF TODAY, RIGHT NOW, YOU'RE EXTRADITED BACK TO YOUR HOMELAND.
SEE, THERE IS AN ARGUMENT THAT SAYS THAT WHEN TONY STARK ARRESTED YOU HE DID SO UNDER THE INFLUENCE OF A SKRULL VIRUS AND THAT MEANS YOU WERE UNLAWFULLY IMPRISONED AND ARE FREE TO GO PENDING FURTHER INTERNATIONAL INVESTIGATION BY A WORLD COURT.
SEE HOW EASY IT IS?
YOU'RE GOING HOME... ON MY DIME.
YOU GOT A BETTER OFFER THAN THAT, TAKE IT.
BUILD YOUR CASTLES. LIVE YOUR LIFE, FEED YOUR PEOPLE.
AND YOU STAY THERE.
WE ALL KNOW THAT OUR BEST MOMENTS HAVE BEEN PRIVATE ONES...
WHILE OUR DEFEATS HAVE BEEN VERY PUBLIC.
I SAY, INSTEAD OF PUSHING AGAINST THAT FATE, EMBRACE IT.
LET'S KEEP OUR WINS QUIET. LET'S KEEP OUR VICTORIES BETWEEN US.
LET'S DO IT IN A WAY THAT WORKS TO OUR STRENGTHS.
MY GUYS.
THEY'RE IN A BUSINESS.
THEY AIN'T GONNA SEE THE UPSIDE FINANCIALLY TO ANYTHING THAT HAS TO DO WITH YOU, OR THE AVENGERS, OR HIM OR WHATEVER SHE IS...
SO I'M GONNA TAKE A PASS.
ACTUALLY, I'LL TELL YOU WHAT YOU AND YOUR MEN ARE GONNA DO...
YOU'RE GONNA REGISTER WITH THE INITIATIVE. YOU'RE GOING LEGIT.
EACH AND EVERY ONE OF YOU.
HA!

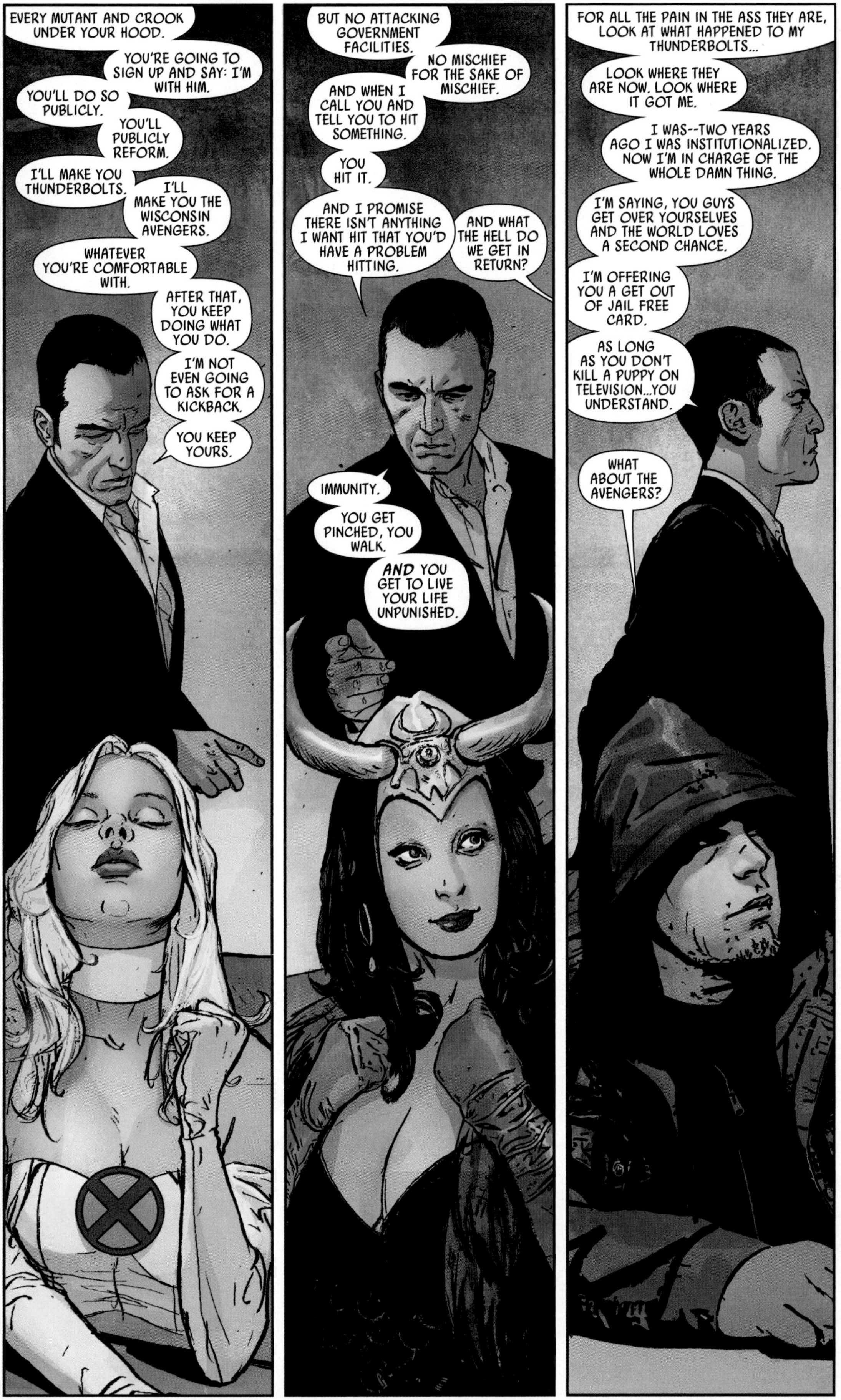
EVERY MUTANT AND CROOK UNDER YOUR HOOD.
YOU'RE GOING TO SIGN UP AND SAY: I'M WITH HIM.
YOU'LL DO SO PUBLICLY.
YOU'LL PUBLICLY REFORM.
I'LL MAKE YOU THUNDERBOLTS.
I'LL MAKE YOU THE WISCONSIN AVENGERS.
WHATEVER YOU'RE COMFORTABLE WITH.
AFTER THAT, YOU KEEP DOING WHAT YOU DO.
I'M NOT EVEN GOING TO ASK FOR A KICKBACK.
YOU KEEP YOURS.
BUT NO ATTACKING GOVERNMENT FACILITIES.
NO MISCHIEF FOR THE SAKE OF MISCHIEF.
AND WHEN I CALL YOU AND TELL YOU TO HIT SOMETHING.
YOU HIT IT.
AND I PROMISE THERE ISN'T ANYTHING I WANT HIT THAT YOU'D HAVE A PROBLEM HITTING.
AND WHAT THE HELL DO WE GET IN RETURN?
IMMUNITY.
YOU GET PINCHED, YOU WALK.
AND YOU GET TO LIVE YOUR LIFE UNPUNISHED.
FOR ALL THE PAIN IN THE ASS THEY ARE, LOOK AT WHAT HAPPENED TO MY THUNDERBOLTS...
LOOK WHERE THEY ARE NOW. LOOK WHERE IT GOT ME.
I WAS--TWO YEARS AGO I WAS INSTITUTIONALIZED. NOW I'M IN CHARGE OF THE WHOLE DAMN THING.
I'M SAYING, YOU GUYS GET OVER YOURSELVES AND THE WORLD LOVES A SECOND CHANCE.
I'M OFFERING YOU A GET OUT OF JAIL FREE CARD.
AS LONG AS YOU DON'T KILL A PUPPY ON TELEVISION...YOU UNDERSTAND.
WHAT ABOUT THE AVENGERS?

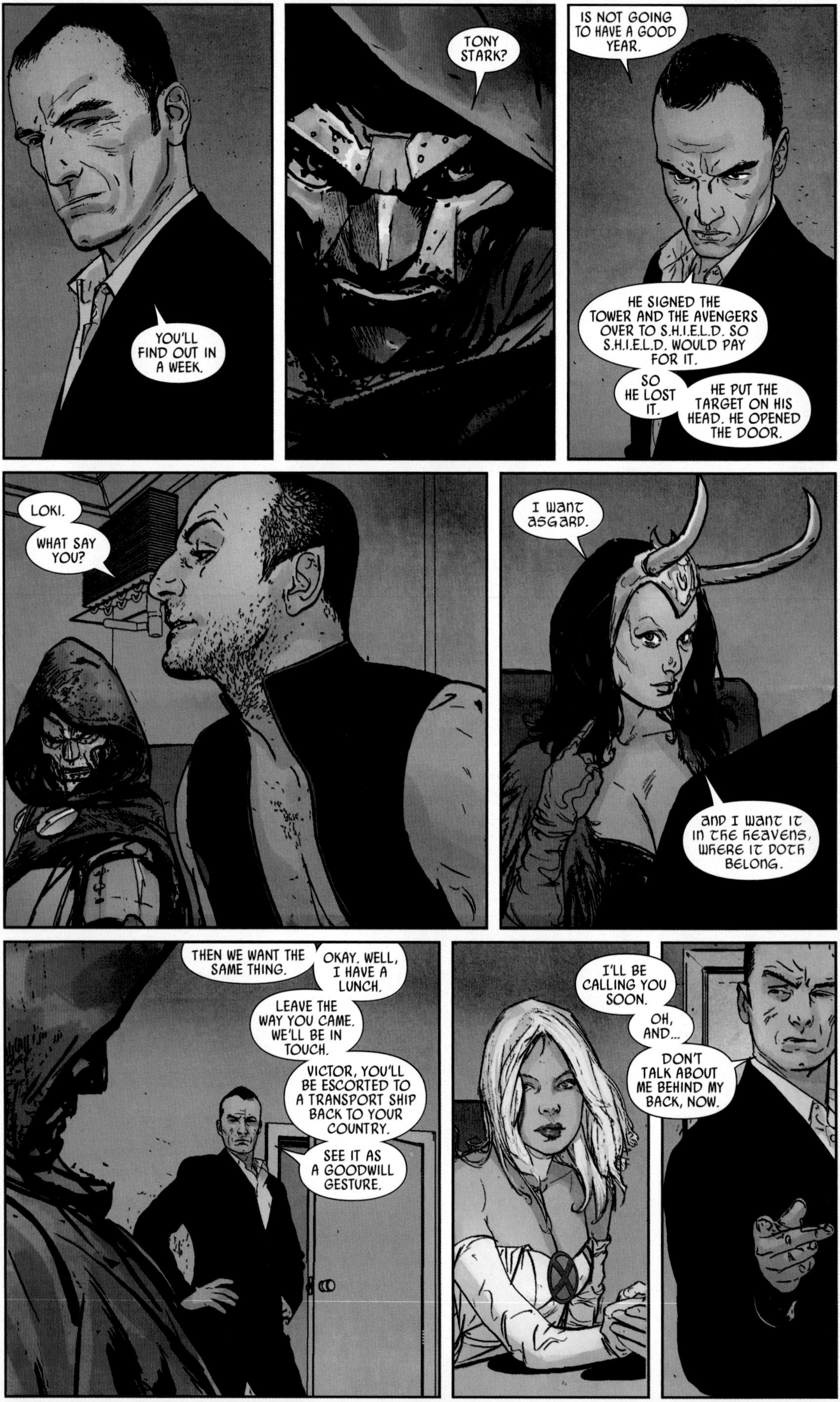
YOU'LL FIND OUT IN A WEEK.
TONY STARK?
IS NOT GOING TO HAVE A GOOD YEAR.
HE SIGNED THE TOWER AND THE AVENGERS OVER TO S.H.I.E.L.D. SO S.H.I.E.L.D. WOULD PAY FOR IT.
SO HE LOST IT.
HE PUT THE TARGET ON HIS HEAD. HE OPENED THE DOOR.
LOKI.
WHAT SAY YOU?
I WANT ASGARD.
AND I WANT IT IN THE HEAVENS, WHERE IT DOTH BELONG.
THEN WE WANT THE SAME THING.
OKAY. WELL, I HAVE A LUNCH.
LEAVE THE WAY YOU CAME. WE'LL BE IN TOUCH.
VICTOR, YOU'LL BE ESCORTED TO A TRANSPORT SHIP BACK TO YOUR COUNTRY.
SEE IT AS A GOODWILL GESTURE.
I'LL BE CALLING YOU SOON.
OH, AND...
DON'T TALK ABOUT ME BEHIND MY BACK, NOW.

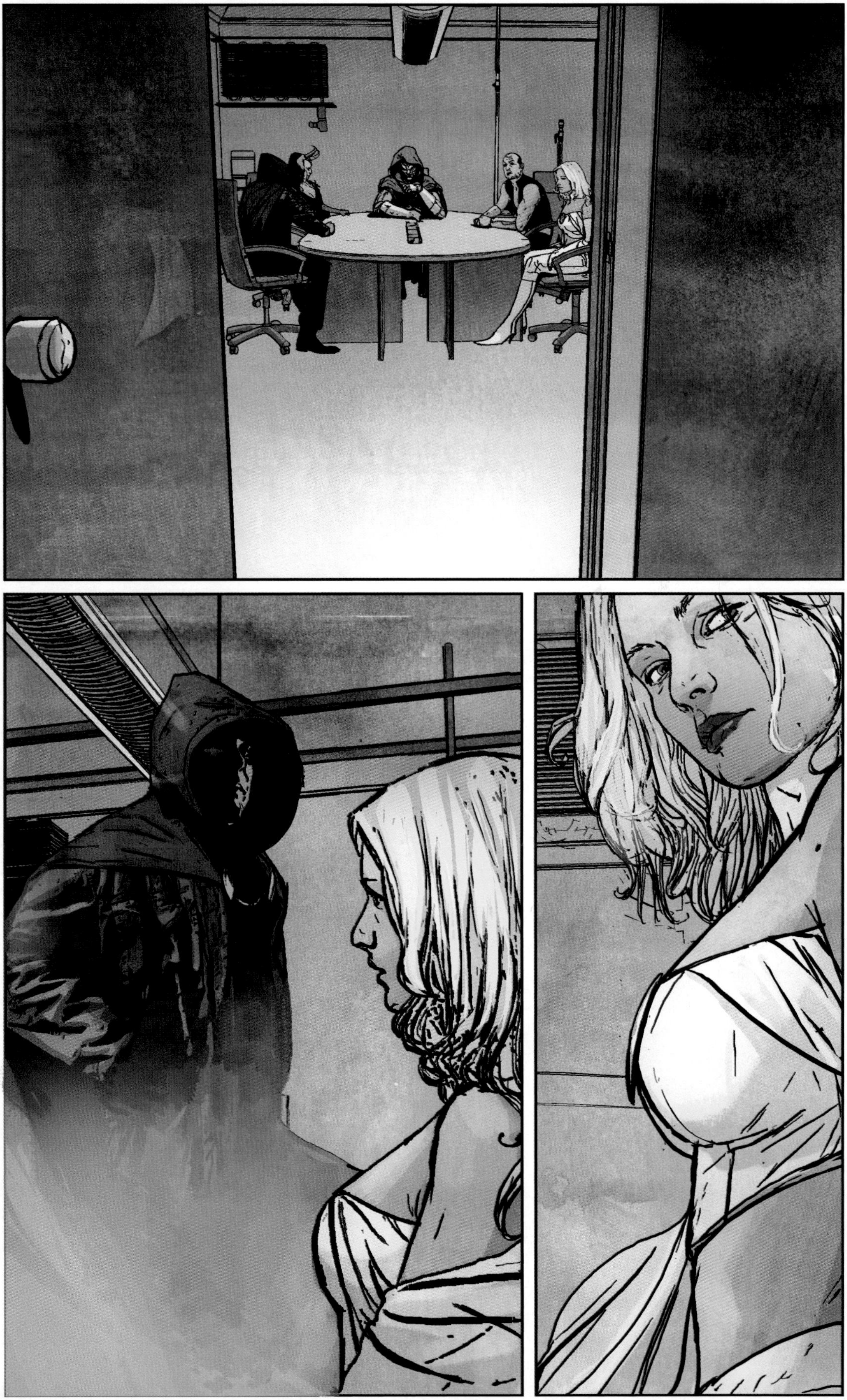

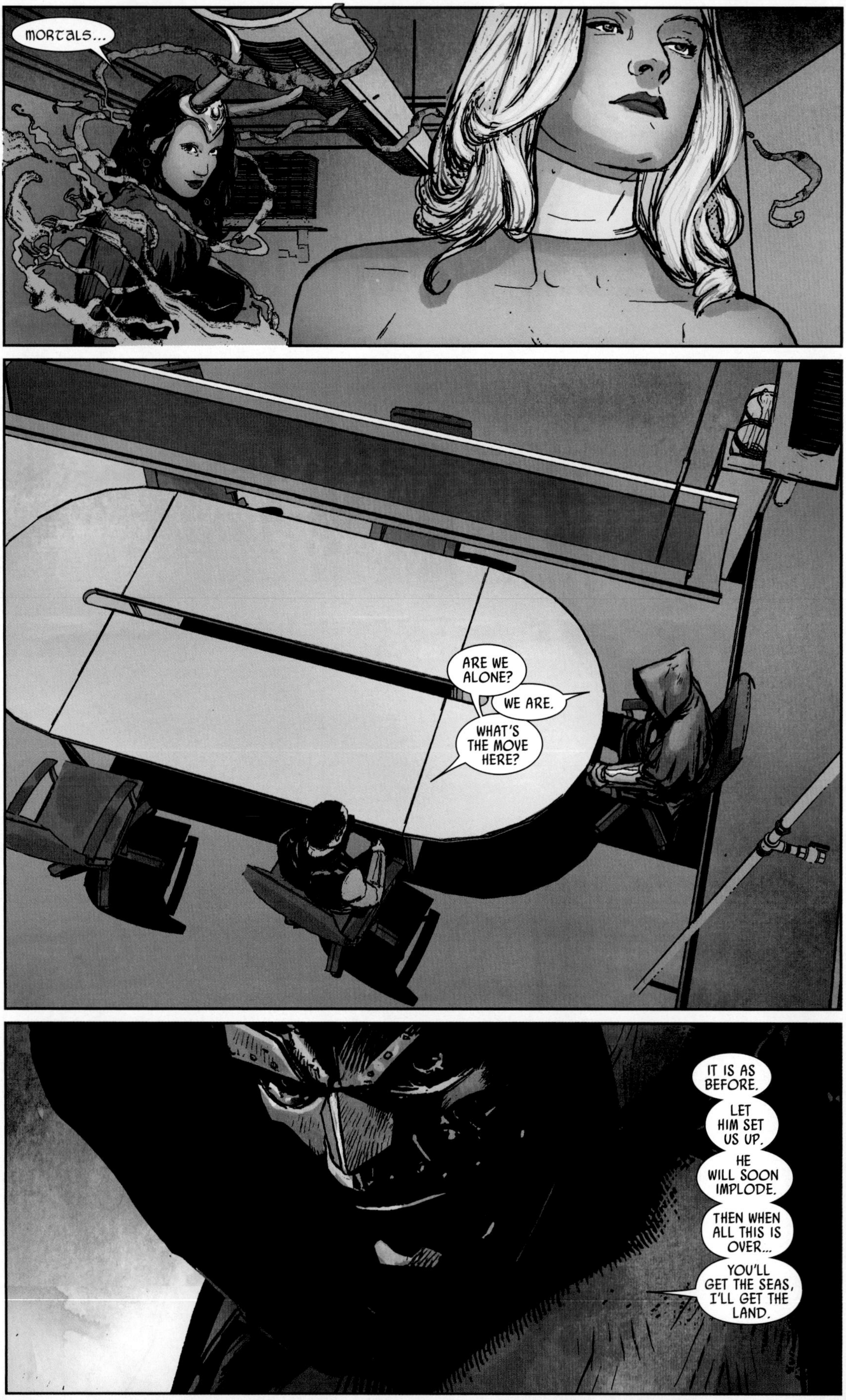
MORTALS...
ARE WE ALONE?
WE ARE.
WHAT'S THE MOVE HERE?
IT IS AS BEFORE.
LET HIM SET US UP.
HE WILL SOON IMPLODE.
THEN WHEN ALL THIS IS OVER...
YOU'LL GET THE SEAS, I'LL GET THE LAND.

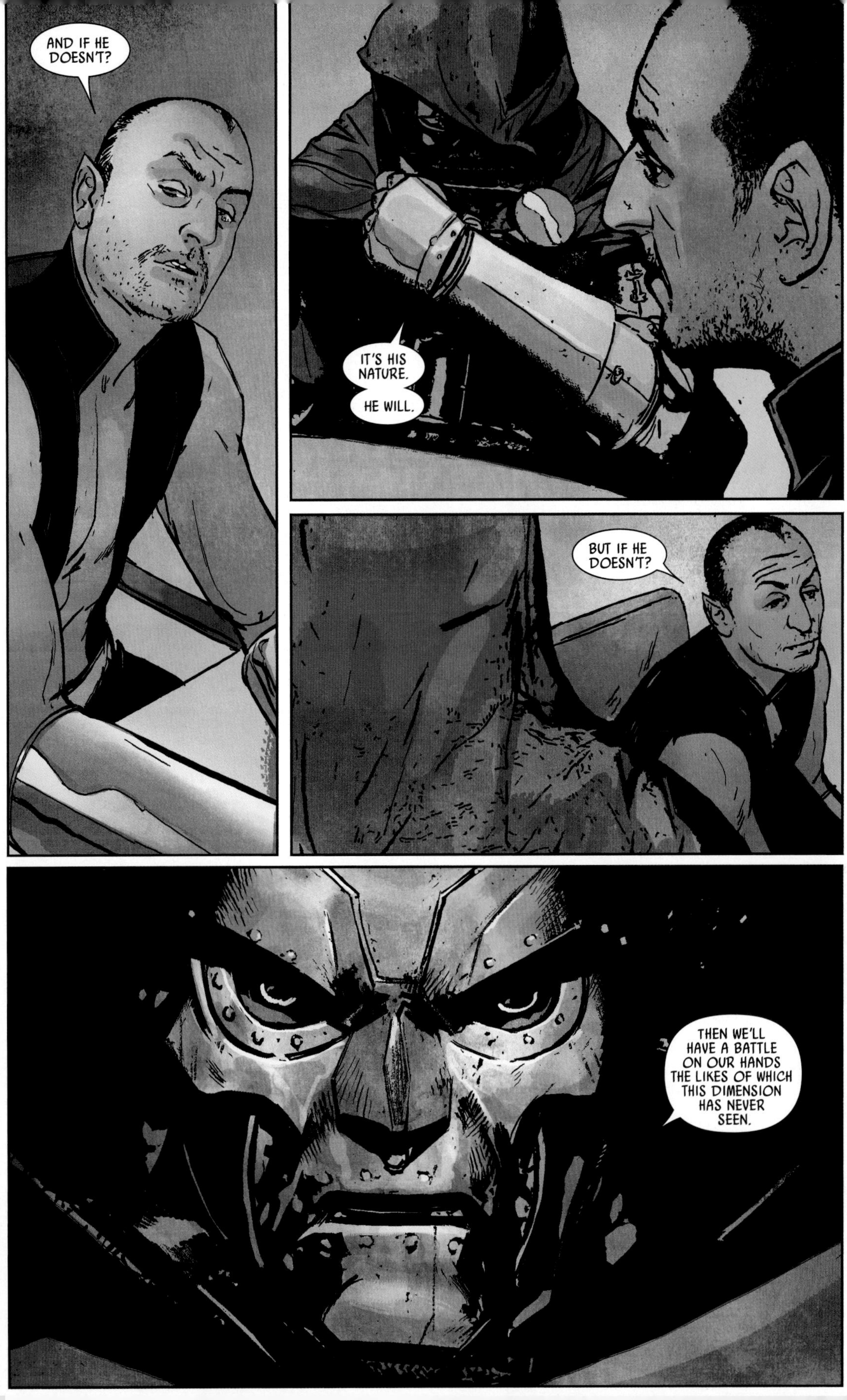
AND IF HE DOESN'T?
IT'S HIS NATURE.
HE WILL.
BUT IF HE DOESN'T?
THEN WE'LL HAVE A BATTLE ON OUR HANDS THE LIKES OF WHICH THIS DIMENSION HAS NEVER SEEN.

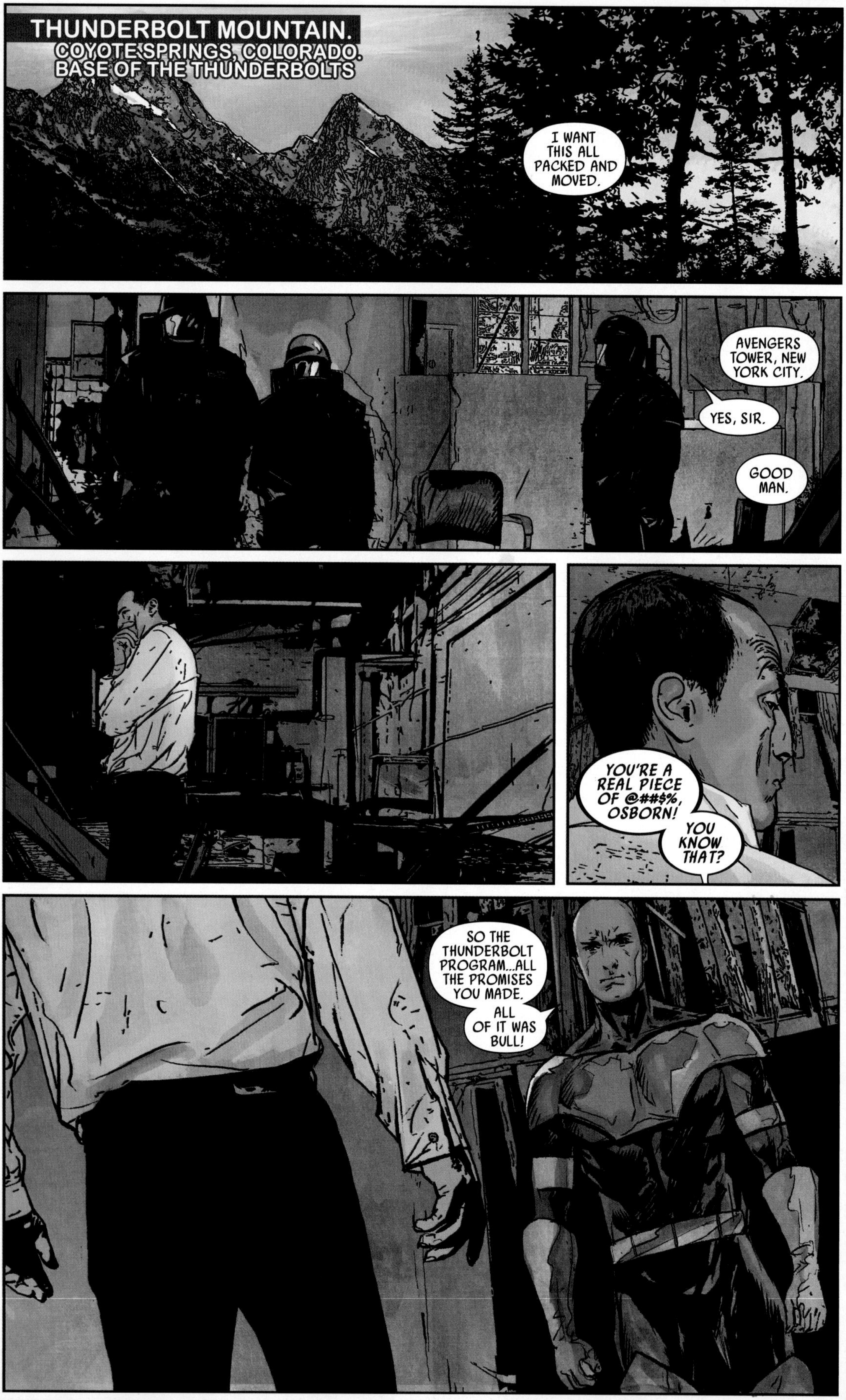
THUNDERBOLT MOUNTAIN.
COYOTE SPRINGS, COLORADO.
BASE OF THE THUNDERBOLTS
I WANT THIS ALL PACKED AND MOVED.
AVENGERS TOWER, NEW YORK CITY.
YES, SIR.
GOOD MAN.
YOU'RE A REAL PIECE OF @##$%, OSBORN!
YOU KNOW THAT?
SO THE THUNDERBOLT PROGRAM...ALL THE PROMISES YOU MADE.
ALL OF IT WAS BULL!

CALM DOWN, SWORDSMAN.

CALM DOWN?! YOU DON'T THINK I KNOW WHAT'S GOING ON?

YOU DON'T THINK I KNOW YOU ALREADY MADE SIDE DEALS WITH HALF THE THUNDERBOLTS TEAM?

WHAT ABOUT ME? WHAT AM I? AM I IN?

I'M NOT, AM I? I GET SCREWED, YOU PIECE OF @#%%.

IT'S COMPLICATED.

WE'RE RESTRUCTURING. WE HAVE TO REEVALUATE ALL THE DIFFERENT--

I KNEW IT! I KNEW YOU'D @#$% ME!

ALL THE WORK I DID FOR YOU! I WAS PROMISED AN OUT.

AM I GETTING IT?

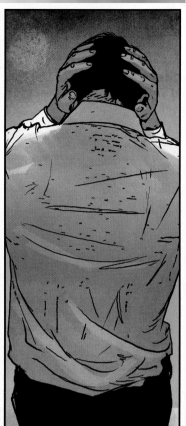

I KNEW IT.

WELL, GUESS WHAT? YOU'RE NOT NICK FURY.

YOU'RE NOT EVEN SANE. YOU'RE A WHACKJOB IN A FANCY SUIT.

AND EVERYONE HERE KNOWS IT, WE ALL KNOW IT.

I'M NOT GOING BACK TO PRISON, GOBLIN!

SETTLE DOWN AND LIS--

I'LL GO PUBLIC, THE @#$% I KNOW YOU DID HERE.

THE @#$$ I KNOW YOU'VE DONE IN YOUR LIFE.

YOU THINK YOU CAN JUST DANCE AROUND LIKE YOU NEVER--

YOU'RE NOT LETTING ME FINISH A SENTENCE.

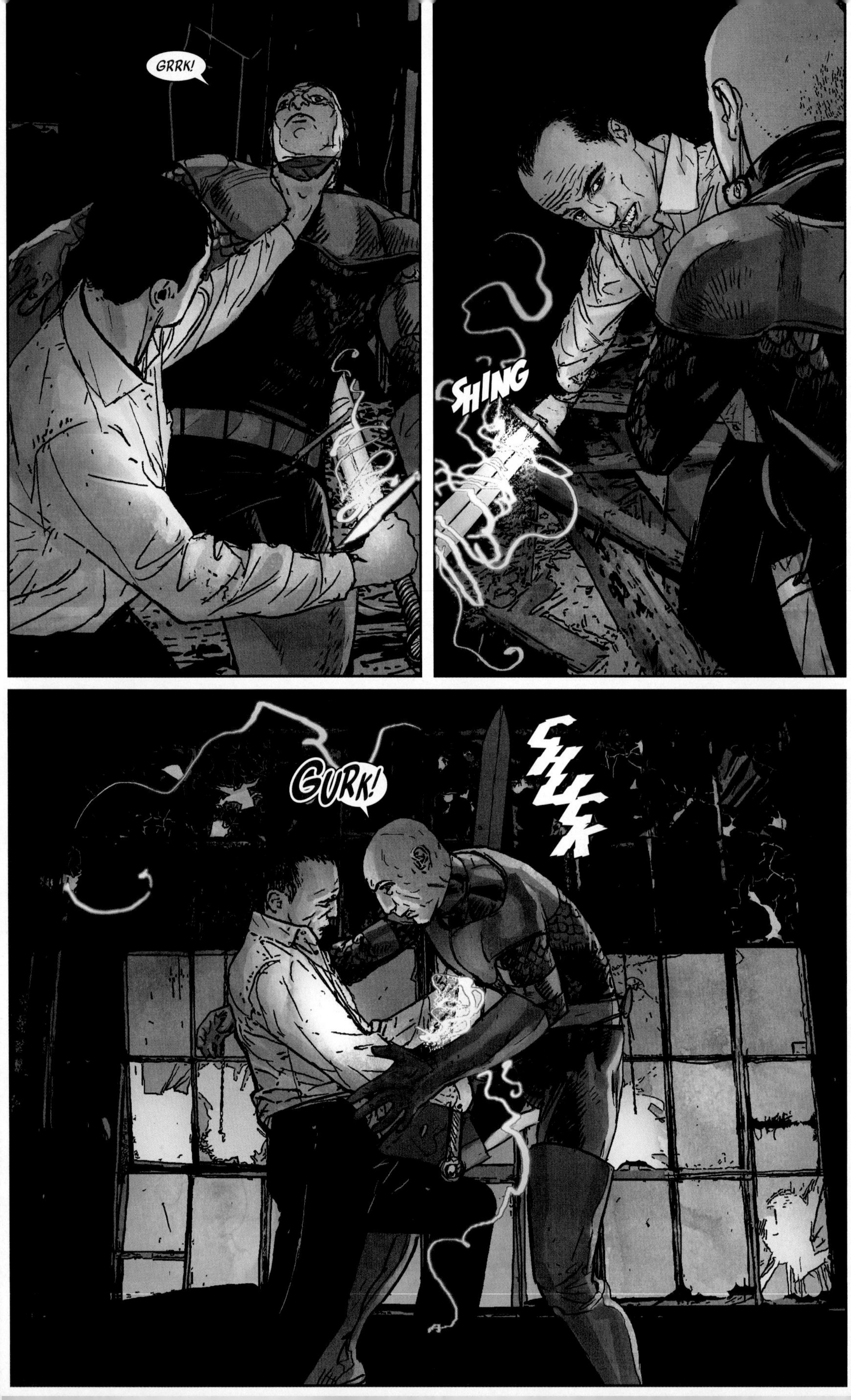
GRRK!
SHING
GURK!
SHUK

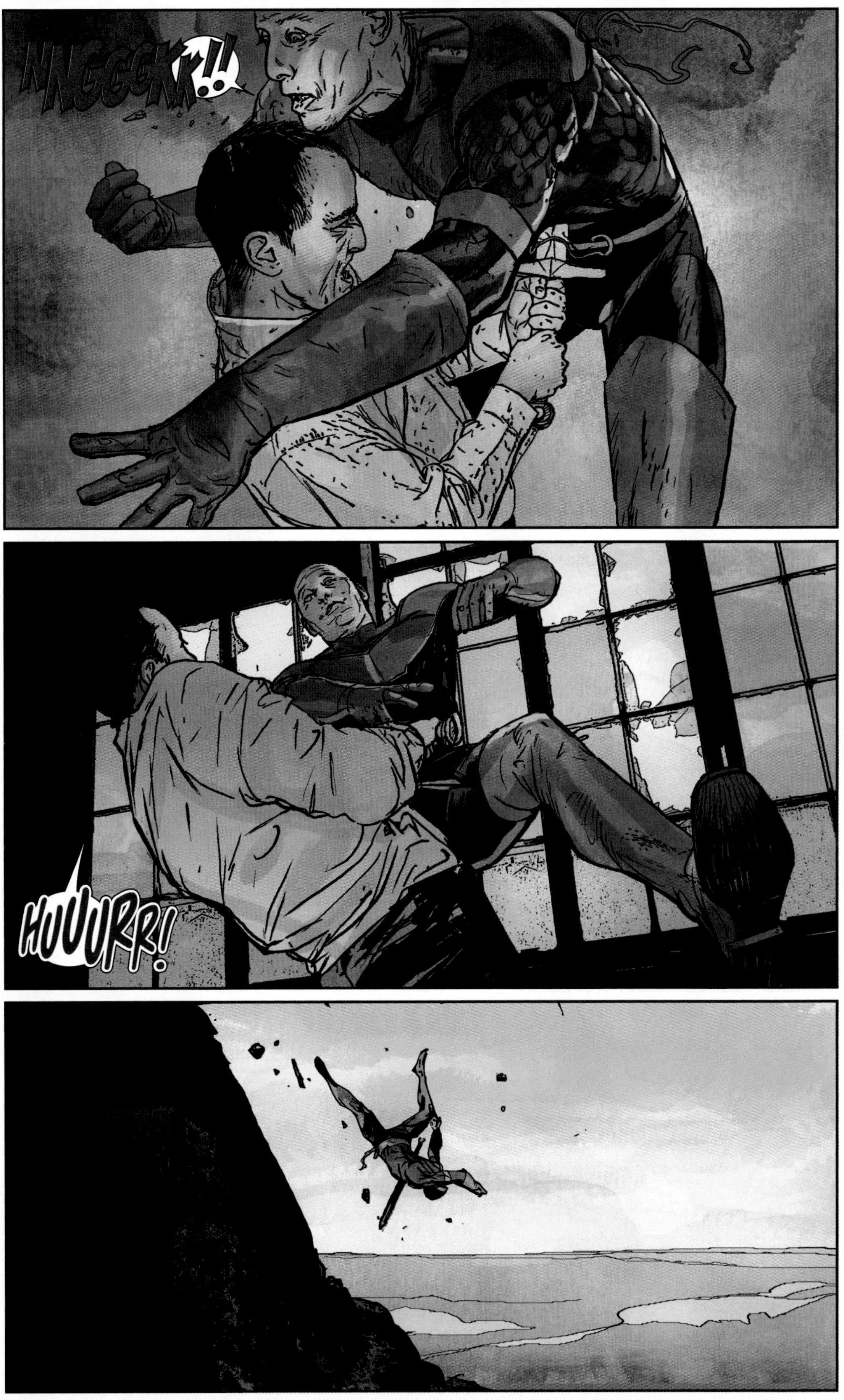
NNGGGKK!!
HUUURR!

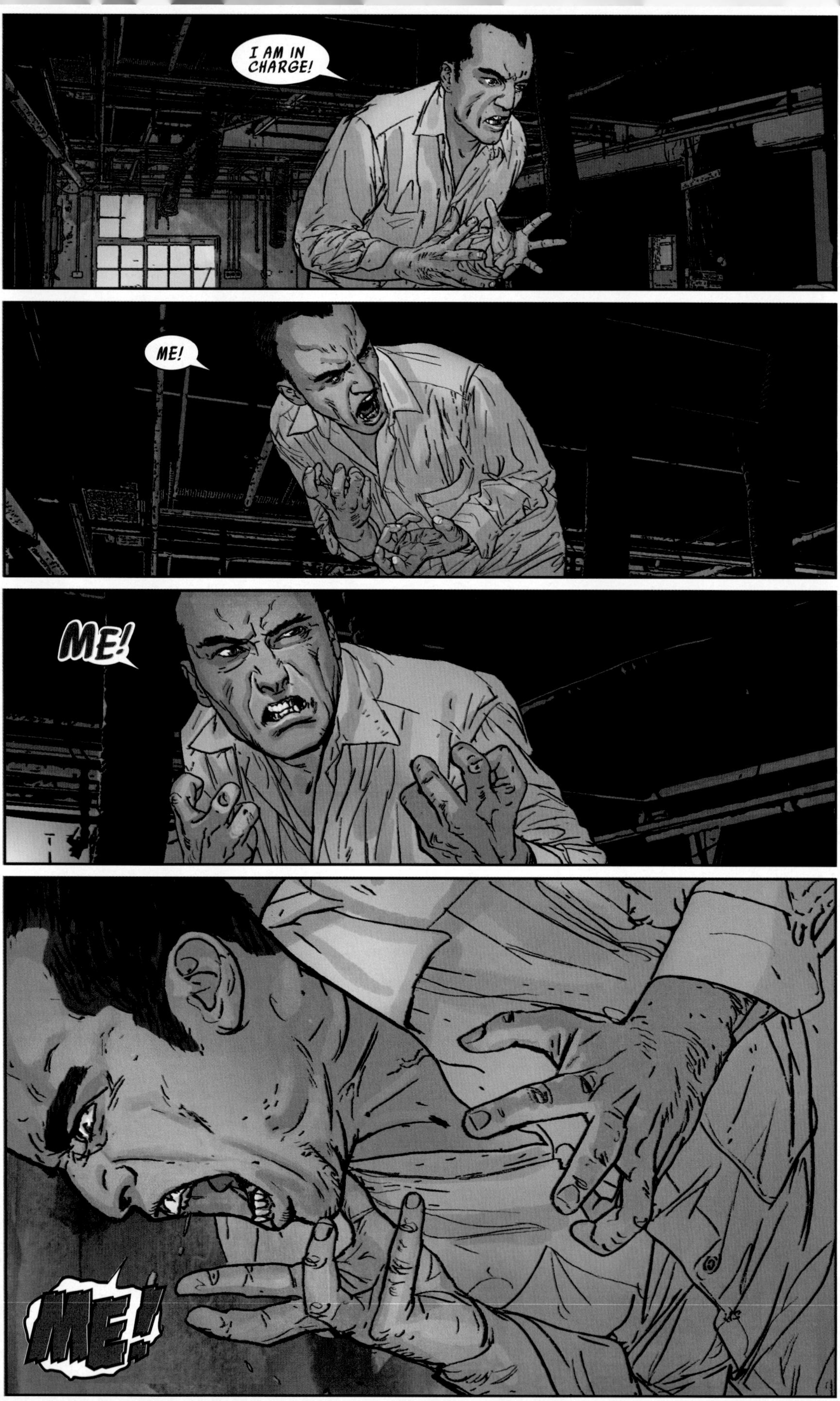
I AM IN CHARGE!
ME!
ME!
ME!

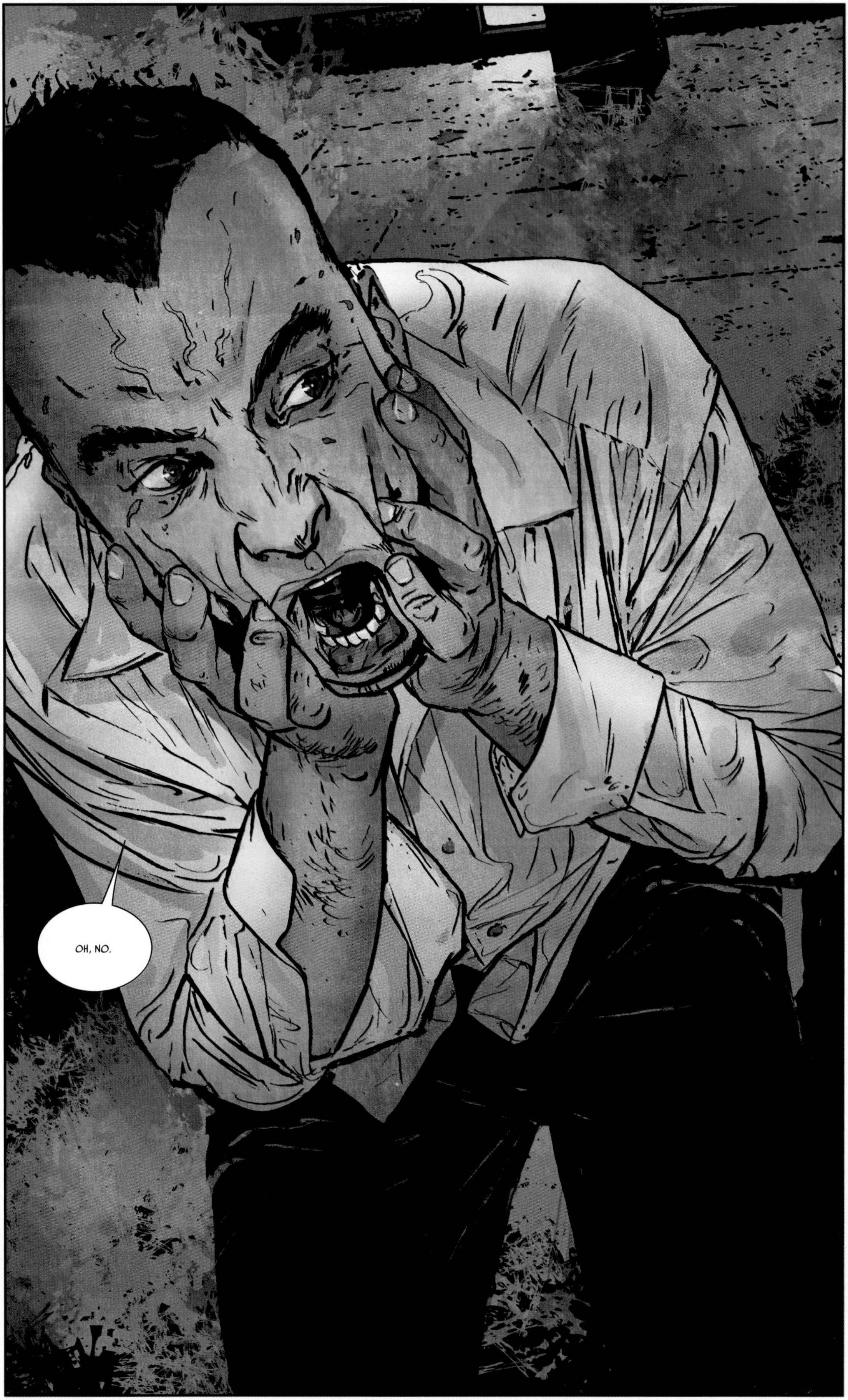
OH, NO.

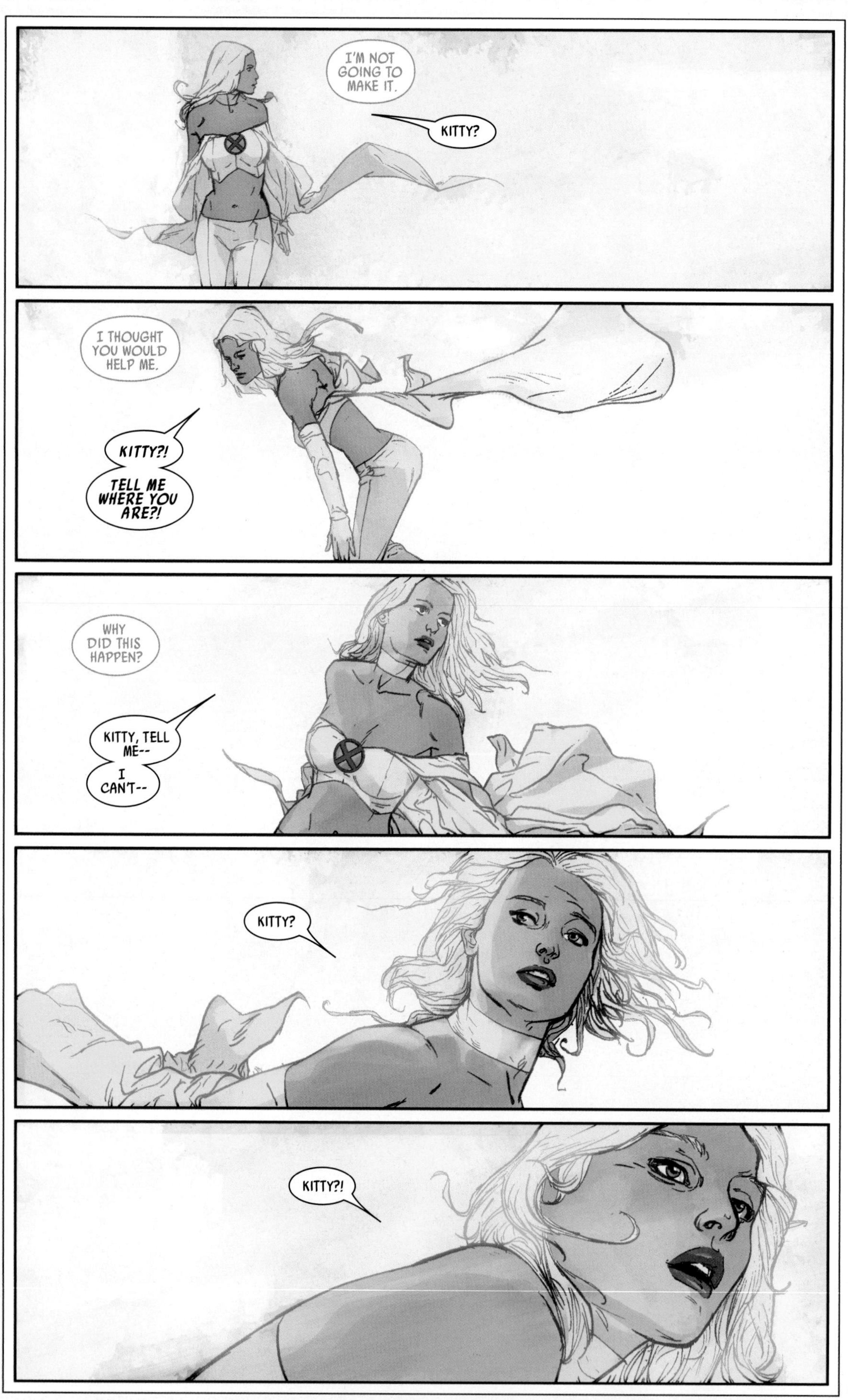
I'M NOT GOING TO MAKE IT.
KITTY?
I THOUGHT YOU WOULD HELP ME.
KITTY?!
TELL ME WHERE YOU ARE?!
WHY DID THIS HAPPEN?
KITTY, TELL ME--
I CAN'T--
KITTY?
KITTY?!

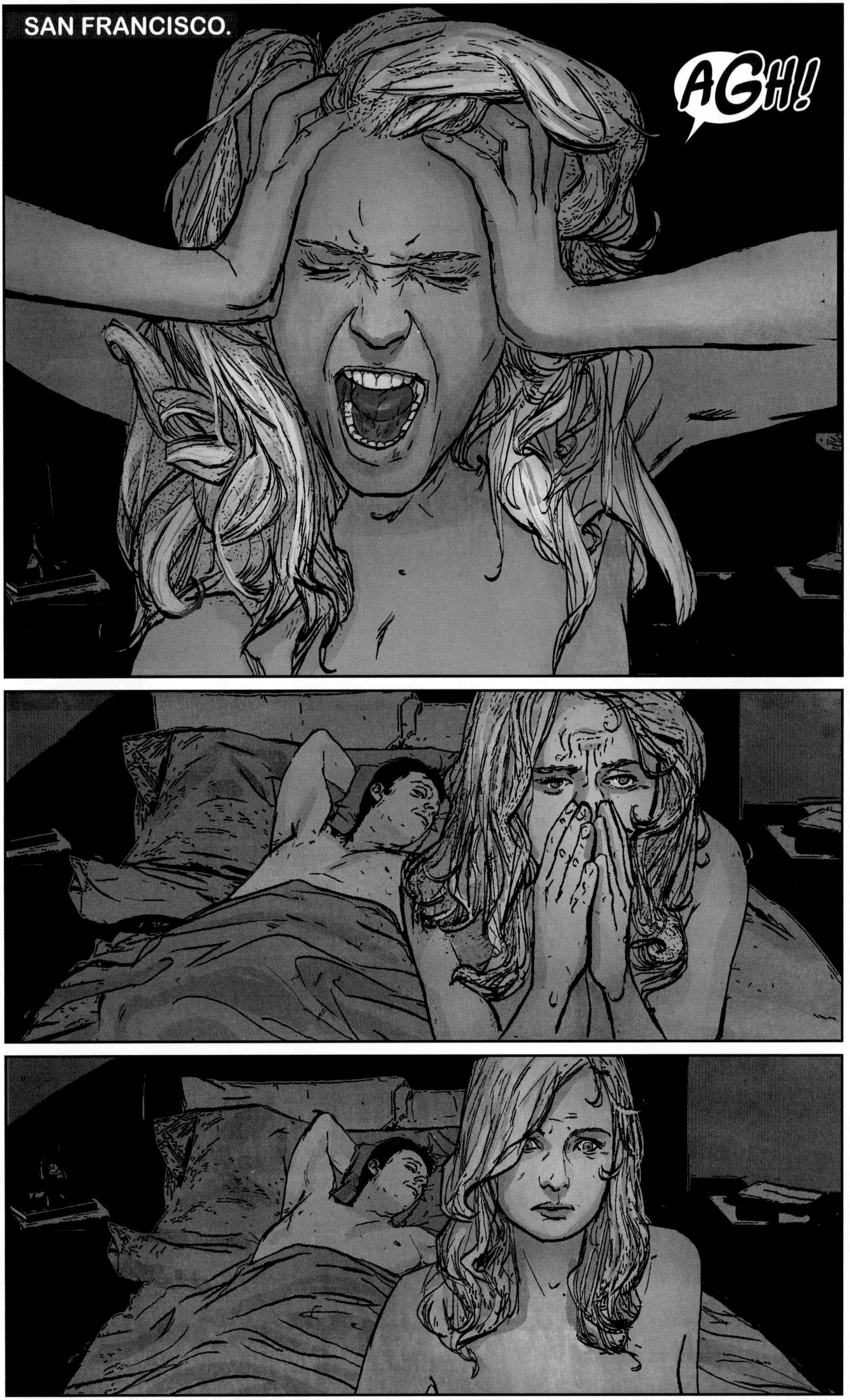
SAN FRANCISCO.
AGH!

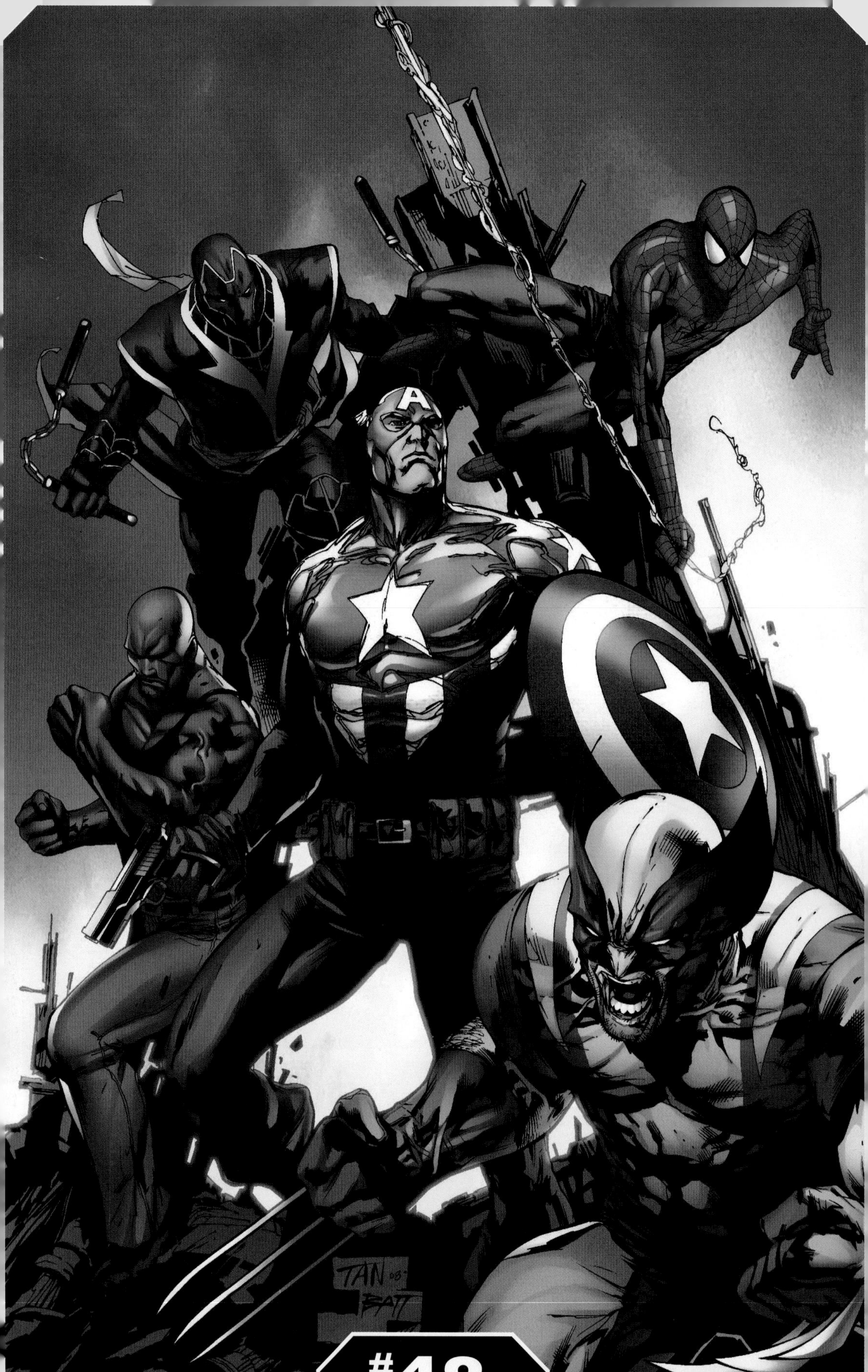

#48

AND THERE CAME A DAY, A DAY UNLIKE ANY OTHER, WHEN EARTH'S MIGHTIEST HEROES FOUND THEMSELVES UNITED AGAINST A COMMON THREAT! ON THAT DAY, THE AVENGERS WERE BORN, TO FIGHT THE FOES NO SINGLE SUPER HERO COULD WITHSTAND!

PREVIOUSLY IN NEW AVENGERS:

THE SHAPE-SHIFTING ALIEN RACE KNOWN AS THE SKRULLS HAS FAILED AT THEIR ATTEMPTED INVASION OF EARTH. BUT THE DAMAGE HAS BEEN DONE.

TONY STARK TOOK THE BLAME FOR THE INVASION AND HAS BEEN STRIPPED OF HIS ROLES AS BOTH LEADER OF THE AVENGERS AND DIRECTOR OF A NOW DEFUNCT S.H.I.E.L.D., WHILE THUNDERBOLTS LEADER AND ONE-TIME SUPER-VILLAIN GREEN GOBLIN NORMAN OSBORN HAS RISEN TO POWER AND BEEN APPOINTED TO REPLACE STARK.

STILL NONE OF THEM, NOT EVEN THE AVENGERS, CAN EVEN KNOW THE FULL EXTENT OF THE INVASION OR WHICH OF THEM WAS -- OR COULD STILL BE -- A SKRULL AGENT.

DURING THE INVASION, THE GROWING PARANOIA CREATES A RIFT IN THE MARRIAGE OF AVENGER LUKE CAGE AND JESSICA JONES. WORRIED FOR THE SAFETY OF THEIR CHILD, JESSICA SEEKS SHELTER AT AVENGERS TOWER, UNDER THE WATCHFUL EYE OF STARK'S BUTLER, JARVIS, TO WAIT OUT THE WORST OF IT.

BUT WHEN THE INVASION'S FINAL BATTLE HIT ITS ZENITH, JESSICA JONES MADE THE SELFLESS DECISION TO LEAVE HER CHILD WITH JARVIS AND FIGHT ALONGSIDE HER HUSBAND. LITTLE DID SHE KNOW, JARVIS WAS ONE OF THE SKRULL AGENTS EMBEDDED WITHIN THE AVENGERS.

BY THE TIME JESSICA FIGURED IT OUT, JARVIS, AND THE BABY, WERE GONE.

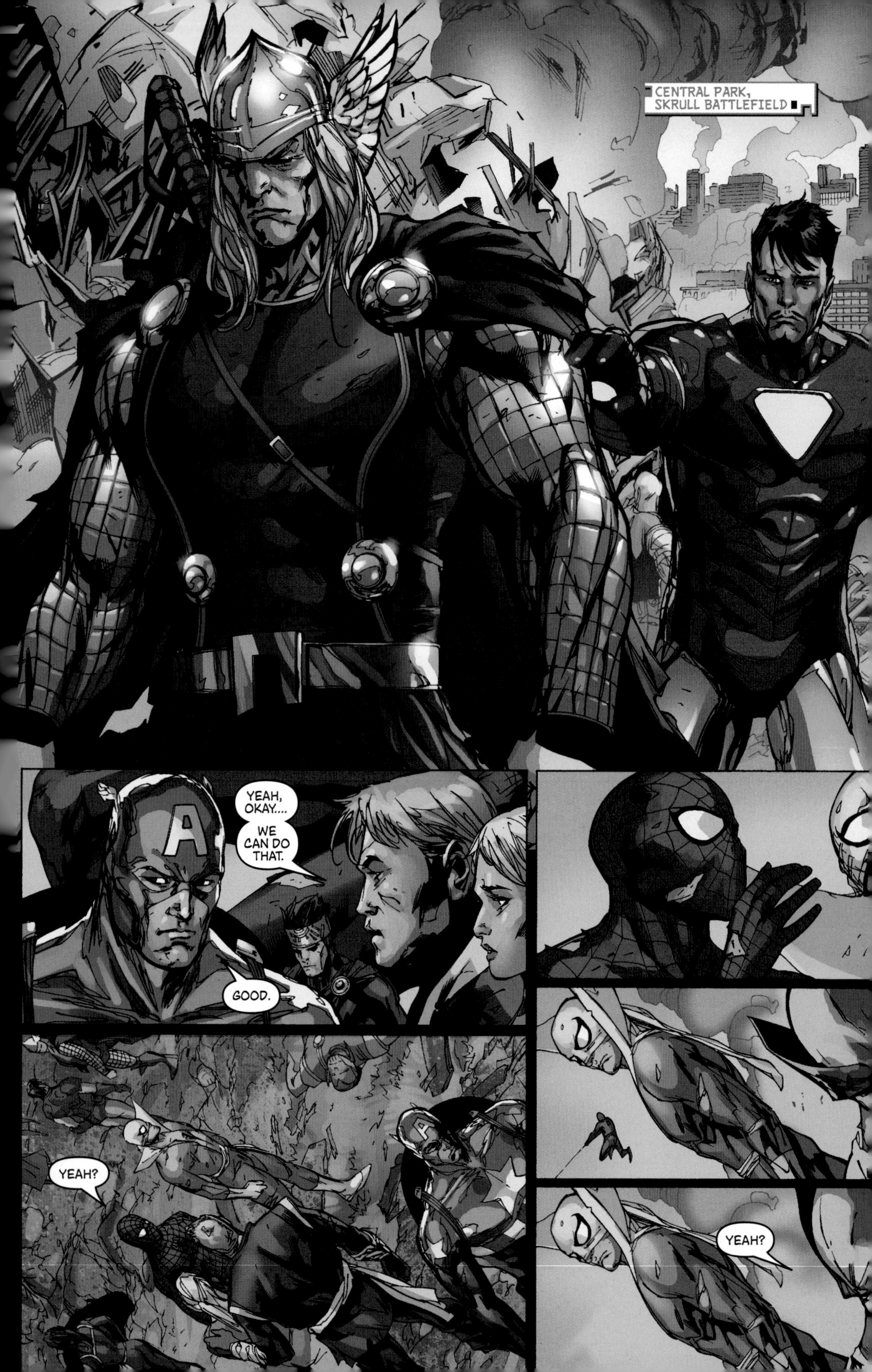
CENTRAL PARK, SKRULL BATTLEFIELD
YEAH, OKAY....
WE CAN DO THAT.
GOOD.
YEAH?
YEAH?

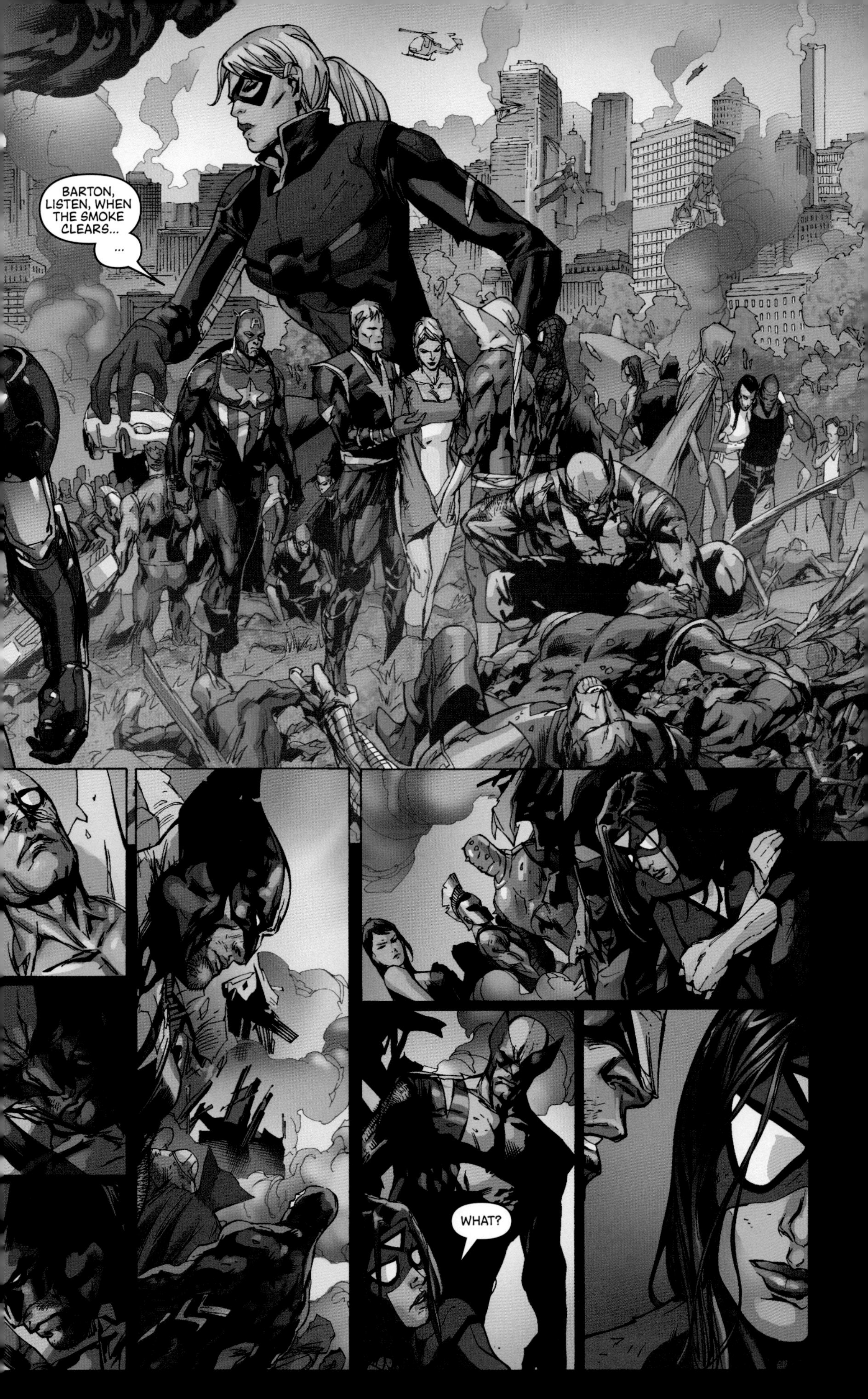
BARTON, LISTEN, WHEN THE SMOKE CLEARS...
...
WHAT?

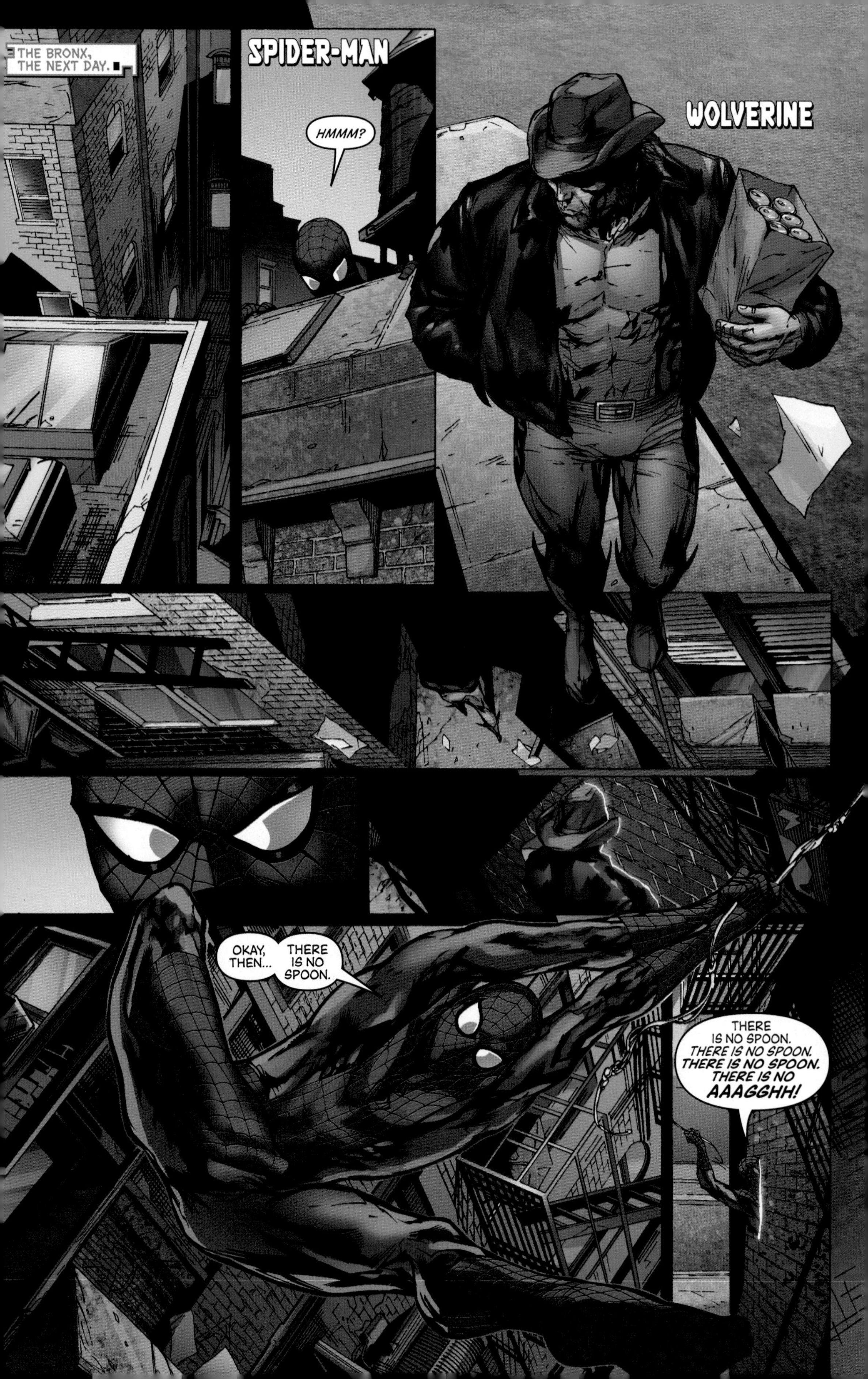
THE BRONX, THE NEXT DAY.
SPIDER-MAN
WOLVERINE
HMMM?
OKAY, THEN...
THERE IS NO SPOON.
THERE IS NO SPOON. THERE IS NO SPOON. THERE IS NO SPOON. THERE IS NO AAAGGHH!

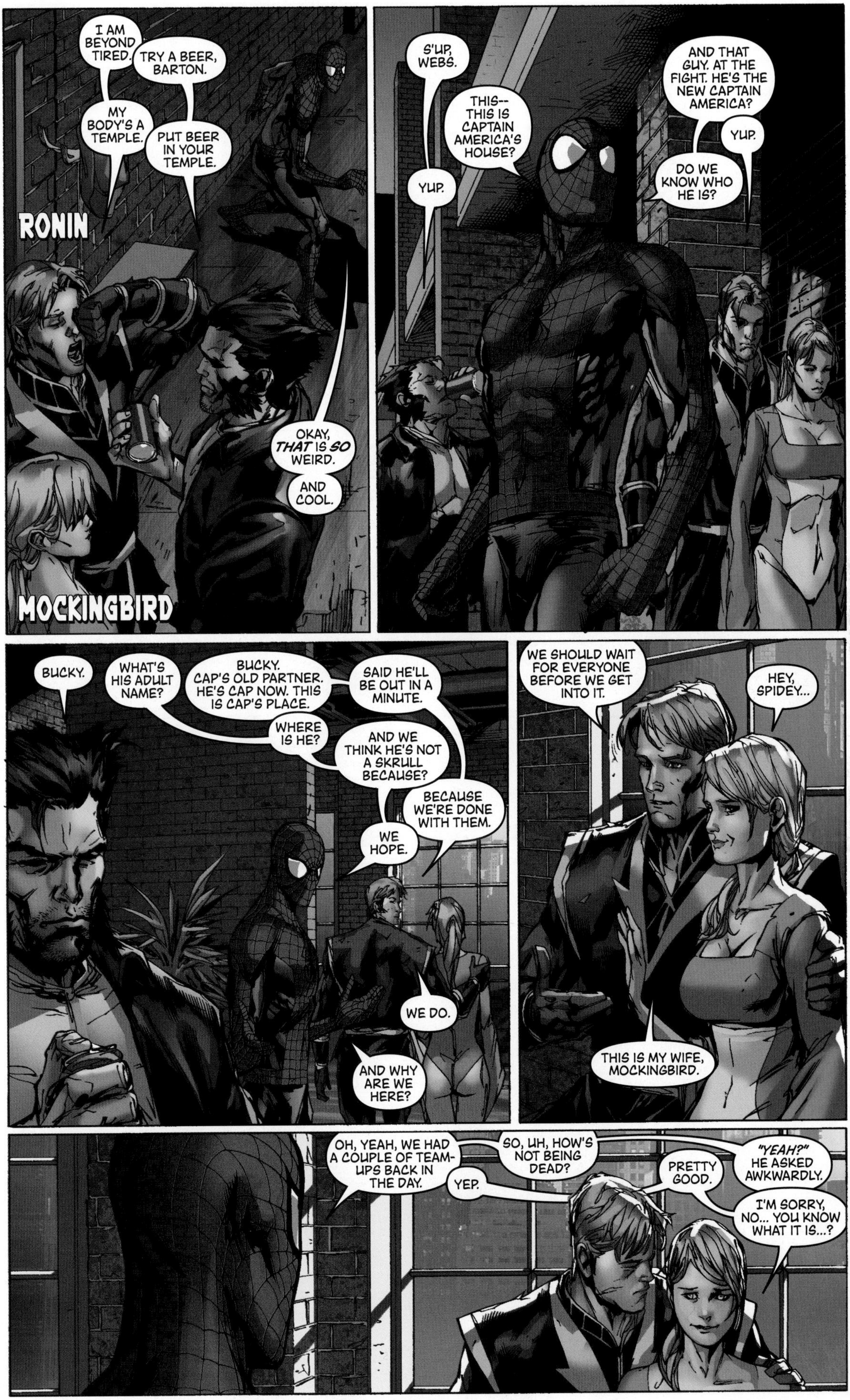

I AM BEYOND TIRED.
TRY A BEER, BARTON.
MY BODY'S A TEMPLE.
PUT BEER IN YOUR TEMPLE.
RONIN
OKAY, *THAT* IS *SO* WEIRD.
AND COOL.
MOCKINGBIRD
S'UP, WEBS.
THIS-- THIS IS CAPTAIN AMERICA'S HOUSE?
YUP.
AND THAT GUY. AT THE FIGHT. HE'S THE NEW CAPTAIN AMERICA?
YUP.
DO WE KNOW WHO HE IS?
BUCKY.
WHAT'S HIS ADULT NAME?
BUCKY. CAP'S OLD PARTNER. HE'S CAP NOW. THIS IS CAP'S PLACE.
WHERE IS HE?
SAID HE'LL BE OUT IN A MINUTE.
AND WE THINK HE'S NOT A SKRULL BECAUSE?
BECAUSE WE'RE DONE WITH THEM.
WE HOPE.
WE DO.
AND WHY ARE WE HERE?
WE SHOULD WAIT FOR EVERYONE BEFORE WE GET INTO IT.
HEY, SPIDEY...
THIS IS MY WIFE, MOCKINGBIRD.
OH, YEAH, WE HAD A COUPLE OF TEAM-UPS BACK IN THE DAY.
YEP.
SO, UH, HOW'S NOT BEING DEAD?
PRETTY GOOD.
"YEAH?" HE ASKED AWKWARDLY.
I'M SORRY, NO... YOU KNOW WHAT IT IS...?

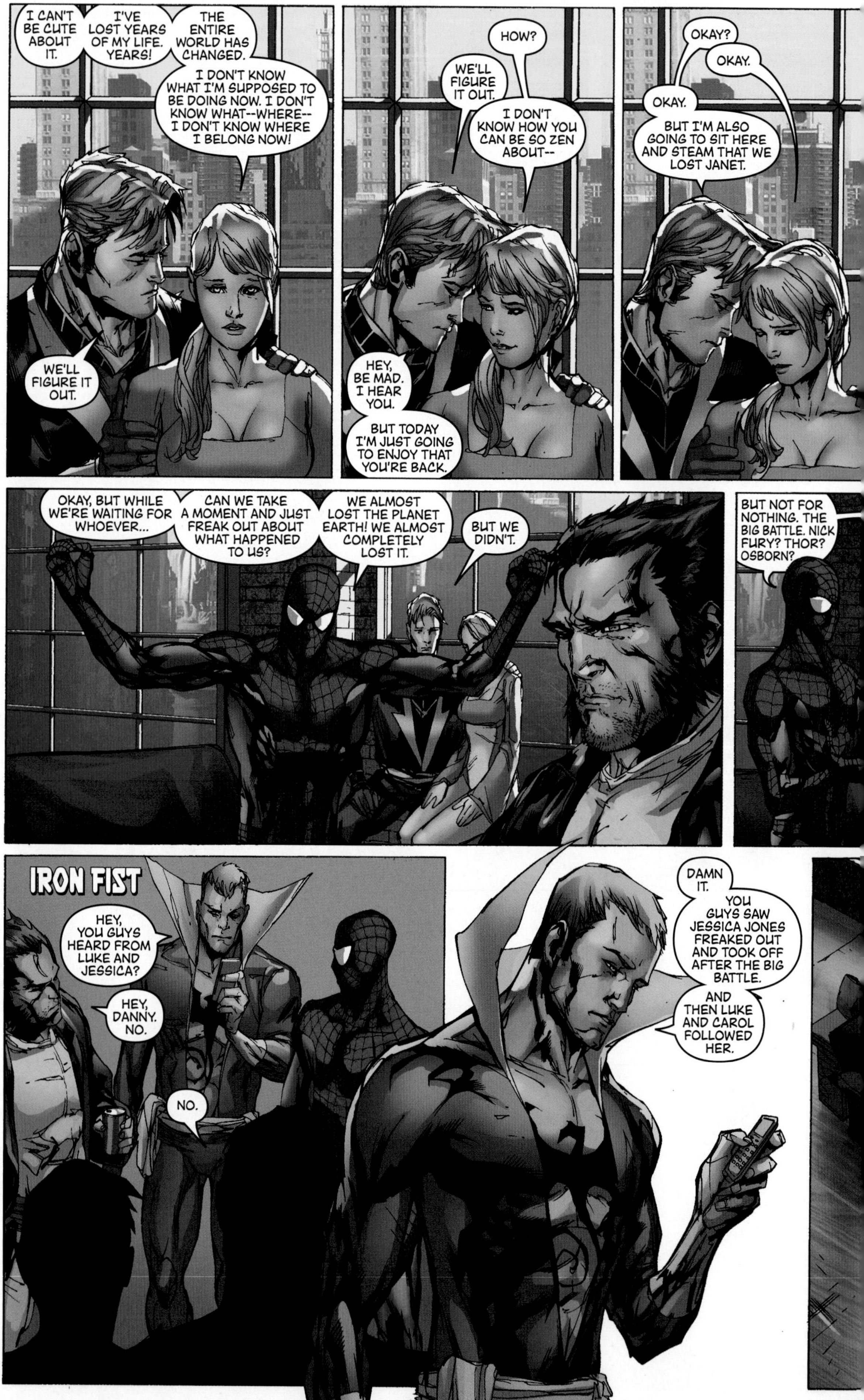
I CAN'T BE CUTE ABOUT IT.
I'VE LOST YEARS OF MY LIFE. YEARS!
THE ENTIRE WORLD HAS CHANGED.
I DON'T KNOW WHAT I'M SUPPOSED TO BE DOING NOW. I DON'T KNOW WHAT--WHERE-- I DON'T KNOW WHERE I BELONG NOW!
WE'LL FIGURE IT OUT.
HOW?
WE'LL FIGURE IT OUT.
I DON'T KNOW HOW YOU CAN BE SO ZEN ABOUT--
HEY, BE MAD. I HEAR YOU.
BUT TODAY I'M JUST GOING TO ENJOY THAT YOU'RE BACK.
OKAY?
OKAY.
OKAY.
BUT I'M ALSO GOING TO SIT HERE AND STEAM THAT WE LOST JANET.
OKAY, BUT WHILE WE'RE WAITING FOR WHOEVER...
CAN WE TAKE A MOMENT AND JUST FREAK OUT ABOUT WHAT HAPPENED TO US?
WE ALMOST LOST THE PLANET EARTH! WE ALMOST COMPLETELY LOST IT.
BUT WE DIDN'T.
BUT NOT FOR NOTHING. THE BIG BATTLE. NICK FURY? THOR? OSBORN?
IRON FIST
HEY, YOU GUYS HEARD FROM LUKE AND JESSICA?
HEY, DANNY. NO.
NO.
DAMN IT.
YOU GUYS SAW JESSICA JONES FREAKED OUT AND TOOK OFF AFTER THE BIG BATTLE.
AND THEN LUKE AND CAROL FOLLOWED HER.

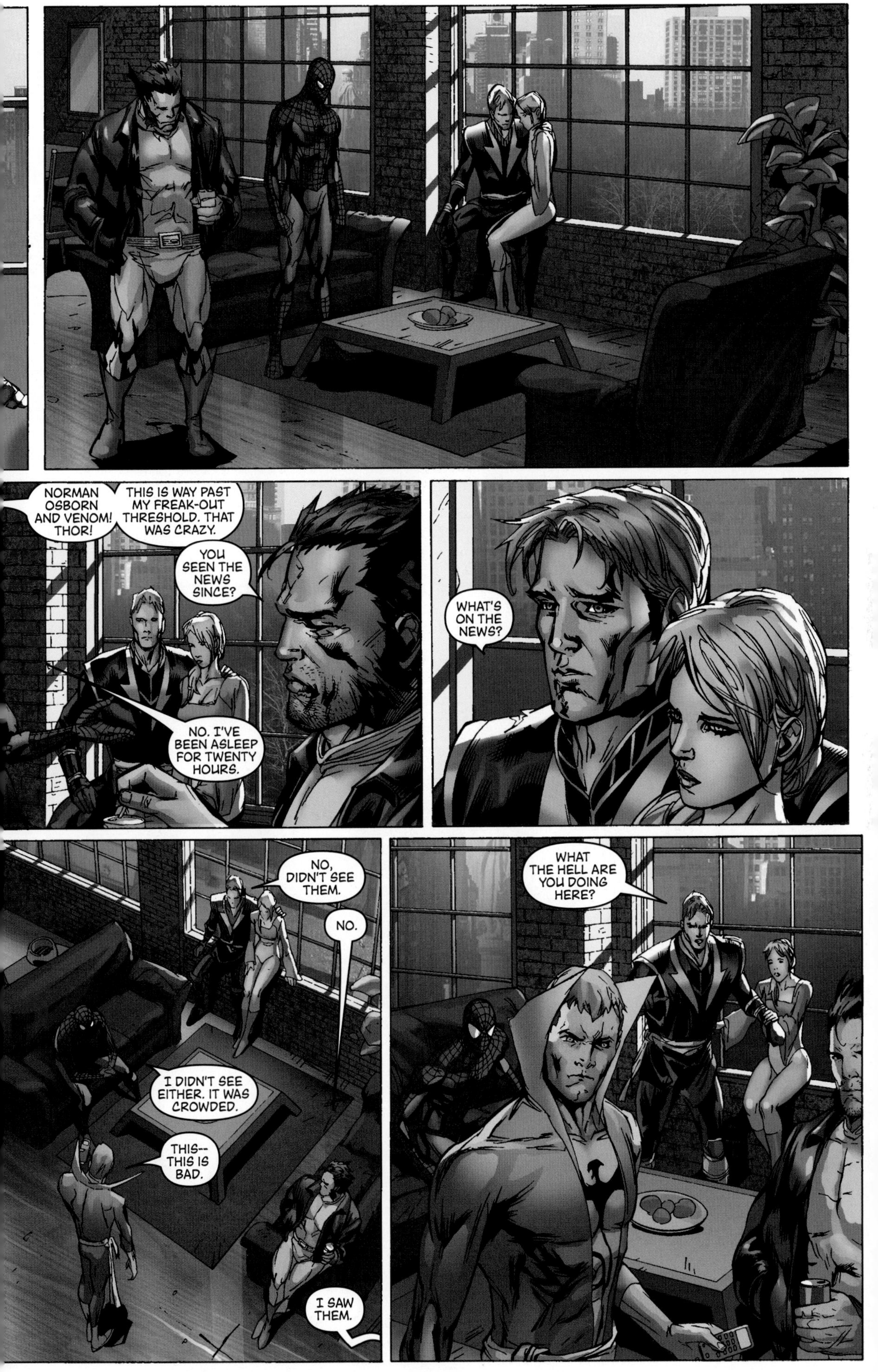
NORMAN OSBORN AND VENOM! THOR!
THIS IS WAY PAST MY FREAK-OUT THRESHOLD. THAT WAS CRAZY.
YOU SEEN THE NEWS SINCE?
NO. I'VE BEEN ASLEEP FOR TWENTY HOURS.
WHAT'S ON THE NEWS?
NO, DIDN'T SEE THEM.
NO.
I DIDN'T SEE EITHER. IT WAS CROWDED.
THIS-- THIS IS BAD.
I SAW THEM.
WHAT THE HELL ARE YOU DOING HERE?

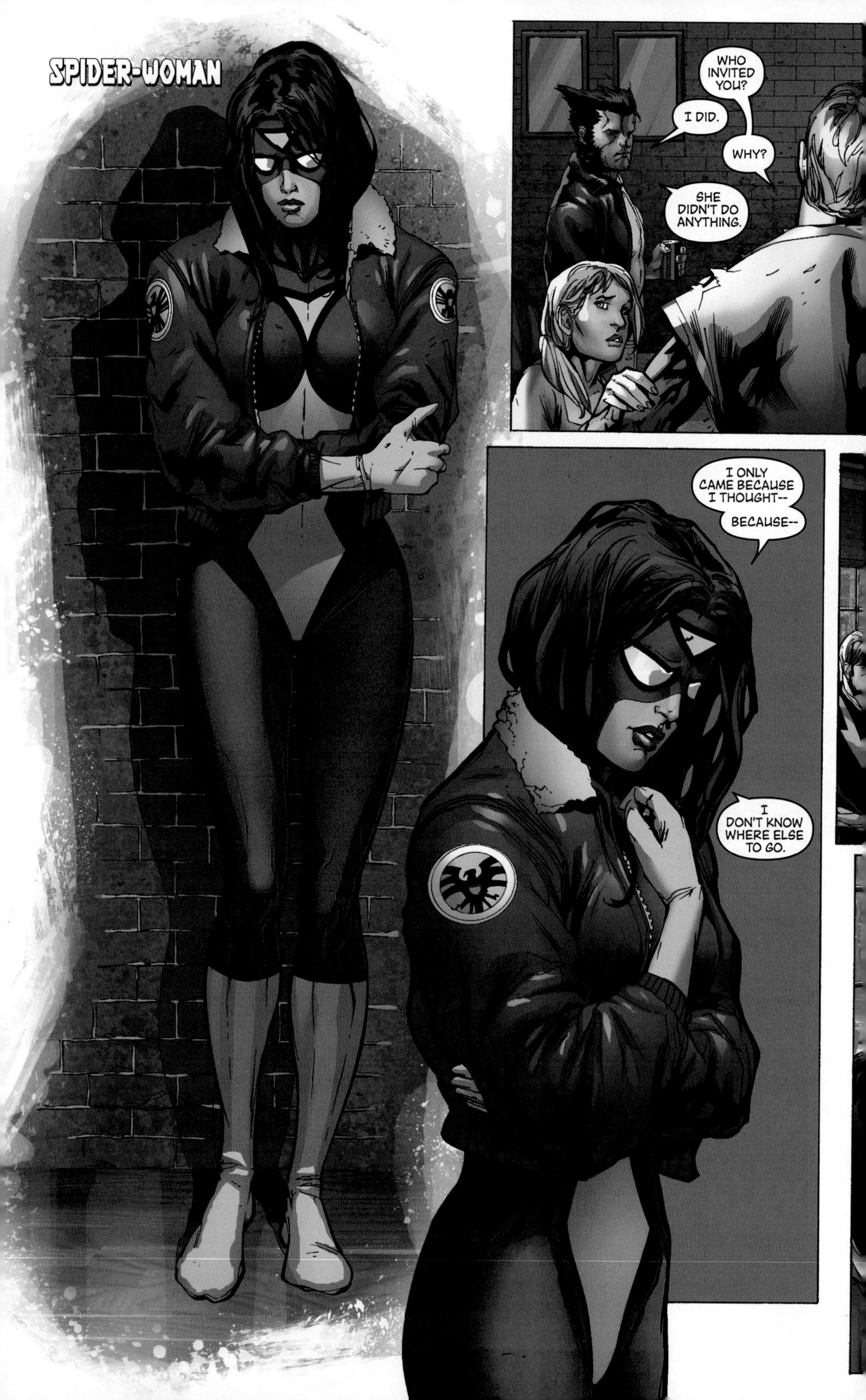
SPIDER-WOMAN
WHO INVITED YOU?
I DID.
WHY?
SHE DIDN'T DO ANYTHING.
I ONLY CAME BECAUSE I THOUGHT--
BECAUSE--
I DON'T KNOW WHERE ELSE TO GO.

UH... HEY, JESSICA.

WASN'T HER.

SKRULLS TOOK HER OUT. TOOK HER PLACE. JUST LIKE THEY DID TO YOUR WIFE, ONLY WORSE.

SHE GOT IT THE WORST OF ALL OF US.

I'LL GO.

NO. DON'T.

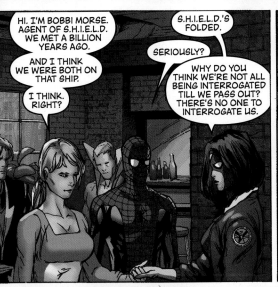

HI. I'M BOBBI MORSE. AGENT OF S.H.I.E.L.D. WE MET A BILLION YEARS AGO.

AND I THINK WE WERE BOTH ON THAT SHIP.

I THINK. RIGHT?

S.H.I.E.L.D.'S FOLDED.

SERIOUSLY?

WHY DO YOU THINK WE'RE NOT ALL BEING INTERROGATED TILL WE PASS OUT? THERE'S NO ONE TO INTERROGATE US.

TOLD YOU, TURN ON THE TV.

IF S.H.I.E.L.D. IS GONE, WHO'S TAPPING OUR PHONES?

IS FURY BACK IN CHARGE?

DON'T THINK SO. THAT I WOULD HAVE HEARD ABOUT.

IS *THIS* EVERYBODY THEN?

NO. LUKE CAGE AND I'M BETTIN' CAROL DANVERS ARE GOING TO NEED TO BE HERE TOO.

SHE'S WITH TONY STARK.

NOT SO MUCH.

SERIOUSLY? IS THERE A TV IN HERE? INTERWEBS?

WELL, WE CAN WAIT FOR EVERYONE ELSE, BUT LISTEN...

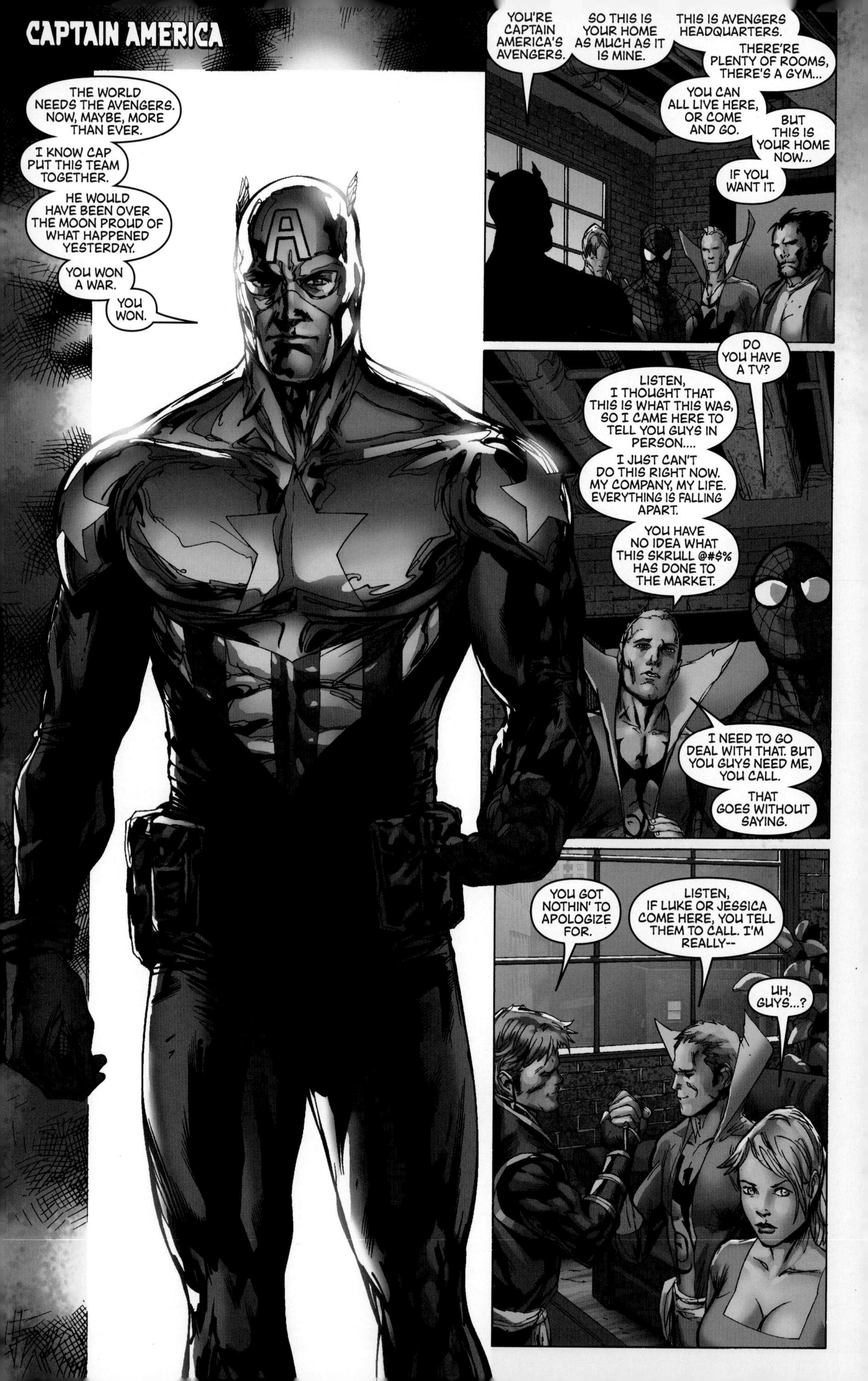
CAPTAIN AMERICA
THE WORLD NEEDS THE AVENGERS. NOW, MAYBE, MORE THAN EVER.
I KNOW CAP PUT THIS TEAM TOGETHER.
HE WOULD HAVE BEEN OVER THE MOON PROUD OF WHAT HAPPENED YESTERDAY.
YOU WON A WAR.
YOU WON.
YOU'RE CAPTAIN AMERICA'S AVENGERS.
SO THIS IS YOUR HOME AS MUCH AS IT IS MINE.
THIS IS AVENGERS HEADQUARTERS.
THERE'RE PLENTY OF ROOMS, THERE'S A GYM...
YOU CAN ALL LIVE HERE, OR COME AND GO.
BUT THIS IS YOUR HOME NOW...
IF YOU WANT IT.
DO YOU HAVE A TV?
LISTEN, I THOUGHT THAT THIS IS WHAT THIS WAS, SO I CAME HERE TO TELL YOU GUYS IN PERSON....
I JUST CAN'T DO THIS RIGHT NOW. MY COMPANY, MY LIFE. EVERYTHING IS FALLING APART.
YOU HAVE NO IDEA WHAT THIS SKRULL @#$% HAS DONE TO THE MARKET.
I NEED TO GO DEAL WITH THAT. BUT YOU GUYS NEED ME, YOU CALL.
THAT GOES WITHOUT SAYING.
YOU GOT NOTHIN' TO APOLOGIZE FOR.
LISTEN, IF LUKE OR JESSICA COME HERE, YOU TELL THEM TO CALL. I'M REALLY--
UH, GUYS...?

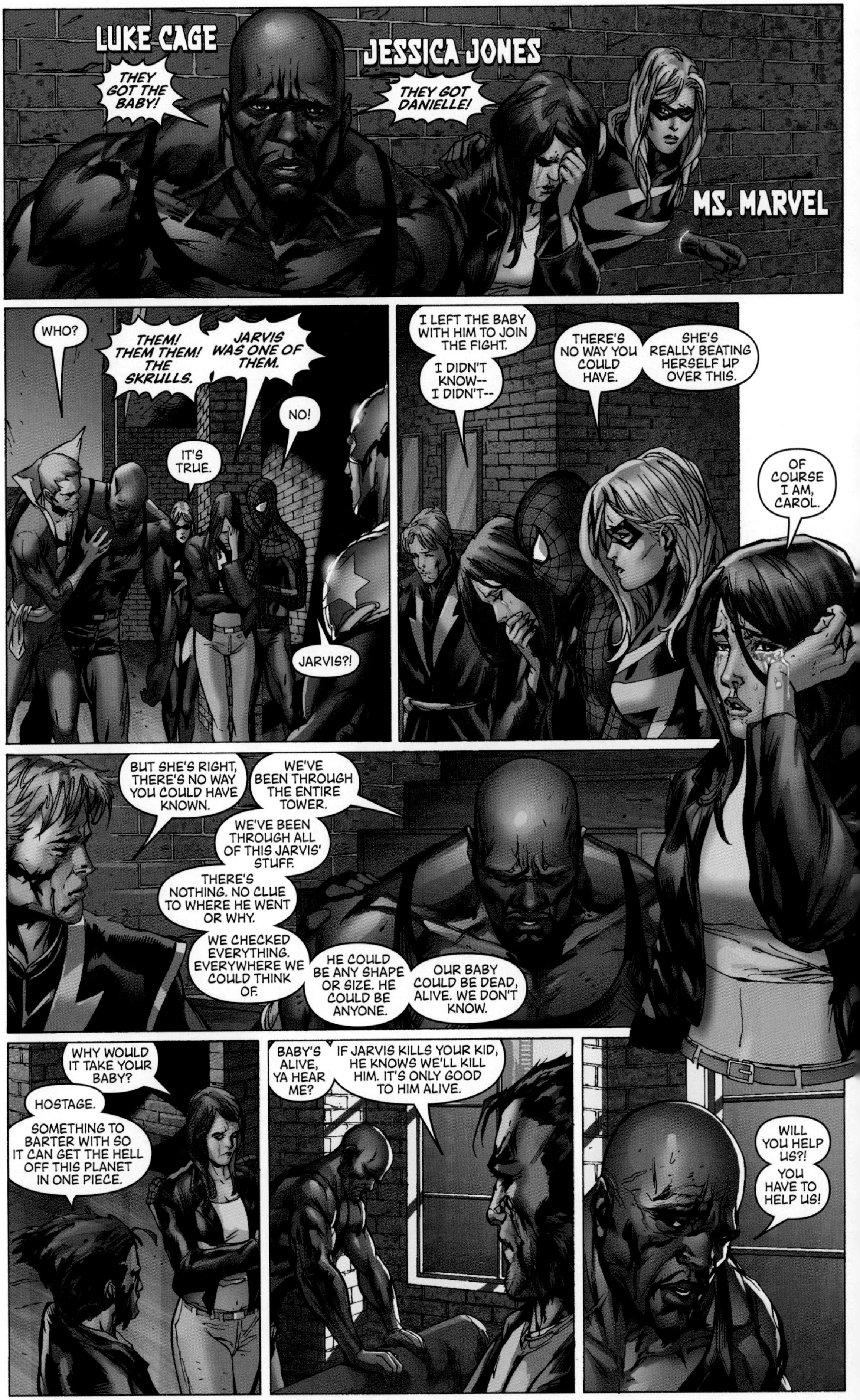
LUKE CAGE
THEY GOT THE BABY!
JESSICA JONES
THEY GOT DANIELLE!
MS. MARVEL
WHO?
THEM! THEM THEM! THE SKRULLS.
JARVIS WAS ONE OF THEM.
NO!
IT'S TRUE.
JARVIS?!
I LEFT THE BABY WITH HIM TO JOIN THE FIGHT.
I DIDN'T KNOW-- I DIDN'T--
THERE'S NO WAY YOU COULD HAVE.
SHE'S REALLY BEATING HERSELF UP OVER THIS.
OF COURSE I AM, CAROL.
BUT SHE'S RIGHT, THERE'S NO WAY YOU COULD HAVE KNOWN.
WE'VE BEEN THROUGH THE ENTIRE TOWER.
WE'VE BEEN THROUGH ALL OF THIS JARVIS' STUFF.
THERE'S NOTHING. NO CLUE TO WHERE HE WENT OR WHY.
WE CHECKED EVERYTHING. EVERYWHERE WE COULD THINK OF.
HE COULD BE ANY SHAPE OR SIZE. HE COULD BE ANYONE.
OUR BABY COULD BE DEAD, ALIVE. WE DON'T KNOW.
WHY WOULD IT TAKE YOUR BABY?
HOSTAGE.
SOMETHING TO BARTER WITH SO IT CAN GET THE HELL OFF THIS PLANET IN ONE PIECE.
BABY'S ALIVE, YA HEAR ME?
IF JARVIS KILLS YOUR KID, HE KNOWS WE'LL KILL HIM. IT'S ONLY GOOD TO HIM ALIVE.
WILL YOU HELP US?!
YOU HAVE TO HELP US!

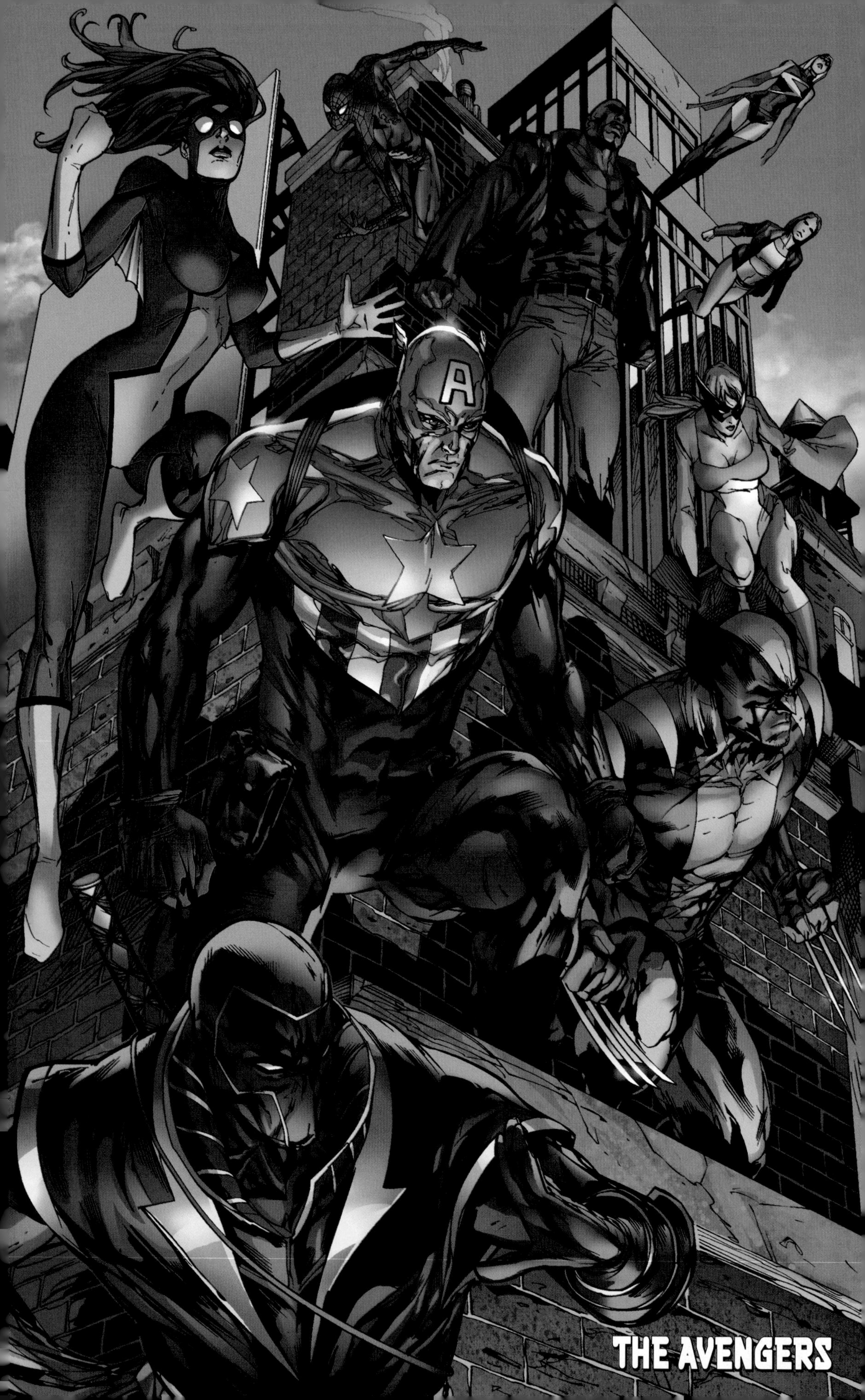
THE AVENGERS

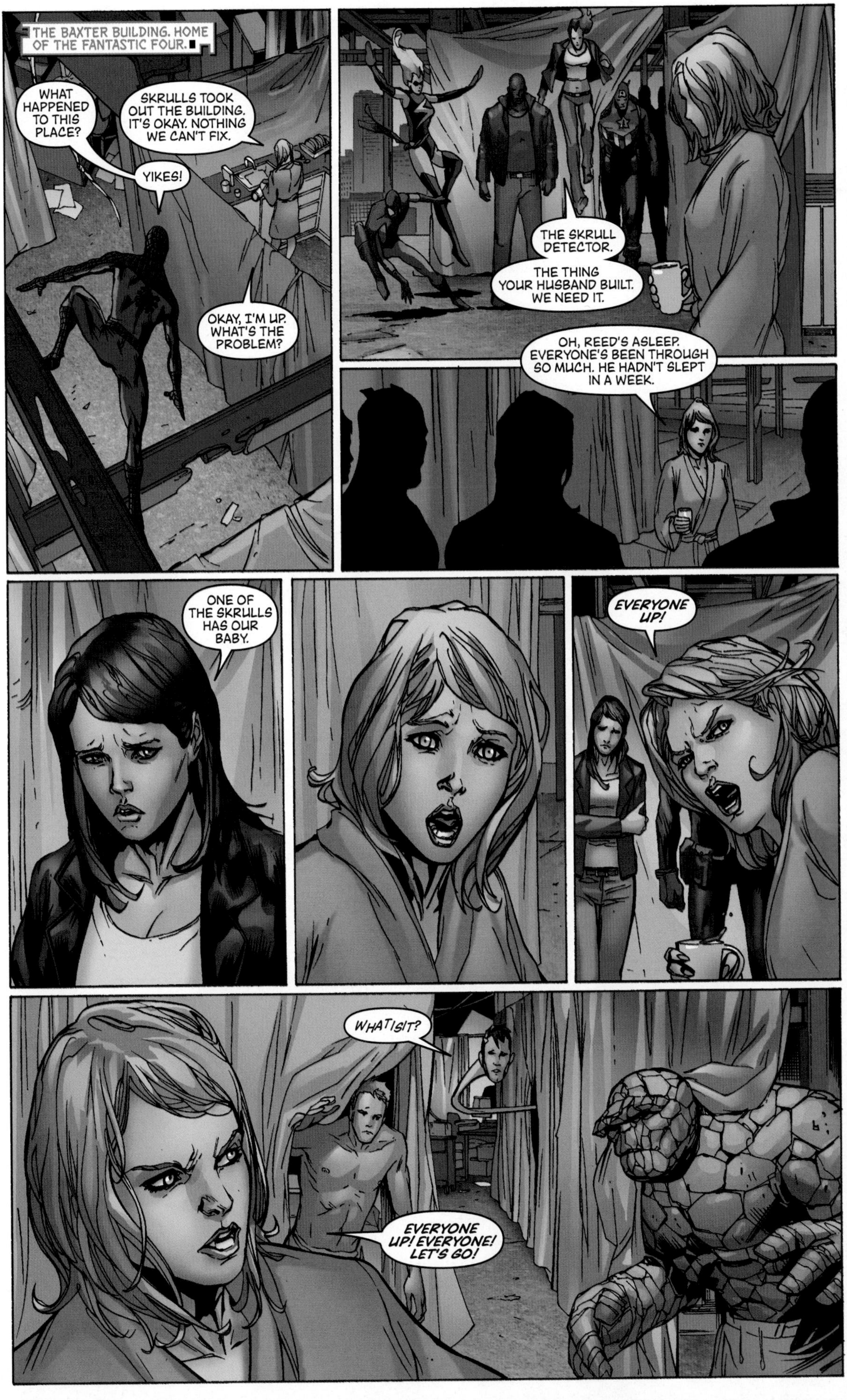
THE BAXTER BUILDING. HOME OF THE FANTASTIC FOUR.
WHAT HAPPENED TO THIS PLACE?
SKRULLS TOOK OUT THE BUILDING. IT'S OKAY. NOTHING WE CAN'T FIX.
YIKES!
OKAY, I'M UP. WHAT'S THE PROBLEM?
THE SKRULL DETECTOR.
THE THING YOUR HUSBAND BUILT. WE NEED IT.
OH, REED'S ASLEEP. EVERYONE'S BEEN THROUGH SO MUCH. HE HADN'T SLEPT IN A WEEK.
ONE OF THE SKRULLS HAS OUR BABY.
EVERYONE UP!
WHAT IS IT?
EVERYONE UP! EVERYONE! LET'S GO!

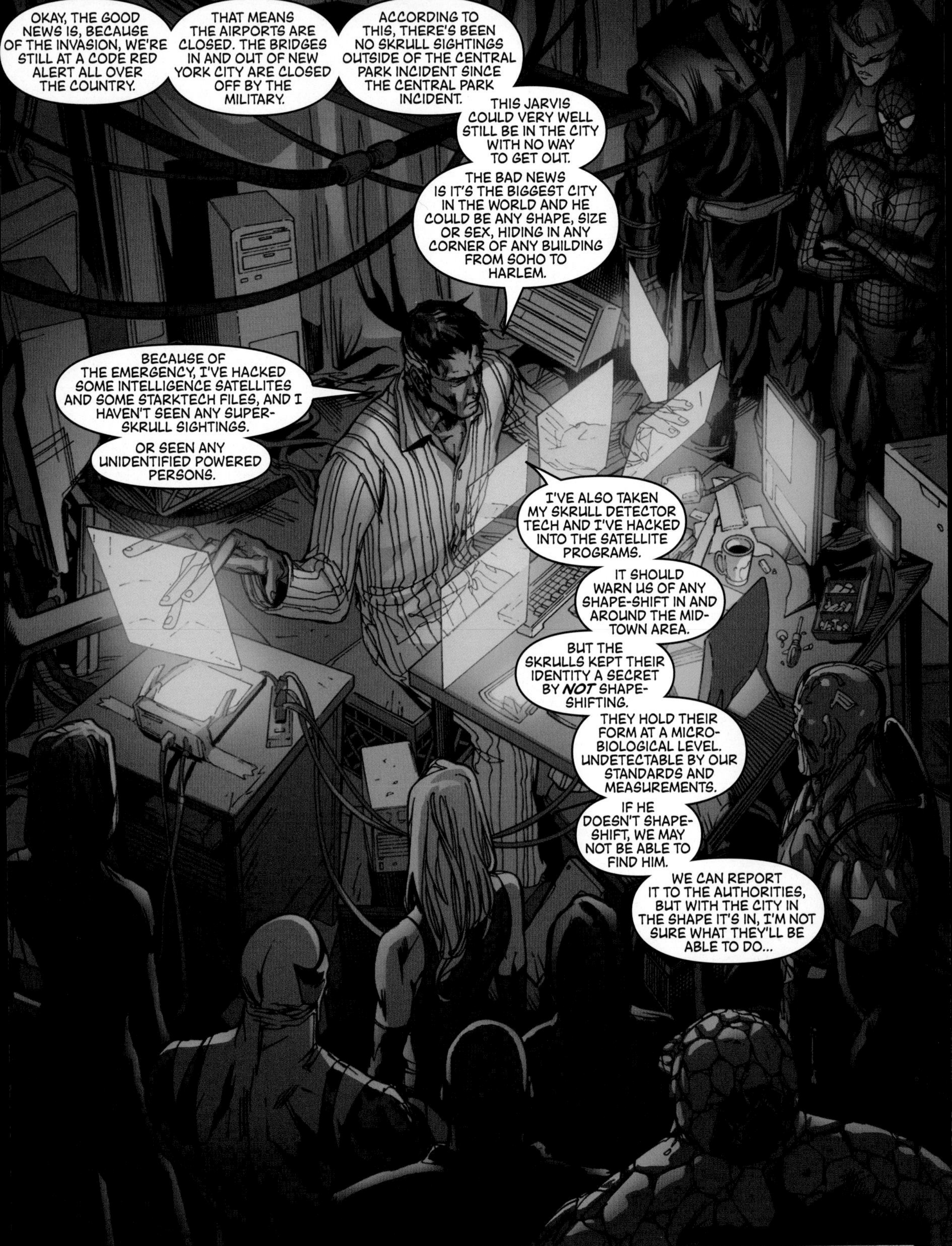
OKAY, THE GOOD NEWS IS, BECAUSE OF THE INVASION, WE'RE STILL AT A CODE RED ALERT ALL OVER THE COUNTRY.
THAT MEANS THE AIRPORTS ARE CLOSED. THE BRIDGES IN AND OUT OF NEW YORK CITY ARE CLOSED OFF BY THE MILITARY.
ACCORDING TO THIS, THERE'S BEEN NO SKRULL SIGHTINGS OUTSIDE OF THE CENTRAL PARK INCIDENT SINCE THE CENTRAL PARK INCIDENT.
THIS JARVIS COULD VERY WELL STILL BE IN THE CITY WITH NO WAY TO GET OUT.
THE BAD NEWS IS IT'S THE BIGGEST CITY IN THE WORLD AND HE COULD BE ANY SHAPE, SIZE OR SEX, HIDING IN ANY CORNER OF ANY BUILDING FROM SOHO TO HARLEM.
BECAUSE OF THE EMERGENCY, I'VE HACKED SOME INTELLIGENCE SATELLITES AND SOME STARKTECH FILES, AND I HAVEN'T SEEN ANY SUPER-SKRULL SIGHTINGS.
OR SEEN ANY UNIDENTIFIED POWERED PERSONS.
I'VE ALSO TAKEN MY SKRULL DETECTOR TECH AND I'VE HACKED INTO THE SATELLITE PROGRAMS.
IT SHOULD WARN US OF ANY SHAPE-SHIFT IN AND AROUND THE MID-TOWN AREA.
BUT THE SKRULLS KEPT THEIR IDENTITY A SECRET BY ***NOT*** SHAPE-SHIFTING.
THEY HOLD THEIR FORM AT A MICRO-BIOLOGICAL LEVEL. UNDETECTABLE BY OUR STANDARDS AND MEASUREMENTS.
IF HE DOESN'T SHAPE-SHIFT, WE MAY NOT BE ABLE TO FIND HIM.
WE CAN REPORT IT TO THE AUTHORITIES, BUT WITH THE CITY IN THE SHAPE IT'S IN, I'M NOT SURE WHAT THEY'LL BE ABLE TO DO...

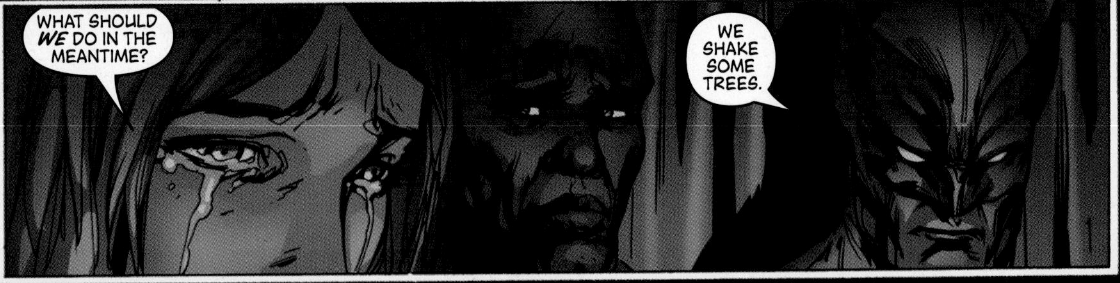
WHAT SHOULD ***WE*** DO IN THE MEANTIME?
WE SHAKE SOME TREES.

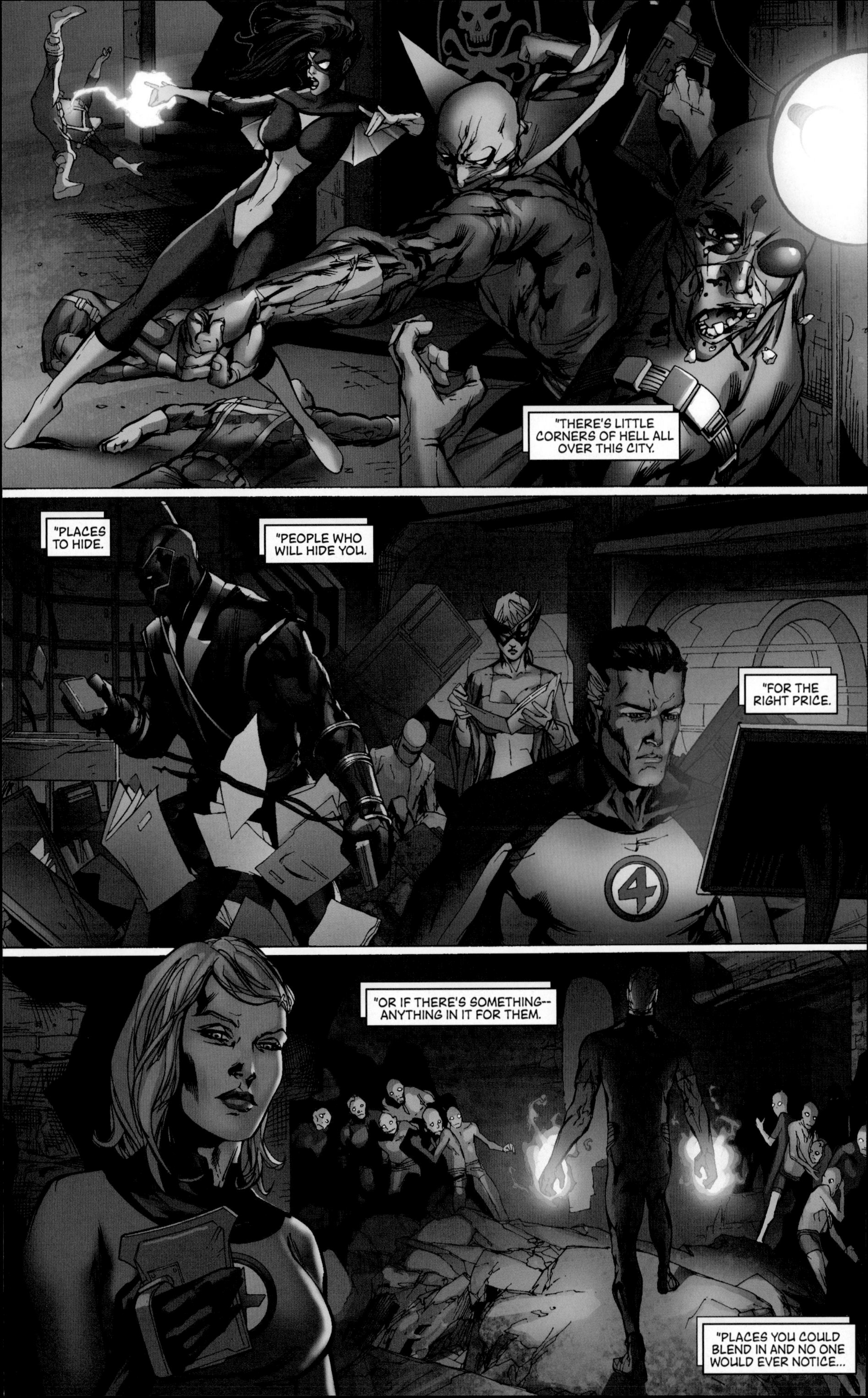

"THERE'S LITTLE CORNERS OF HELL ALL OVER THIS CITY.
"PLACES TO HIDE.
"PEOPLE WHO WILL HIDE YOU.
"FOR THE RIGHT PRICE.
"OR IF THERE'S SOMETHING-- ANYTHING IN IT FOR THEM.
"PLACES YOU COULD BLEND IN AND NO ONE WOULD EVER NOTICE...

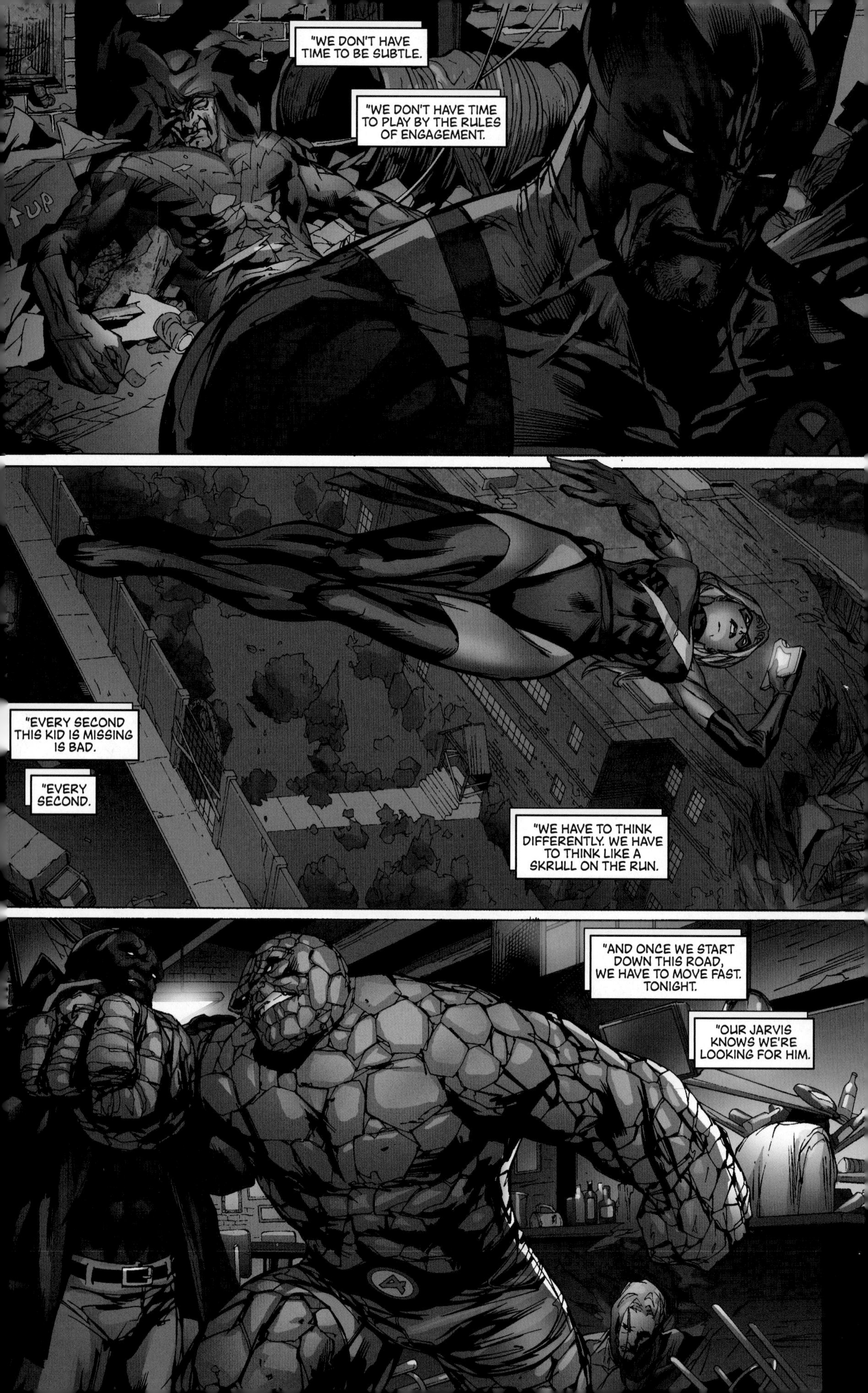
"WE DON'T HAVE TIME TO BE SUBTLE.
"WE DON'T HAVE TIME TO PLAY BY THE RULES OF ENGAGEMENT.
UP
"EVERY SECOND THIS KID IS MISSING IS BAD.
"EVERY SECOND.
"WE HAVE TO THINK DIFFERENTLY. WE HAVE TO THINK LIKE A SKRULL ON THE RUN.
"AND ONCE WE START DOWN THIS ROAD, WE HAVE TO MOVE FAST. TONIGHT.
"OUR JARVIS KNOWS WE'RE LOOKING FOR HIM.

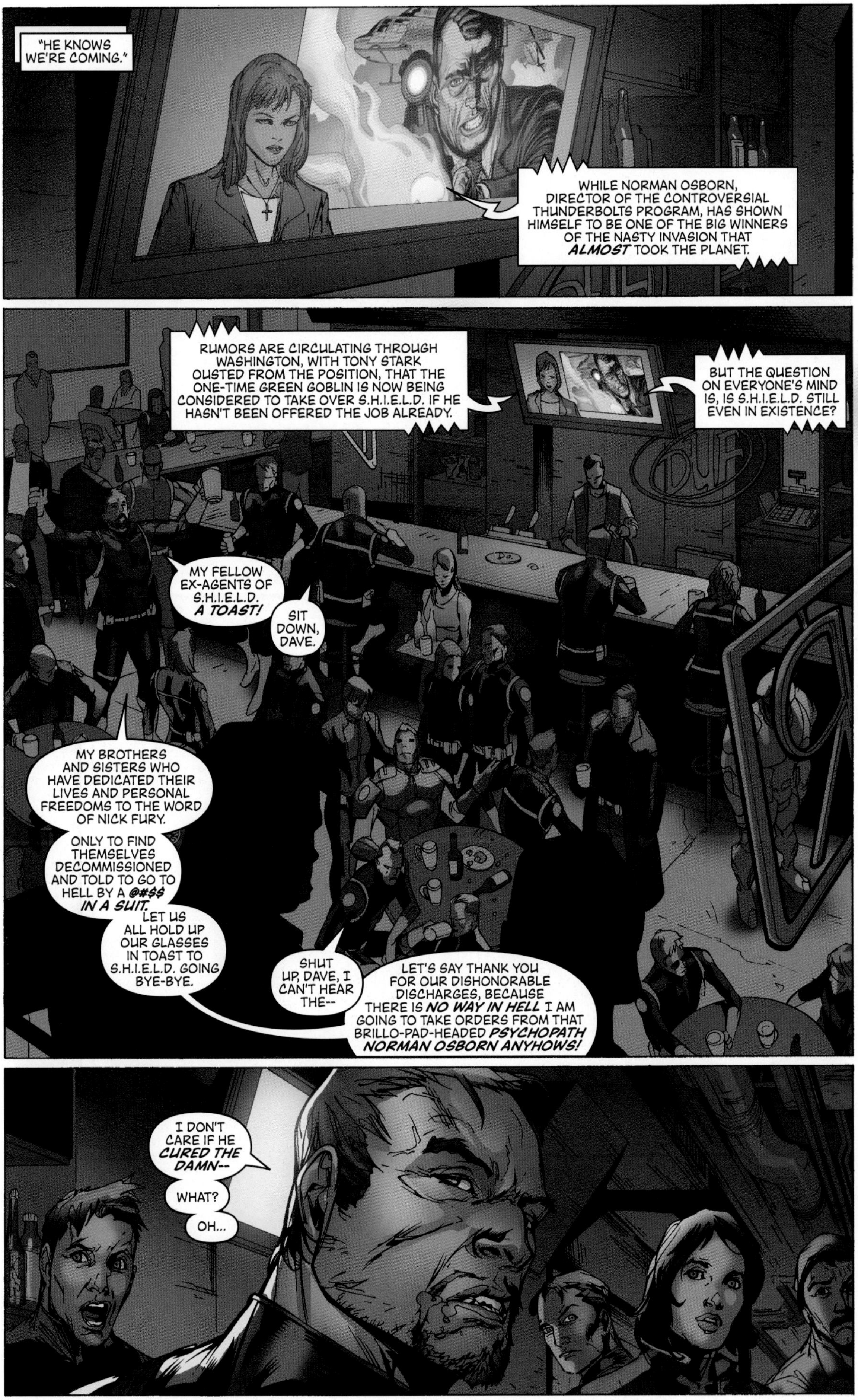
"HE KNOWS WE'RE COMING."
WHILE NORMAN OSBORN, DIRECTOR OF THE CONTROVERSIAL THUNDERBOLTS PROGRAM, HAS SHOWN HIMSELF TO BE ONE OF THE BIG WINNERS OF THE NASTY INVASION THAT *ALMOST* TOOK THE PLANET.
RUMORS ARE CIRCULATING THROUGH WASHINGTON, WITH TONY STARK OUSTED FROM THE POSITION, THAT THE ONE-TIME GREEN GOBLIN IS NOW BEING CONSIDERED TO TAKE OVER S.H.I.E.L.D. IF HE HASN'T BEEN OFFERED THE JOB ALREADY.
BUT THE QUESTION ON EVERYONE'S MIND IS, IS S.H.I.E.L.D. STILL EVEN IN EXISTENCE?
MY FELLOW EX-AGENTS OF S.H.I.E.L.D. *A TOAST!*
SIT DOWN, DAVE.
MY BROTHERS AND SISTERS WHO HAVE DEDICATED THEIR LIVES AND PERSONAL FREEDOMS TO THE WORD OF NICK FURY.
ONLY TO FIND THEMSELVES DECOMMISSIONED AND TOLD TO GO TO HELL BY A *@#$$ IN A SUIT.*
LET US ALL HOLD UP OUR GLASSES IN TOAST TO S.H.I.E.L.D. GOING BYE-BYE.
SHUT UP, DAVE, I CAN'T HEAR THE--
LET'S SAY THANK YOU FOR OUR DISHONORABLE DISCHARGES, BECAUSE THERE IS *NO WAY IN HELL* I AM GOING TO TAKE ORDERS FROM THAT BRILLO-PAD-HEADED *PSYCHOPATH NORMAN OSBORN ANYHOWS!*
I DON'T CARE IF HE *CURED THE DAMN--*
WHAT?
OH...

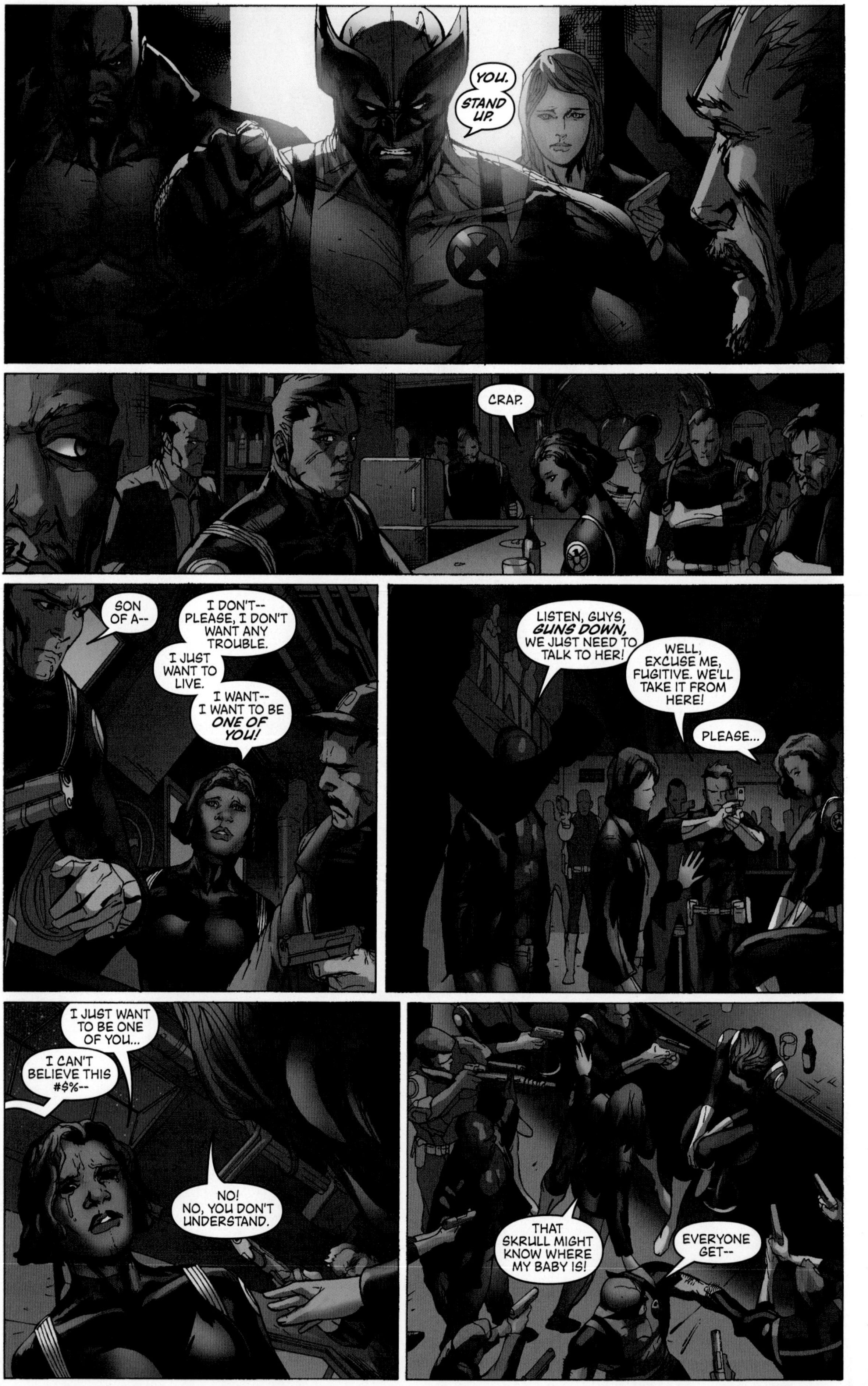
YOU.
STAND UP.
CRAP.
SON OF A--
I DON'T-- PLEASE, I DON'T WANT ANY TROUBLE.
I JUST WANT TO LIVE.
I WANT-- I WANT TO BE *ONE OF YOU!*
LISTEN, GUYS, *GUNS DOWN,* WE JUST NEED TO TALK TO HER!
WELL, EXCUSE ME, FUGITIVE. WE'LL TAKE IT FROM HERE!
PLEASE...
I JUST WANT TO BE ONE OF YOU...
I CAN'T BELIEVE THIS #$%--
NO! NO, YOU DON'T UNDERSTAND.
THAT SKRULL MIGHT KNOW WHERE MY BABY IS!
EVERYONE GET--

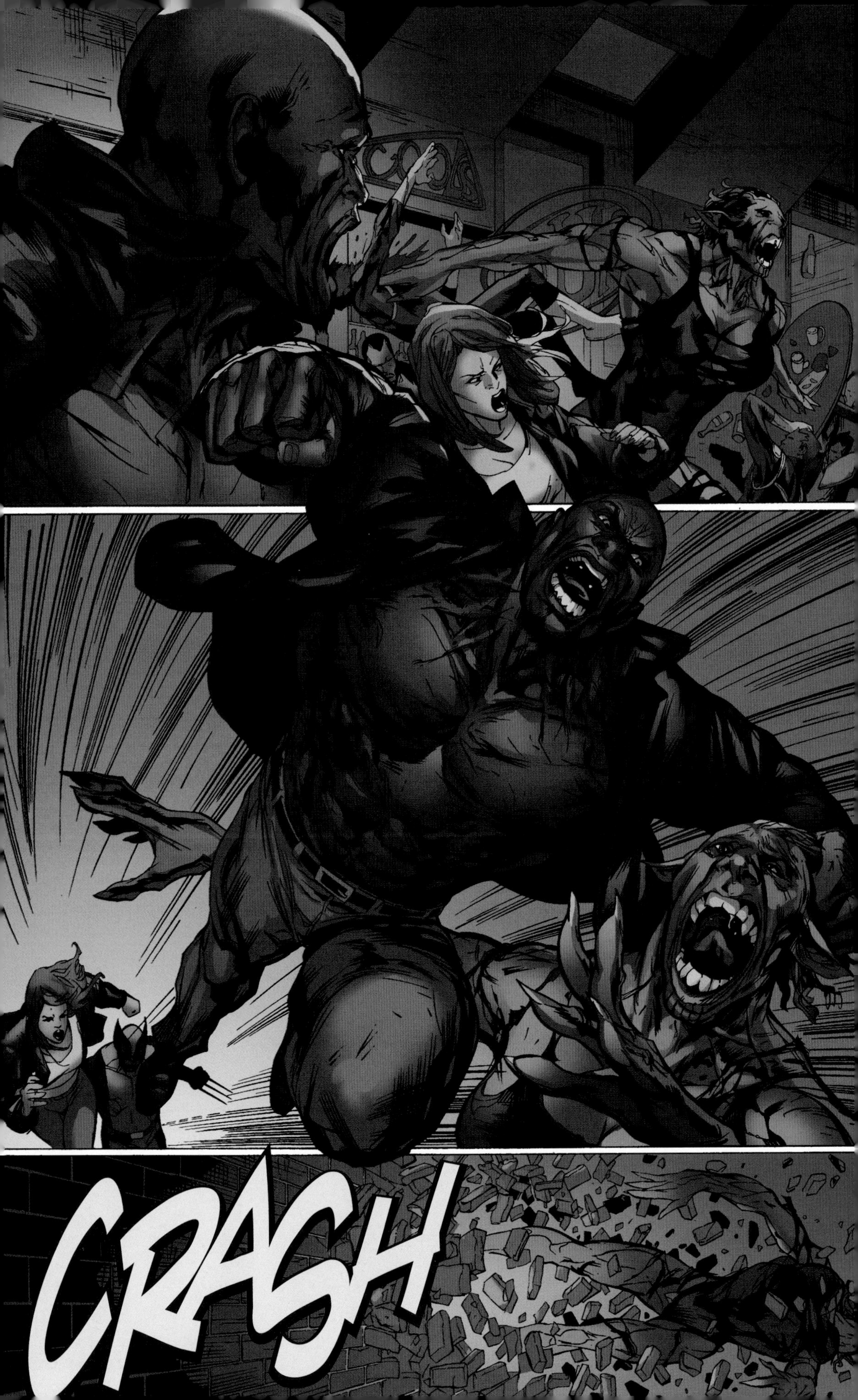
CRASH

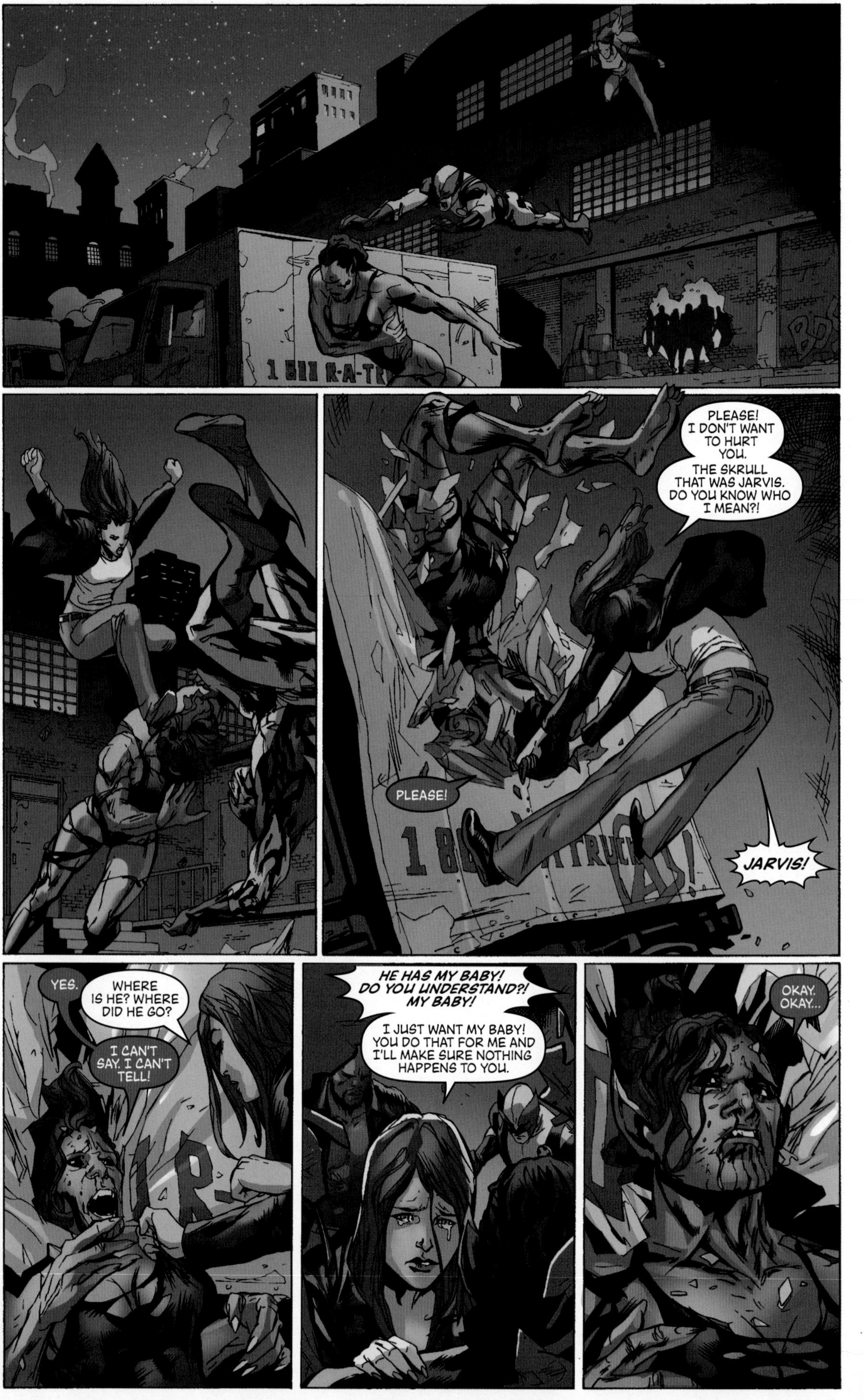
1 8 R-A-T
PLEASE! I DON'T WANT TO HURT YOU. THE SKRULL THAT WAS JARVIS. DO YOU KNOW WHO I MEAN?!
PLEASE!
JARVIS!
YES.
WHERE IS HE? WHERE DID HE GO?
I CAN'T SAY. I CAN'T TELL!
HE HAS MY BABY! DO YOU UNDERSTAND?! MY BABY!
I JUST WANT MY BABY! YOU DO THAT FOR ME AND I'LL MAKE SURE NOTHING HAPPENS TO YOU.
OKAY. OKAY...

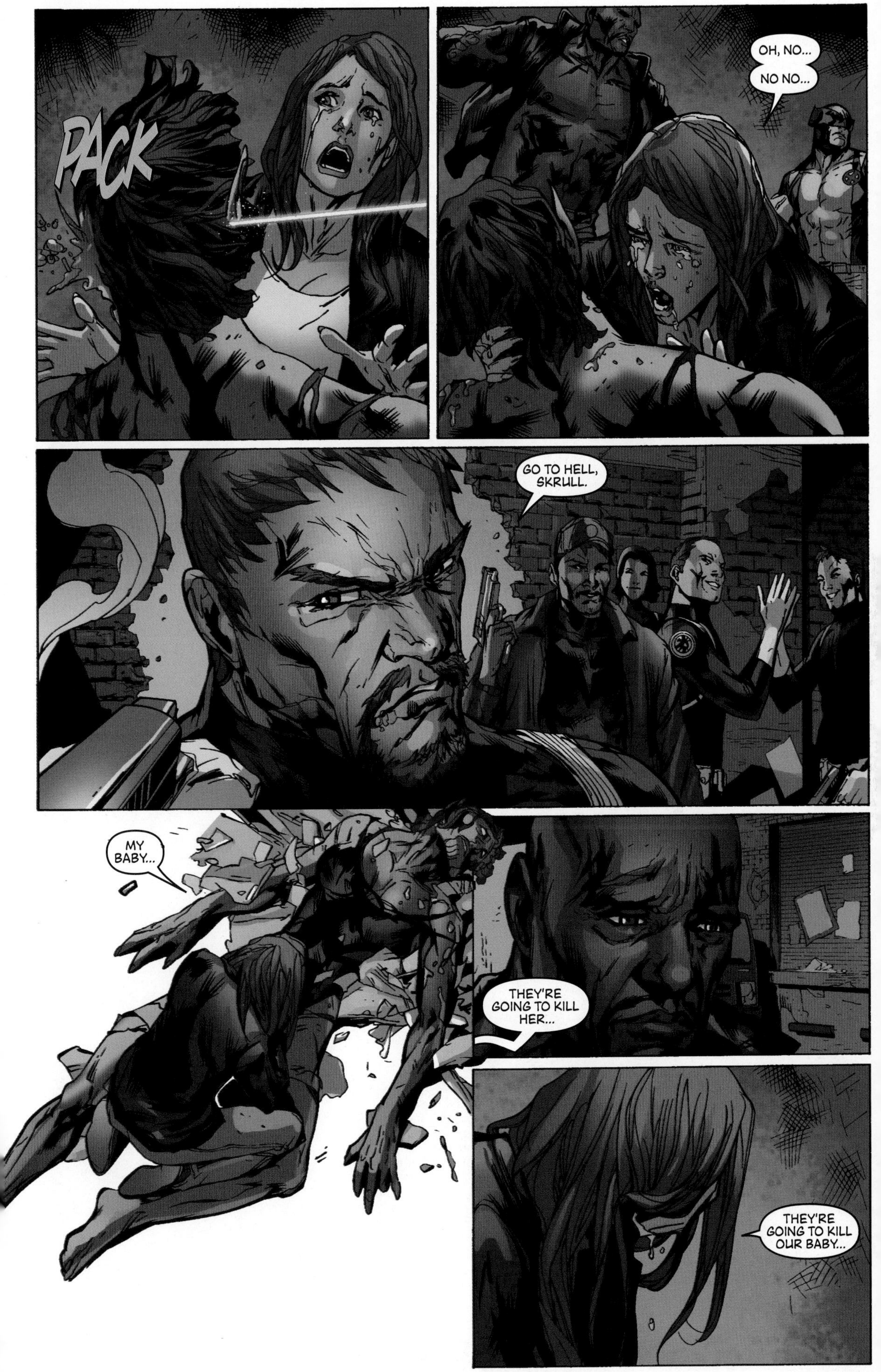
PACK
OH, NO...
NO NO...
GO TO HELL, SKRULL.
MY BABY...
THEY'RE GOING TO KILL HER...
THEY'RE GOING TO KILL OUR BABY...

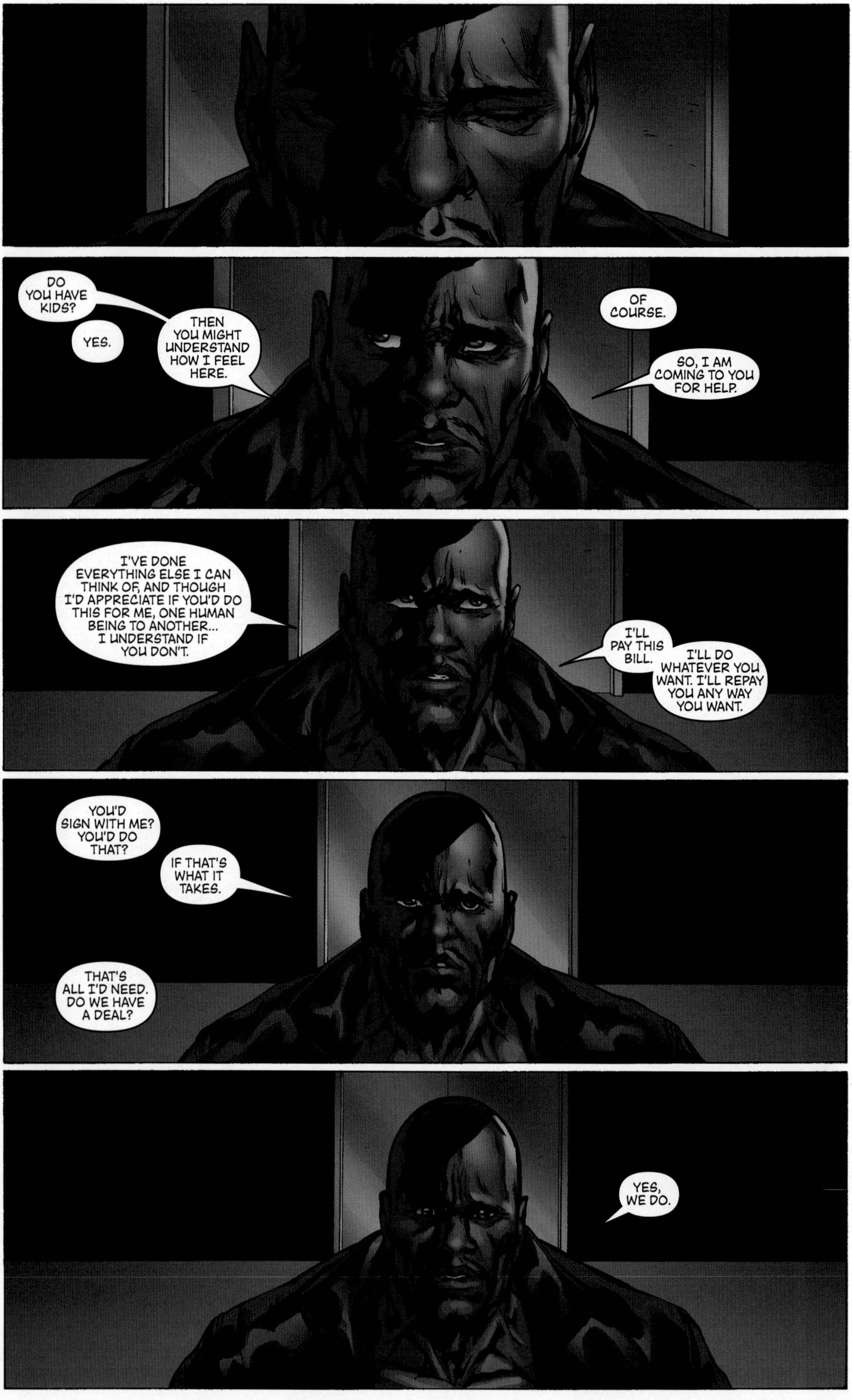
DO YOU HAVE KIDS?
YES.
THEN YOU MIGHT UNDERSTAND HOW I FEEL HERE.
OF COURSE.
SO, I AM COMING TO YOU FOR HELP.
I'VE DONE EVERYTHING ELSE I CAN THINK OF, AND THOUGH I'D APPRECIATE IF YOU'D DO THIS FOR ME, ONE HUMAN BEING TO ANOTHER... I UNDERSTAND IF YOU DON'T.
I'LL PAY THIS BILL.
I'LL DO WHATEVER YOU WANT. I'LL REPAY YOU ANY WAY YOU WANT.
YOU'D SIGN WITH ME? YOU'D DO THAT?
IF THAT'S WHAT IT TAKES.
THAT'S ALL I'D NEED. DO WE HAVE A DEAL?
YES, WE DO.

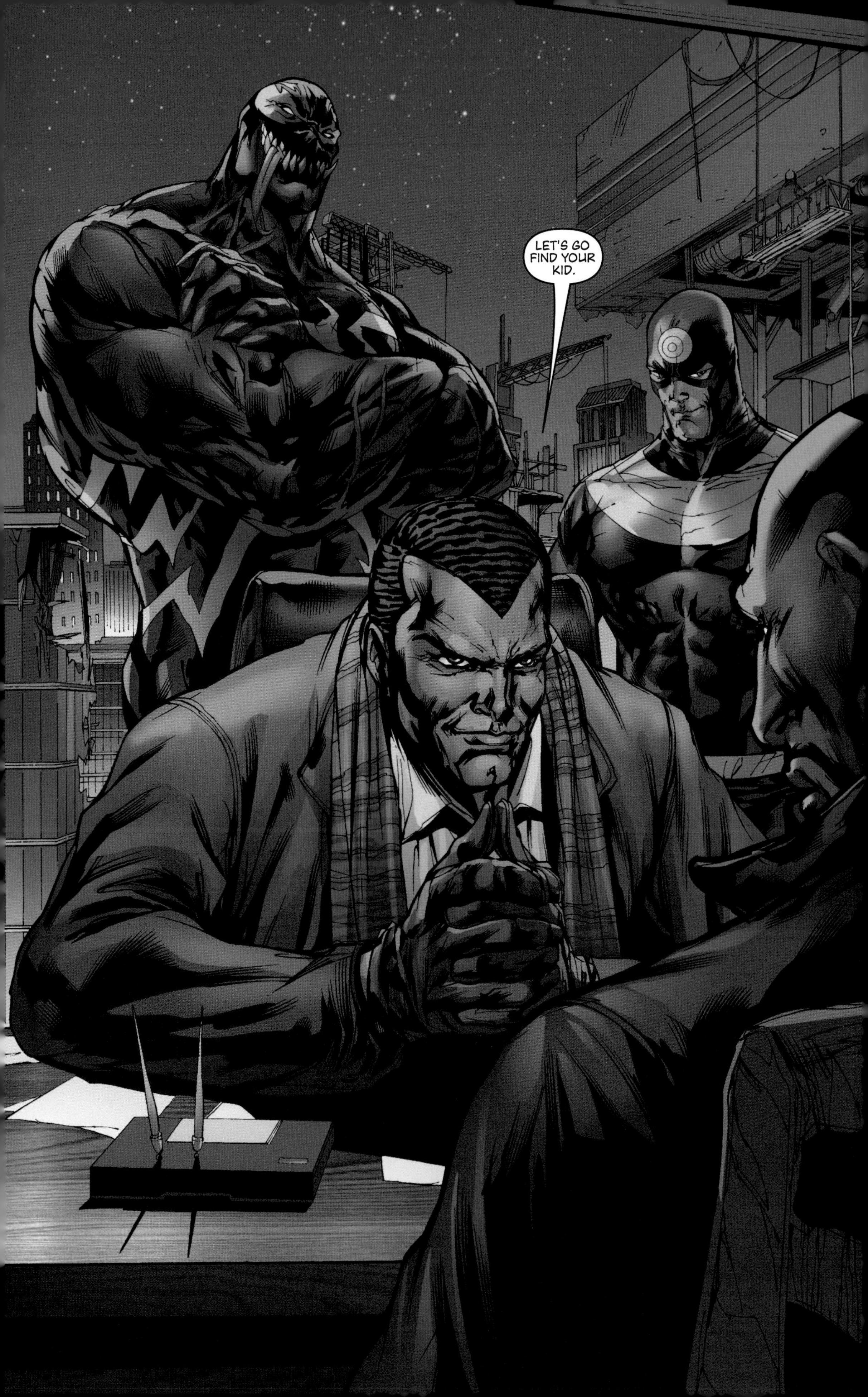
LET'S GO FIND YOUR KID.

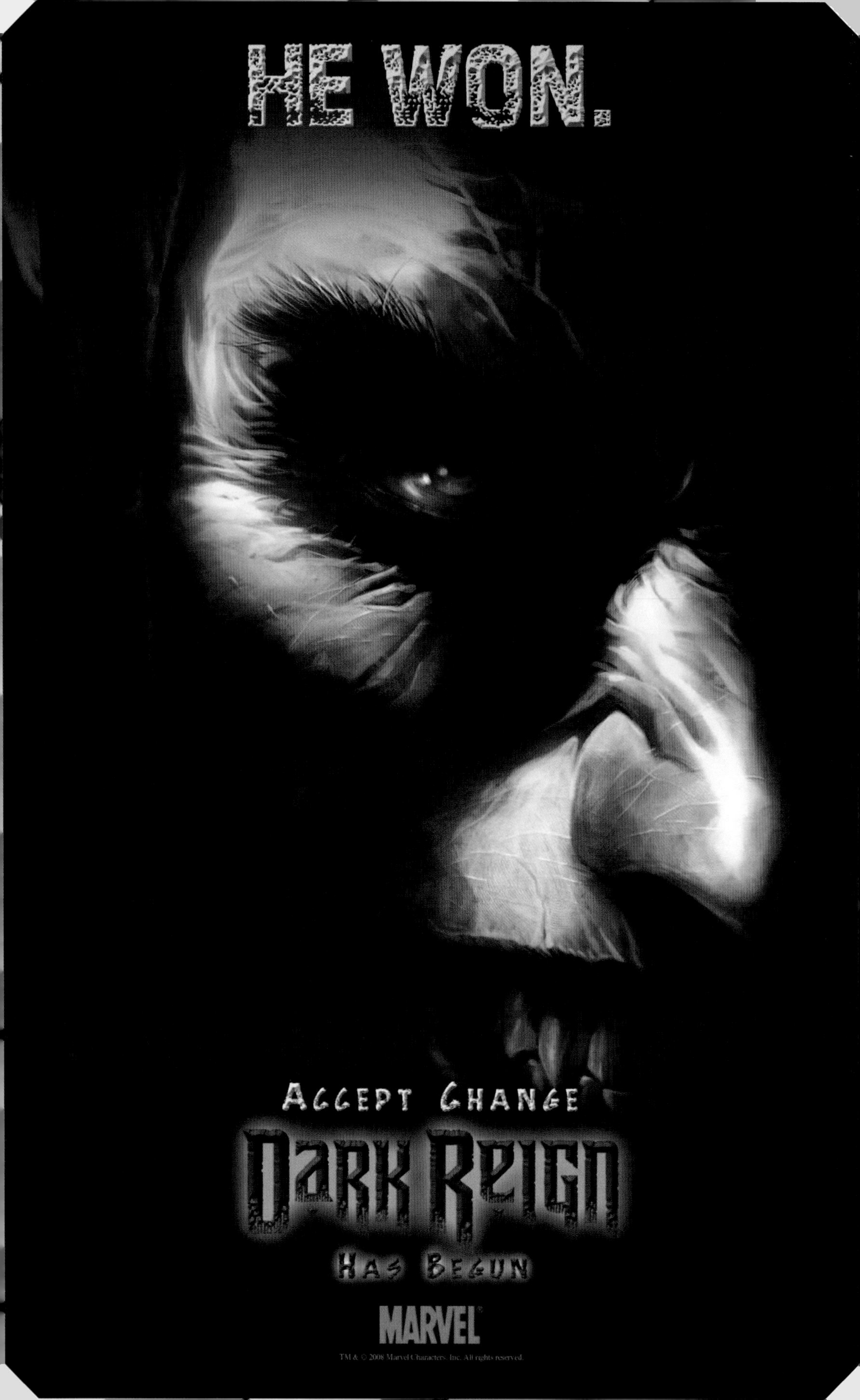
HE WON.
ACCEPT CHANGE
DARK REIGN
HAS BEGUN
MARVEL
TM & © 2008 Marvel Characters, Inc. All rights reserved.

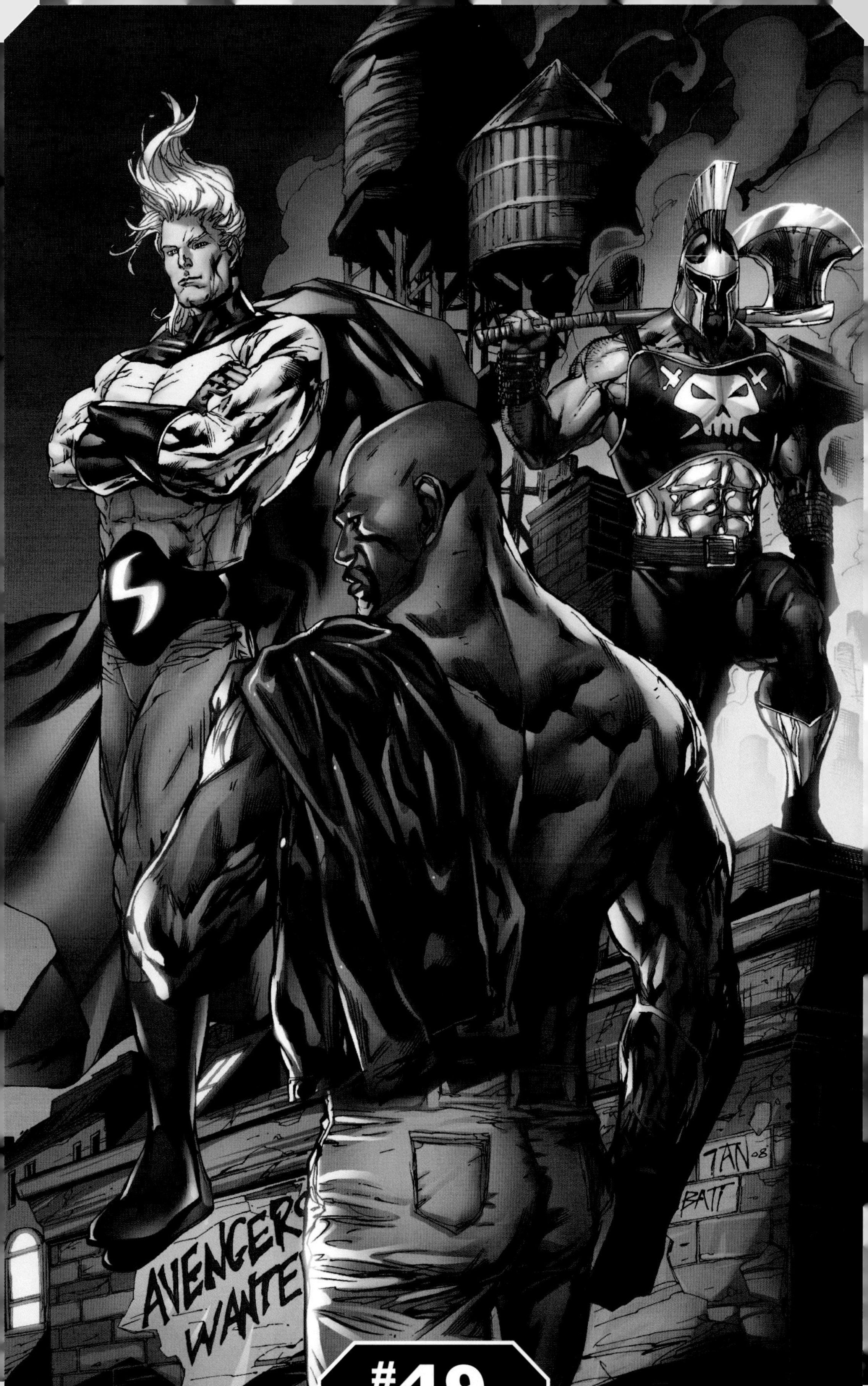
AVENGERS
WANTE
TAN '08
BATT

#49

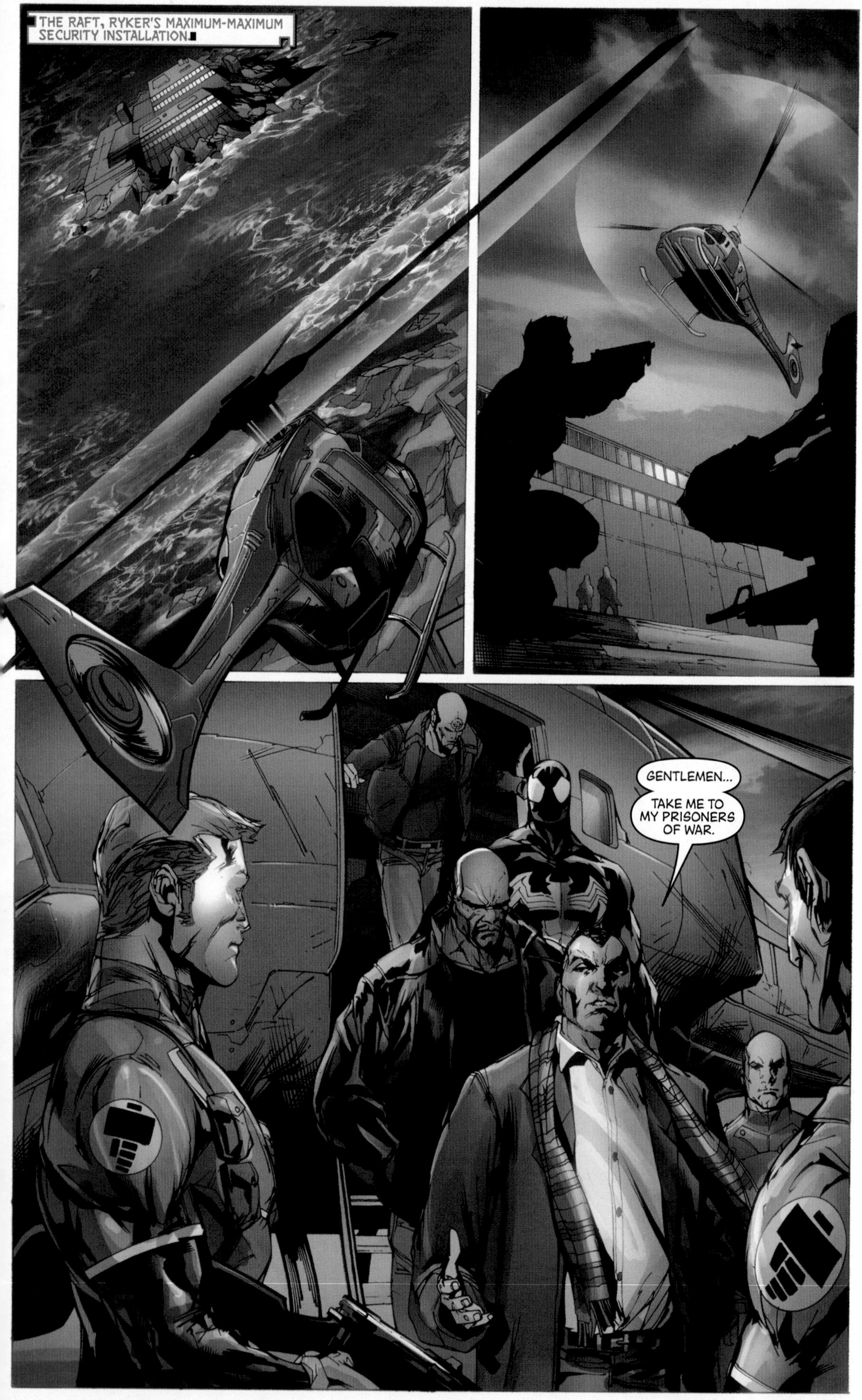
THE RAFT, RYKER'S MAXIMUM-MAXIMUM SECURITY INSTALLATION.
GENTLEMEN...
TAKE ME TO MY PRISONERS OF WAR.

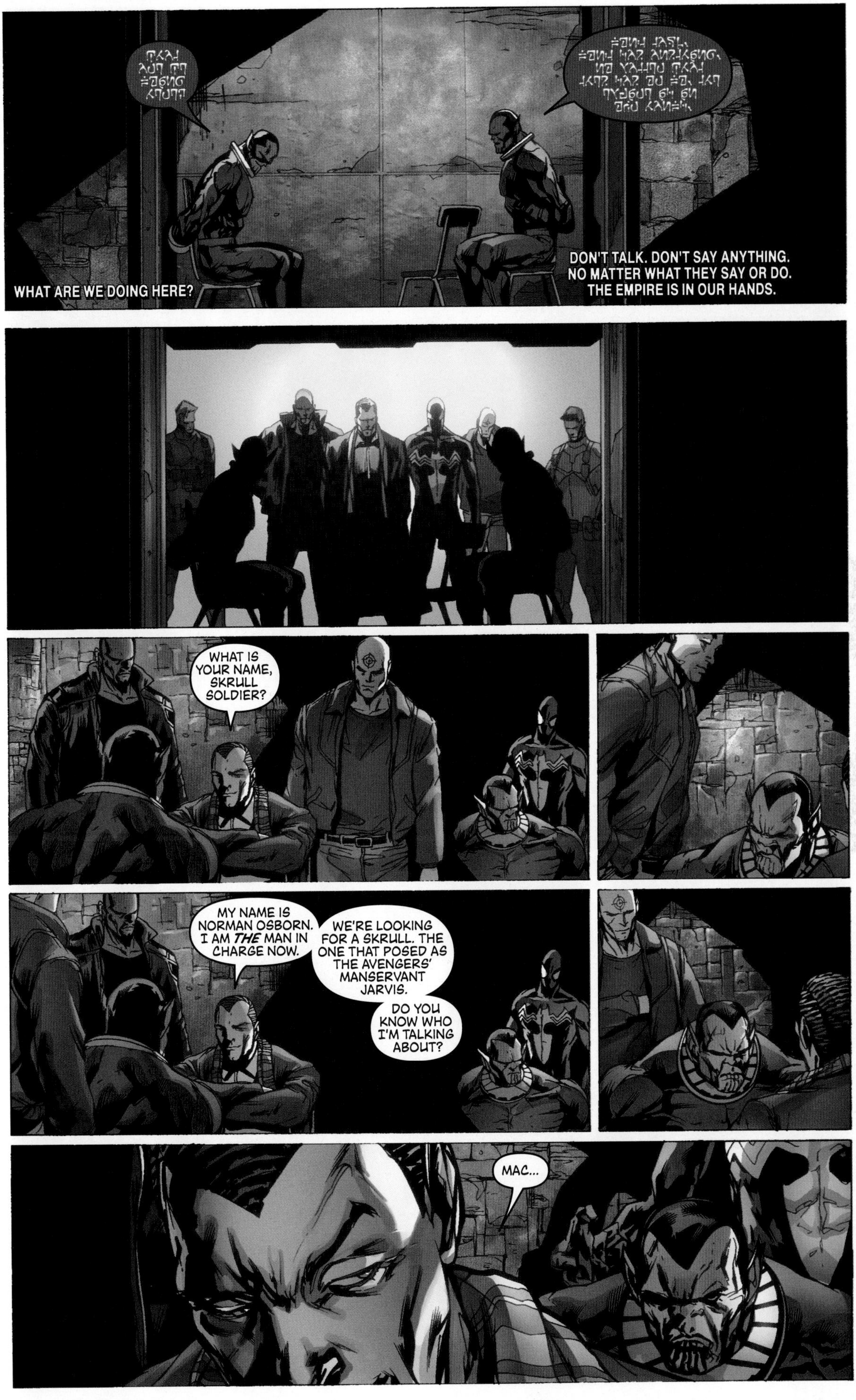
WHAT ARE WE DOING HERE?
DON'T TALK. DON'T SAY ANYTHING. NO MATTER WHAT THEY SAY OR DO. THE EMPIRE IS IN OUR HANDS.
WHAT IS YOUR NAME, SKRULL SOLDIER?
MY NAME IS NORMAN OSBORN. I AM *THE* MAN IN CHARGE NOW.
WE'RE LOOKING FOR A SKRULL. THE ONE THAT POSED AS THE AVENGERS' MANSERVANT JARVIS.
DO YOU KNOW WHO I'M TALKING ABOUT?
MAC...

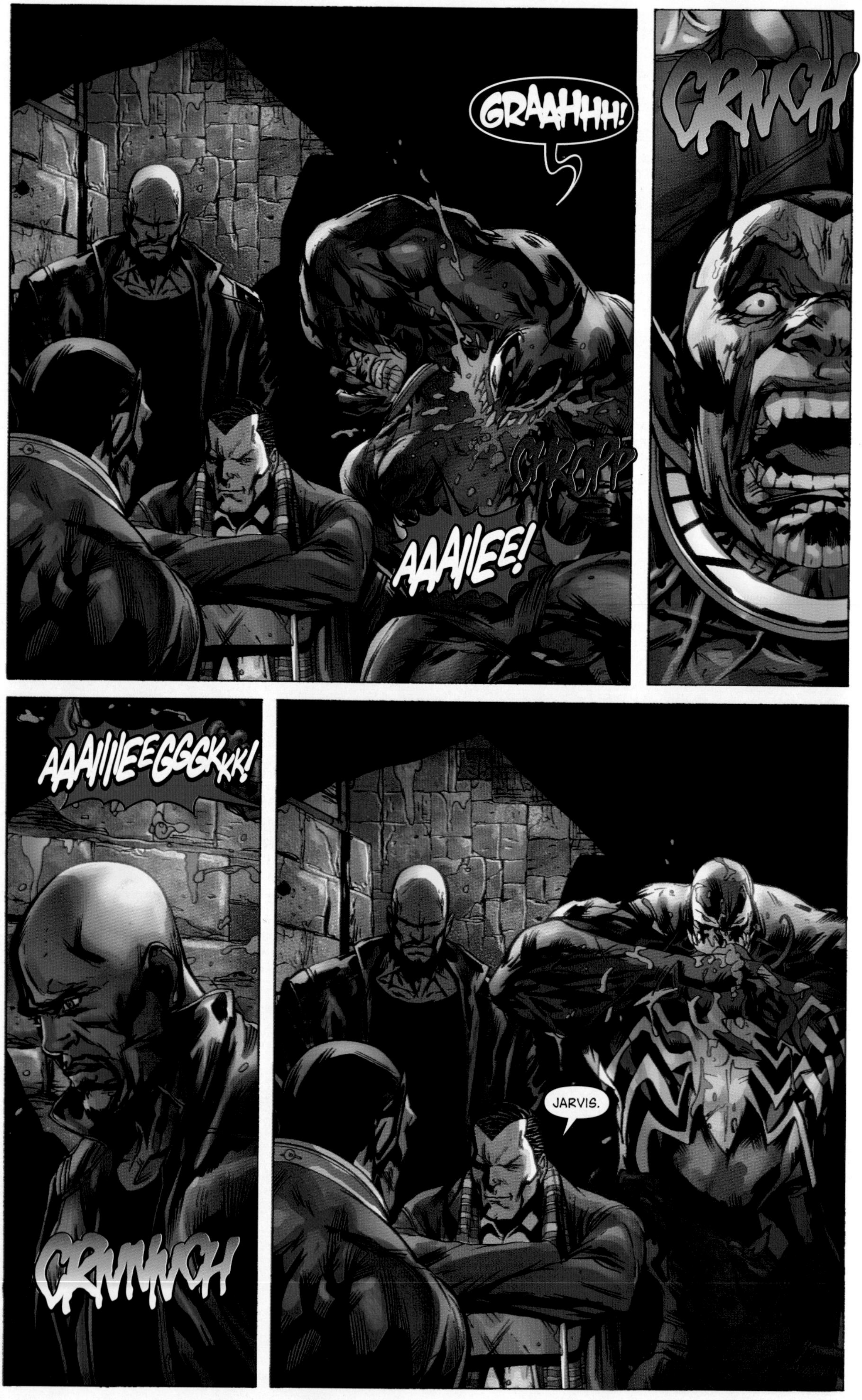
GRAAHHH!
CHOMP
AAAIIEE!
CRUNCH
AAAIIIIEEGGGKKK!
CRUNNCH
JARVIS.

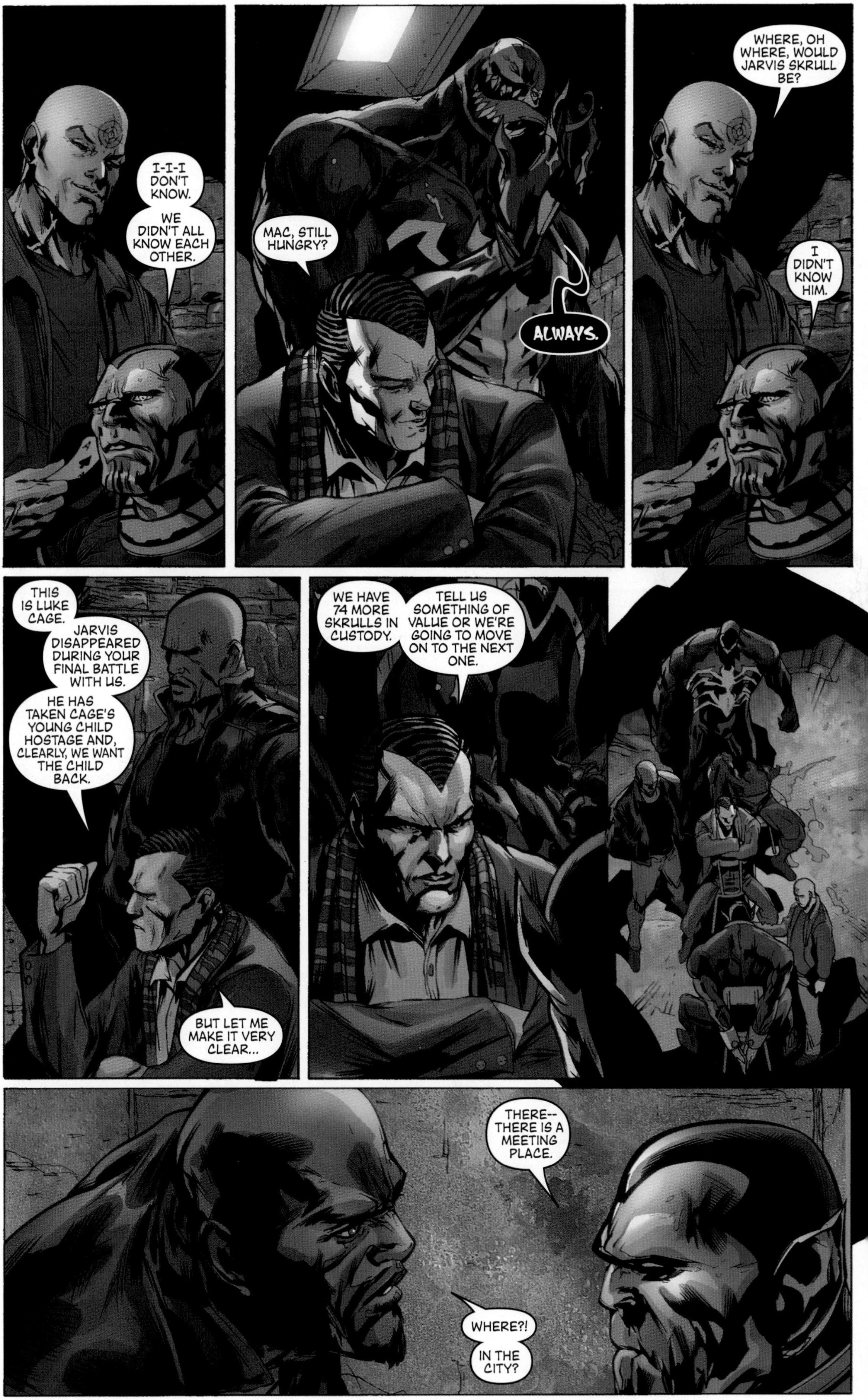
I-I-I DON'T KNOW.
WE DIDN'T ALL KNOW EACH OTHER.
MAC, STILL HUNGRY?
ALWAYS.
WHERE, OH WHERE, WOULD JARVIS SKRULL BE?
I DIDN'T KNOW HIM.
THIS IS LUKE CAGE.
JARVIS DISAPPEARED DURING YOUR FINAL BATTLE WITH US.
HE HAS TAKEN CAGE'S YOUNG CHILD HOSTAGE AND, CLEARLY, WE WANT THE CHILD BACK.
BUT LET ME MAKE IT VERY CLEAR...
WE HAVE 74 MORE SKRULLS IN CUSTODY.
TELL US SOMETHING OF VALUE OR WE'RE GOING TO MOVE ON TO THE NEXT ONE.
THERE-- THERE IS A MEETING PLACE.
WHERE?!
IN THE CITY?

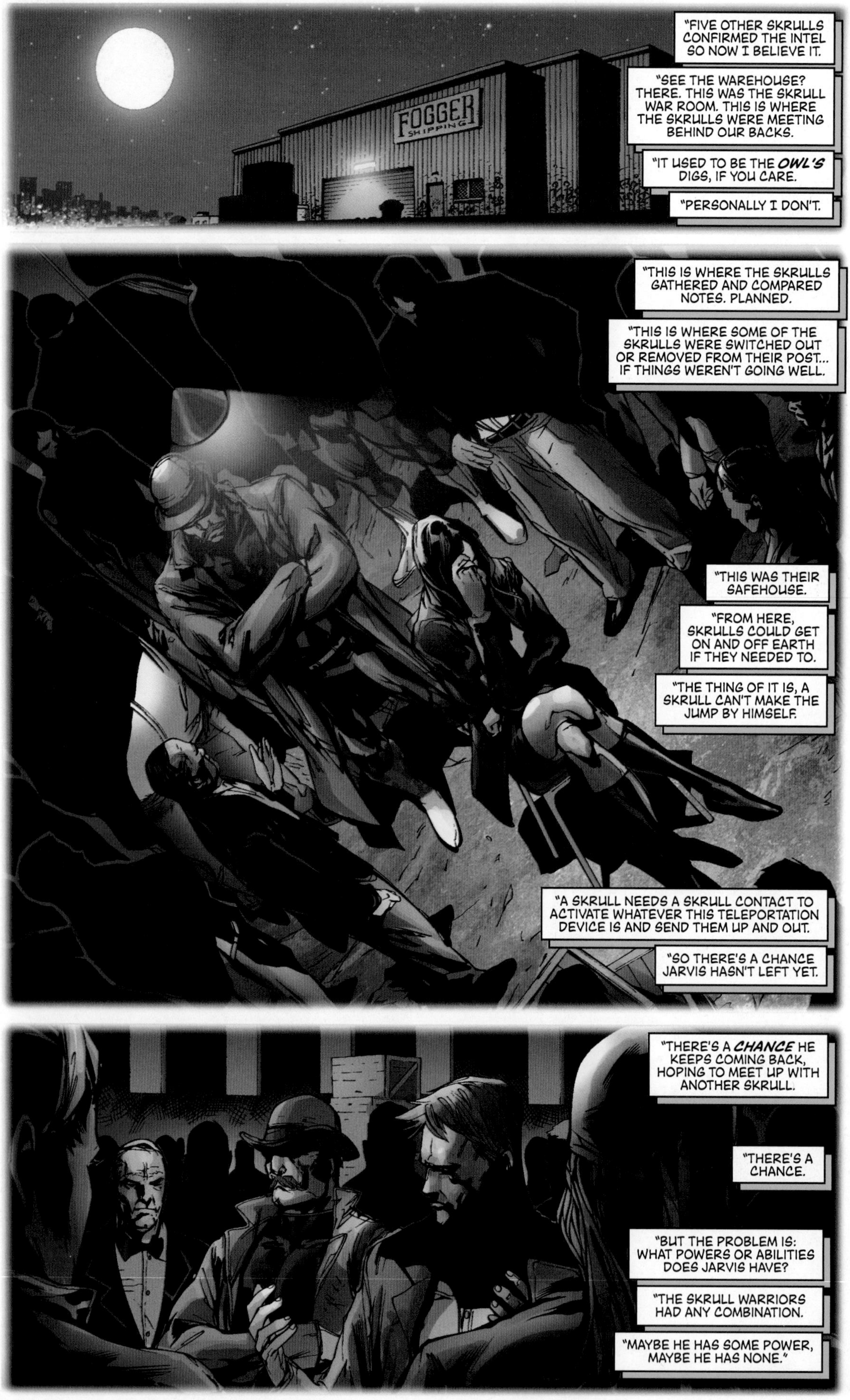
"FIVE OTHER SKRULLS CONFIRMED THE INTEL SO NOW I BELIEVE IT.
FOGGER SHIPPING
"SEE THE WAREHOUSE? THERE. THIS WAS THE SKRULL WAR ROOM. THIS IS WHERE THE SKRULLS WERE MEETING BEHIND OUR BACKS.
"IT USED TO BE THE *OWL'S* DIGS, IF YOU CARE.
"PERSONALLY I DON'T.
"THIS IS WHERE THE SKRULLS GATHERED AND COMPARED NOTES. PLANNED.
"THIS IS WHERE SOME OF THE SKRULLS WERE SWITCHED OUT OR REMOVED FROM THEIR POST... IF THINGS WEREN'T GOING WELL.
"THIS WAS THEIR SAFEHOUSE.
"FROM HERE, SKRULLS COULD GET ON AND OFF EARTH IF THEY NEEDED TO.
"THE THING OF IT IS, A SKRULL CAN'T MAKE THE JUMP BY HIMSELF.
"A SKRULL NEEDS A SKRULL CONTACT TO ACTIVATE WHATEVER THIS TELEPORTATION DEVICE IS AND SEND THEM UP AND OUT.
"SO THERE'S A CHANCE JARVIS HASN'T LEFT YET.
"THERE'S A *CHANCE* HE KEEPS COMING BACK, HOPING TO MEET UP WITH ANOTHER SKRULL.
"THERE'S A CHANCE.
"BUT THE PROBLEM IS: WHAT POWERS OR ABILITIES DOES JARVIS HAVE?
"THE SKRULL WARRIORS HAD ANY COMBINATION.
"MAYBE HE HAS SOME POWER, MAYBE HE HAS NONE."

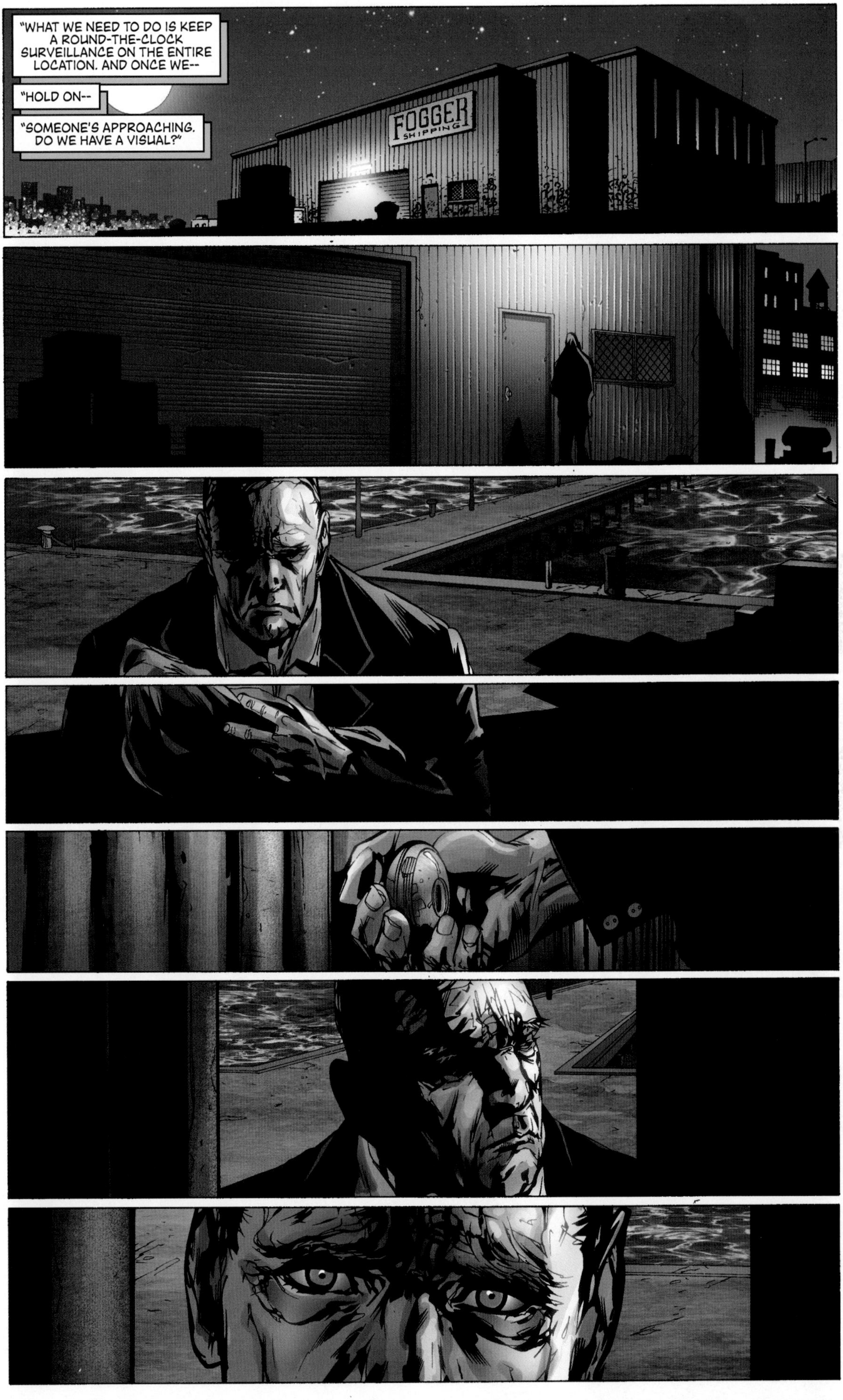
"WHAT WE NEED TO DO IS KEEP A ROUND-THE-CLOCK SURVEILLANCE ON THE ENTIRE LOCATION. AND ONCE WE--
"HOLD ON--
"SOMEONE'S APPROACHING. DO WE HAVE A VISUAL?"
FOGGER SHIPPING

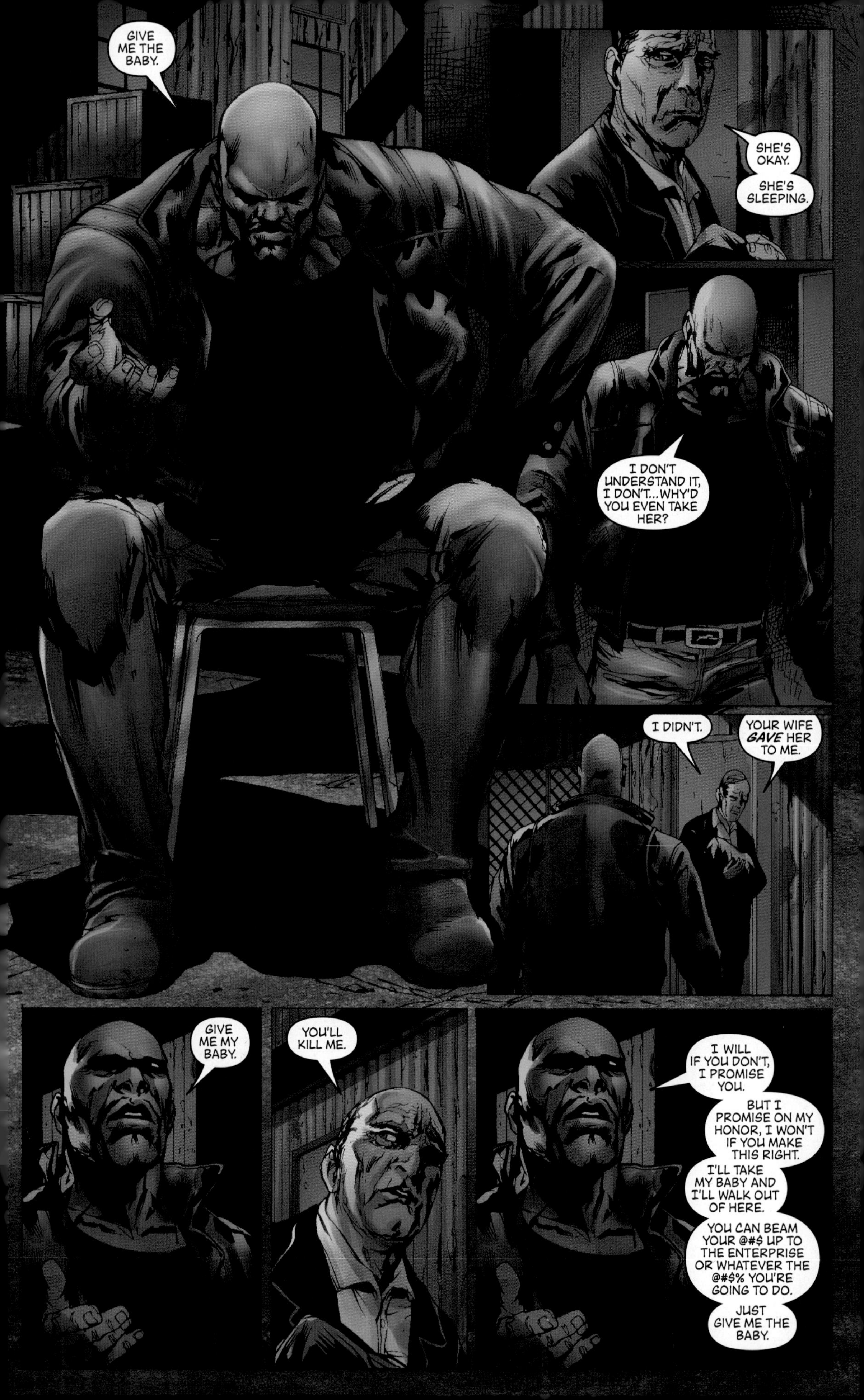
GIVE ME THE BABY.
SHE'S OKAY.
SHE'S SLEEPING.
I DON'T UNDERSTAND IT, I DON'T...WHY'D YOU EVEN TAKE HER?
I DIDN'T.
YOUR WIFE GAVE HER TO ME.
GIVE ME MY BABY.
YOU'LL KILL ME.
I WILL IF YOU DON'T, I PROMISE YOU.
BUT I PROMISE ON MY HONOR, I WON'T IF YOU MAKE THIS RIGHT.
I'LL TAKE MY BABY AND I'LL WALK OUT OF HERE.
YOU CAN BEAM YOUR @#$ UP TO THE ENTERPRISE OR WHATEVER THE @#$% YOU'RE GOING TO DO.
JUST GIVE ME THE BABY.

YOU--YOU DIDN'T COME ALONE.

AIN'T NO ONE ELSE HERE.

YOU TELL OSBORN TO RELEASE THE PRISONERS.

HE--HE RELEASES THEM ALL AND *THEN* YOU GET THE BABY! WE'LL LEAVE. ALL OF US.

THIS AIN'T A SWAP MEET. GIVE ME MY BABY.

MY PEOPLE ARE *DESTROYED!*

NOTHIN' TO DO WITH ME. NOTHING TO DO WITH THAT LITTLE BABY.

I DON'T CARE... ABOUT ANY OF IT. JUST WANT MY KID.

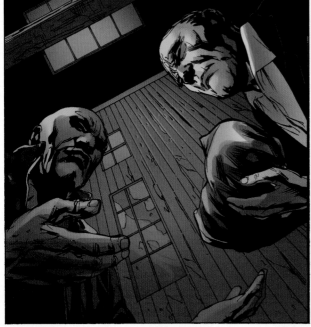

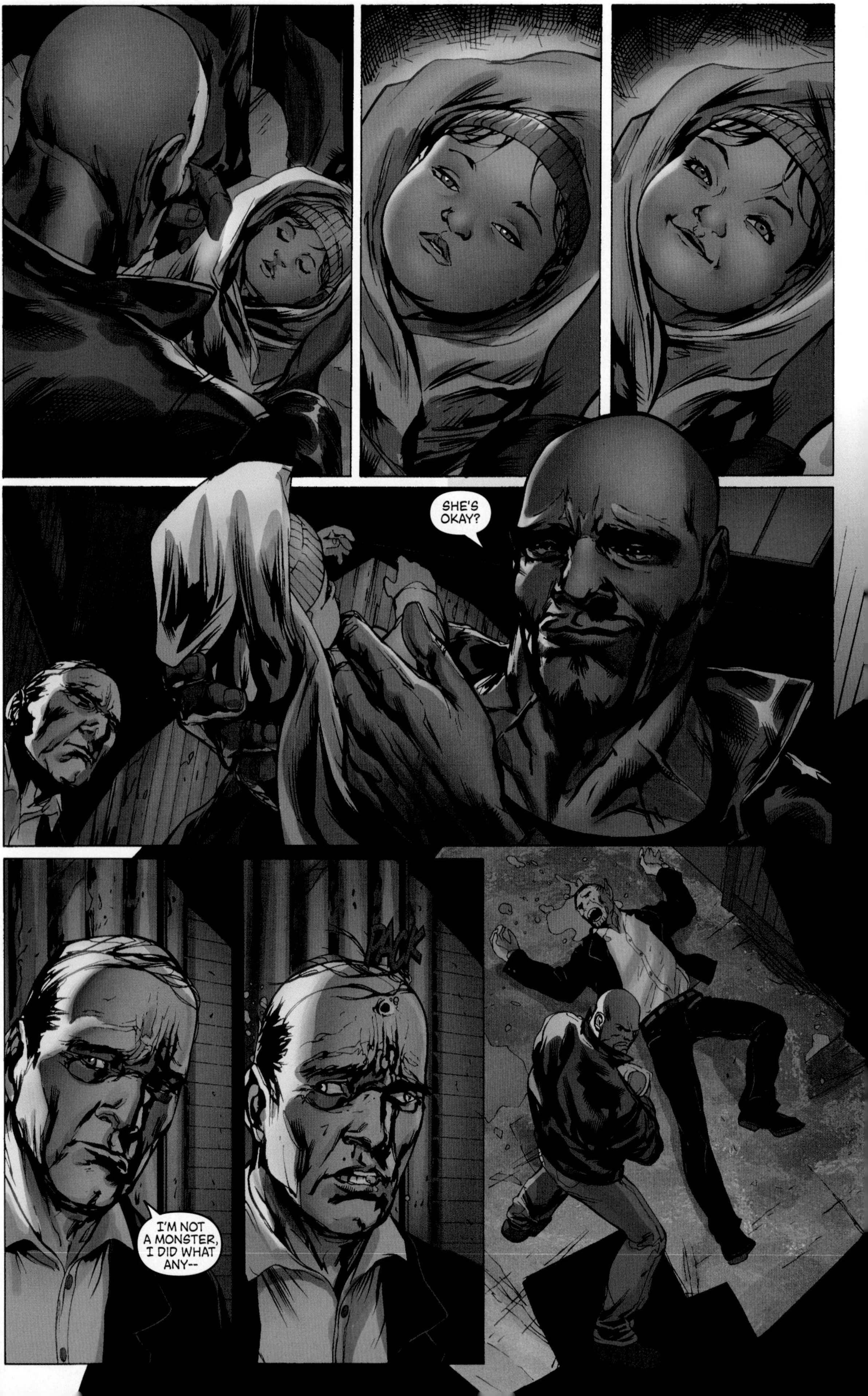
SHE'S OKAY?
I'M NOT A MONSTER, I DID WHAT ANY--

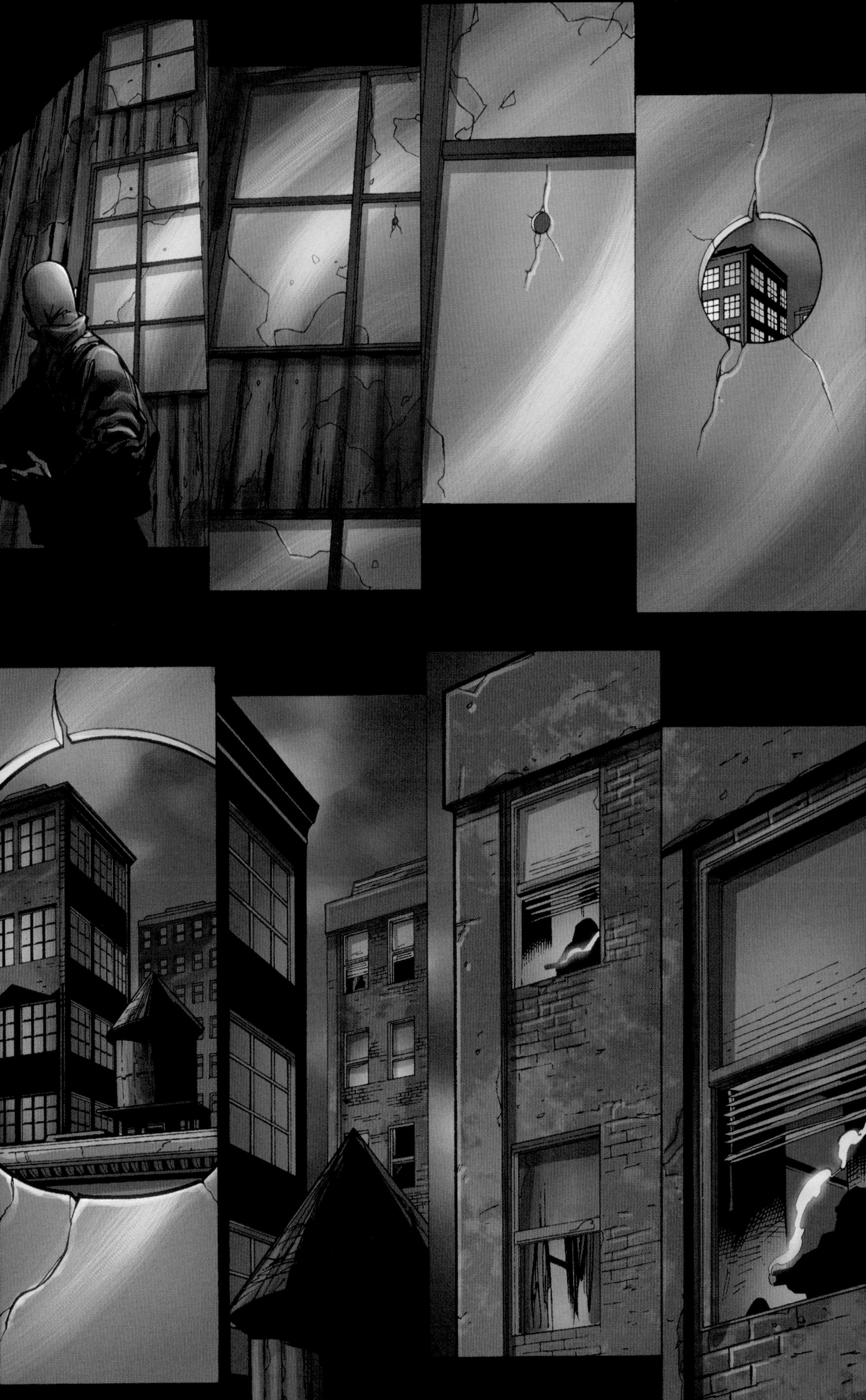

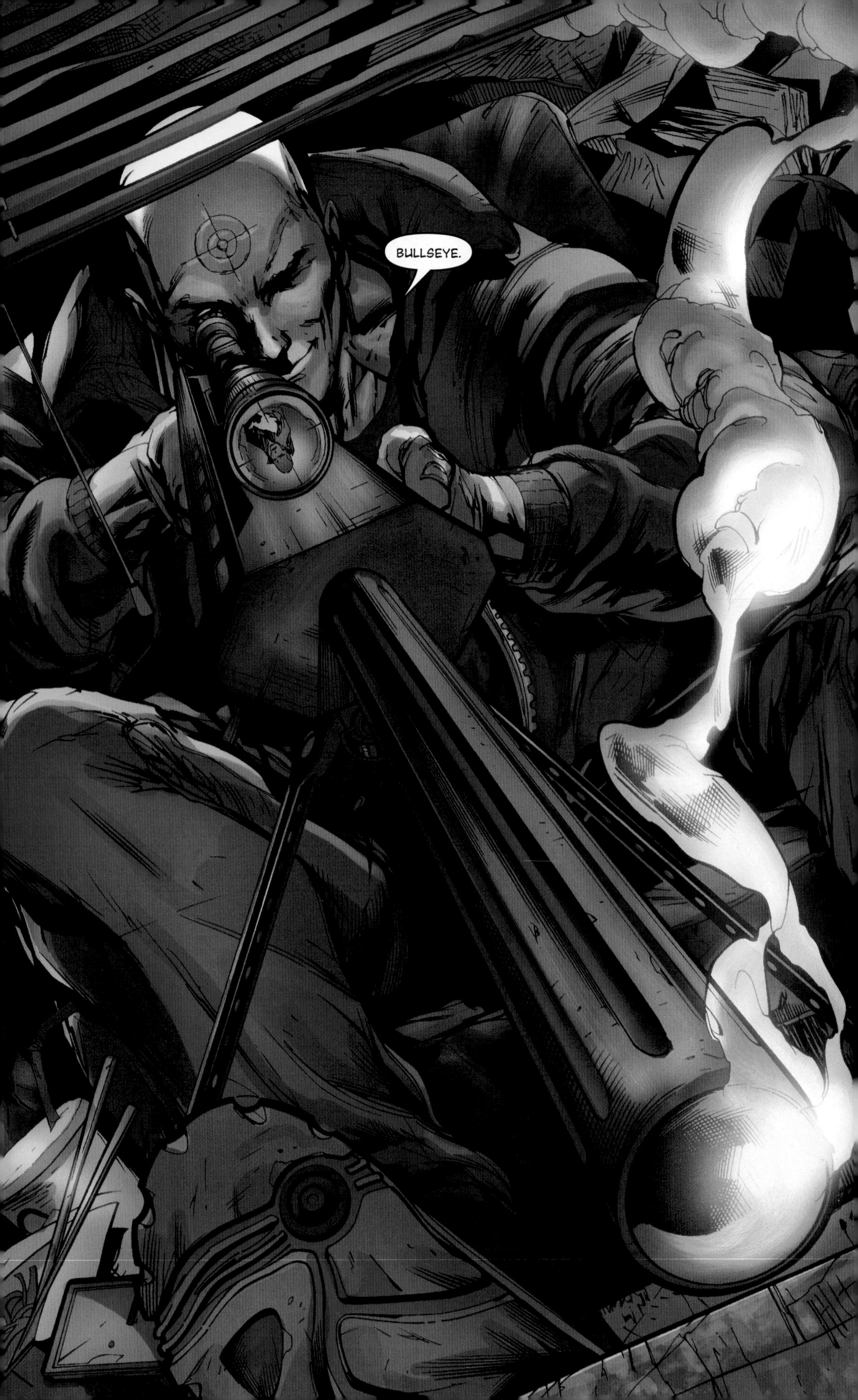
BULLSEYE.

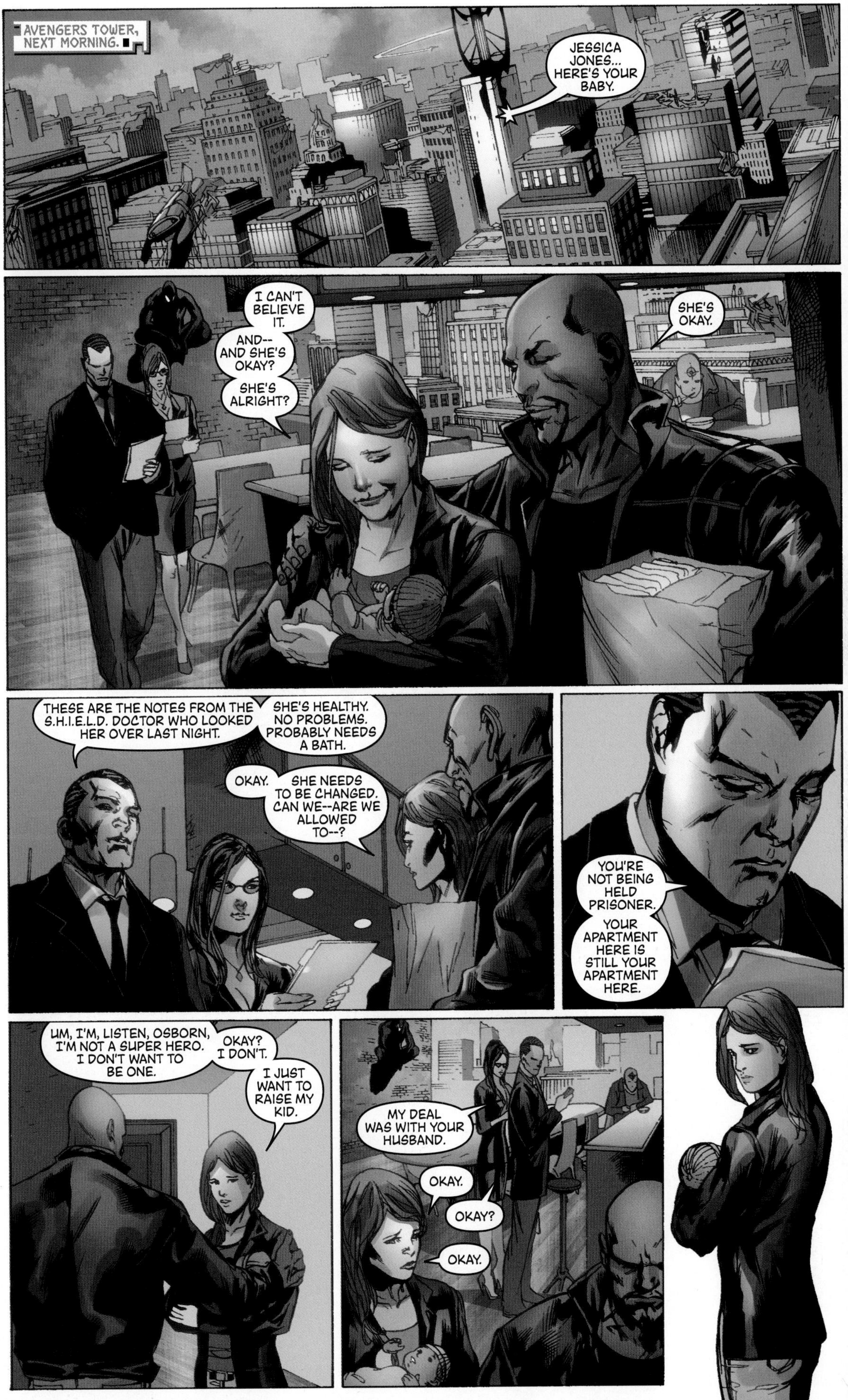
AVENGERS TOWER, NEXT MORNING.
JESSICA JONES... HERE'S YOUR BABY.
I CAN'T BELIEVE IT.
AND-- AND SHE'S OKAY?
SHE'S ALRIGHT?
SHE'S OKAY.
THESE ARE THE NOTES FROM THE S.H.I.E.L.D. DOCTOR WHO LOOKED HER OVER LAST NIGHT.
SHE'S HEALTHY. NO PROBLEMS. PROBABLY NEEDS A BATH.
OKAY.
SHE NEEDS TO BE CHANGED. CAN WE--ARE WE ALLOWED TO--?
YOU'RE NOT BEING HELD PRISONER.
YOUR APARTMENT HERE IS STILL YOUR APARTMENT HERE.
UM, I'M, LISTEN, OSBORN, I'M NOT A SUPER HERO. I DON'T WANT TO BE ONE.
OKAY? I DON'T.
I JUST WANT TO RAISE MY KID.
MY DEAL WAS WITH YOUR HUSBAND.
OKAY.
OKAY?
OKAY.

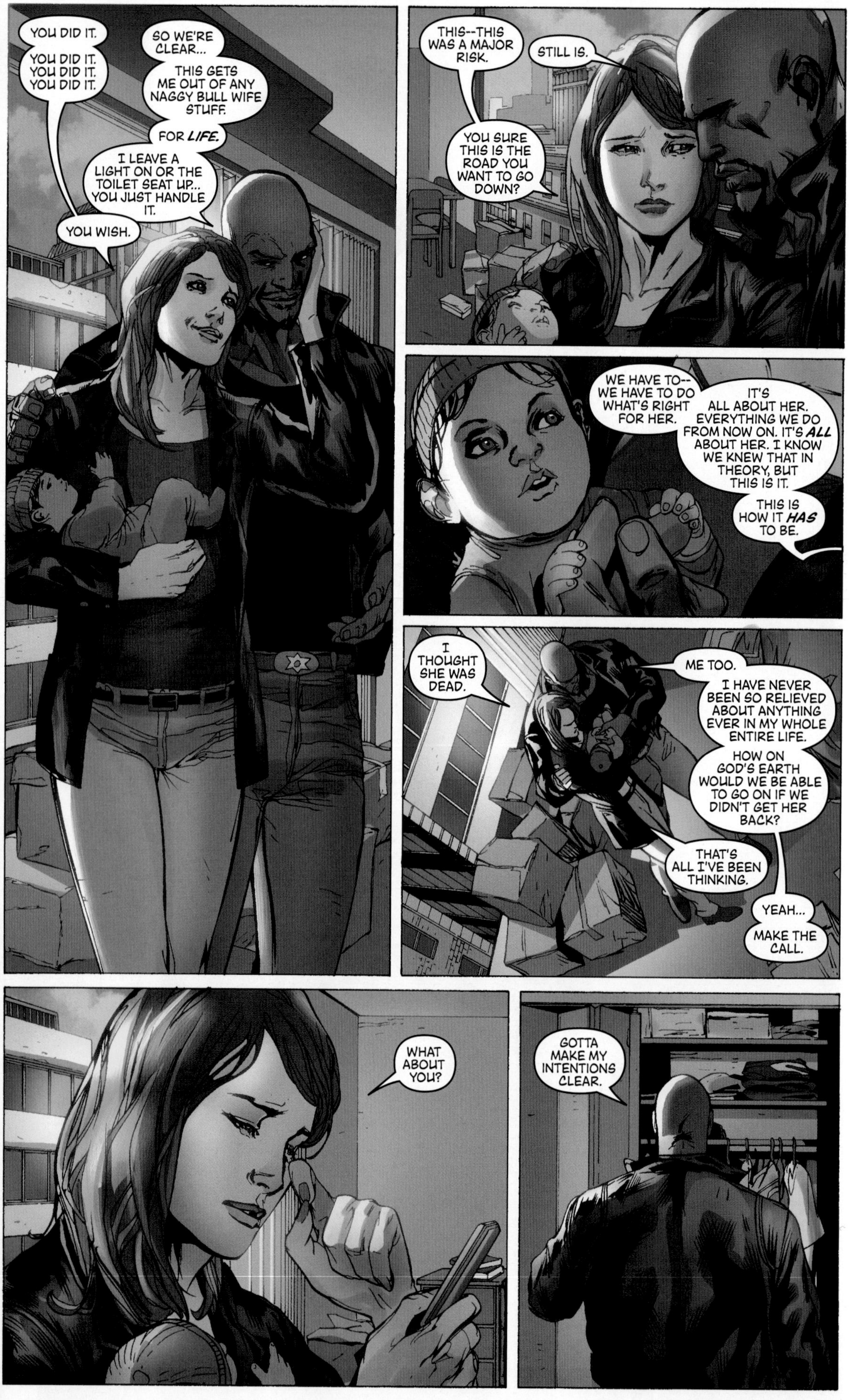

YOU DID IT.
YOU DID IT. YOU DID IT. YOU DID IT.
SO WE'RE CLEAR...
THIS GETS ME OUT OF ANY NAGGY BULL WIFE STUFF.
FOR LIFE.
I LEAVE A LIGHT ON OR THE TOILET SEAT UP... YOU JUST HANDLE IT.
YOU WISH.
THIS--THIS WAS A MAJOR RISK.
STILL IS.
YOU SURE THIS IS THE ROAD YOU WANT TO GO DOWN?
WE HAVE TO-- WE HAVE TO DO WHAT'S RIGHT FOR HER.
IT'S ALL ABOUT HER. EVERYTHING WE DO FROM NOW ON. IT'S ALL ABOUT HER. I KNOW WE KNEW THAT IN THEORY, BUT THIS IS IT.
THIS IS HOW IT HAS TO BE.
I THOUGHT SHE WAS DEAD.
ME TOO.
I HAVE NEVER BEEN SO RELIEVED ABOUT ANYTHING EVER IN MY WHOLE ENTIRE LIFE.
HOW ON GOD'S EARTH WOULD WE BE ABLE TO GO ON IF WE DIDN'T GET HER BACK?
THAT'S ALL I'VE BEEN THINKING.
YEAH...
MAKE THE CALL.
WHAT ABOUT YOU?
GOTTA MAKE MY INTENTIONS CLEAR.

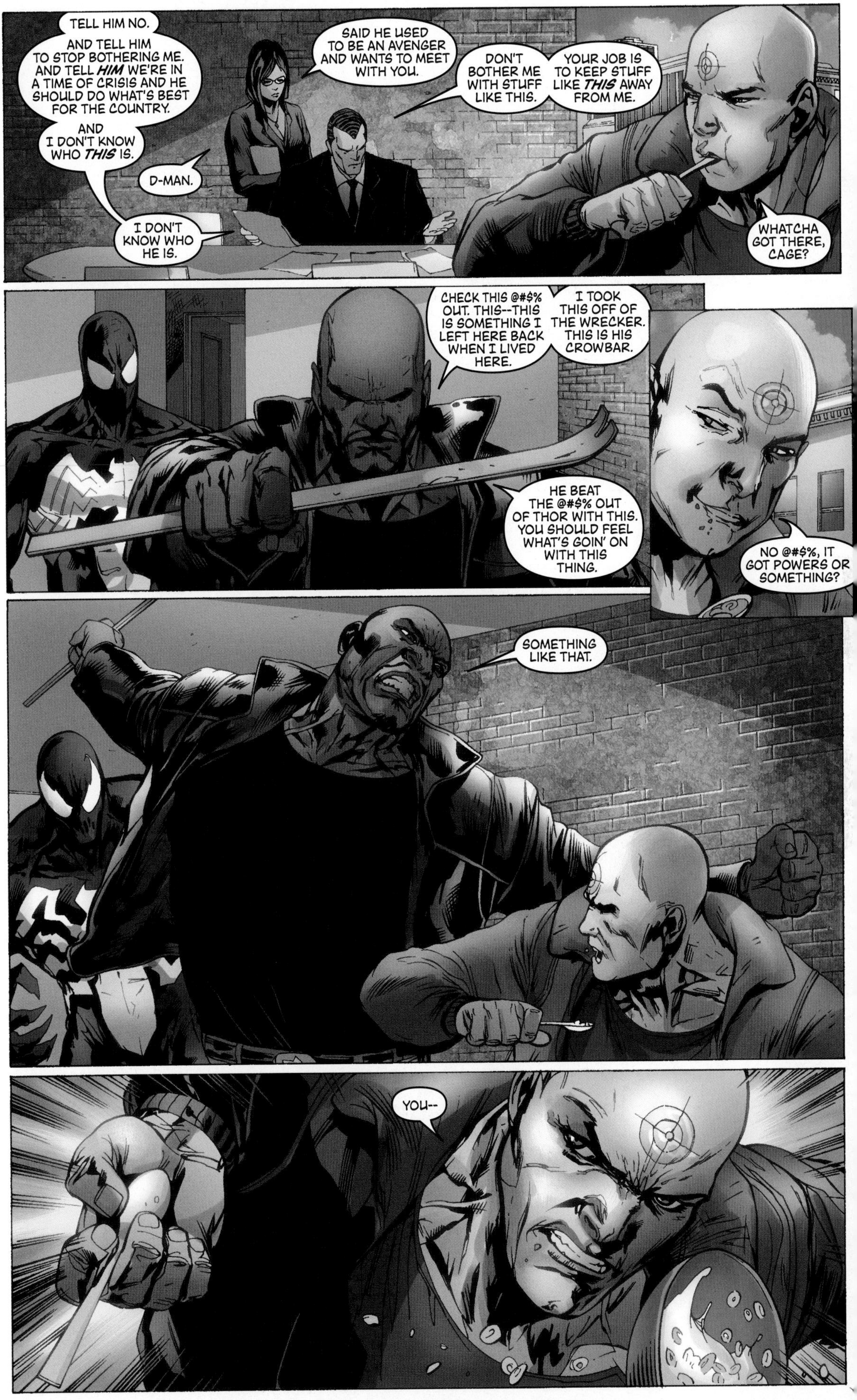
TELL HIM NO.
AND TELL HIM TO STOP BOTHERING ME. AND TELL *HIM* WE'RE IN A TIME OF CRISIS AND HE SHOULD DO WHAT'S BEST FOR THE COUNTRY.
AND I DON'T KNOW WHO *THIS* IS.
SAID HE USED TO BE AN AVENGER AND WANTS TO MEET WITH YOU.
DON'T BOTHER ME WITH STUFF LIKE THIS.
YOUR JOB IS TO KEEP STUFF LIKE *THIS* AWAY FROM ME.
D-MAN.
I DON'T KNOW WHO HE IS.
WHATCHA GOT THERE, CAGE?
CHECK THIS @#$% OUT. THIS--THIS IS SOMETHING I LEFT HERE BACK WHEN I LIVED HERE.
I TOOK THIS OFF OF THE WRECKER. THIS IS HIS CROWBAR.
HE BEAT THE @#$% OUT OF THOR WITH THIS. YOU SHOULD FEEL WHAT'S GOIN' ON WITH THIS THING.
NO @#$%, IT GOT POWERS OR SOMETHING?
SOMETHING LIKE THAT.
YOU--

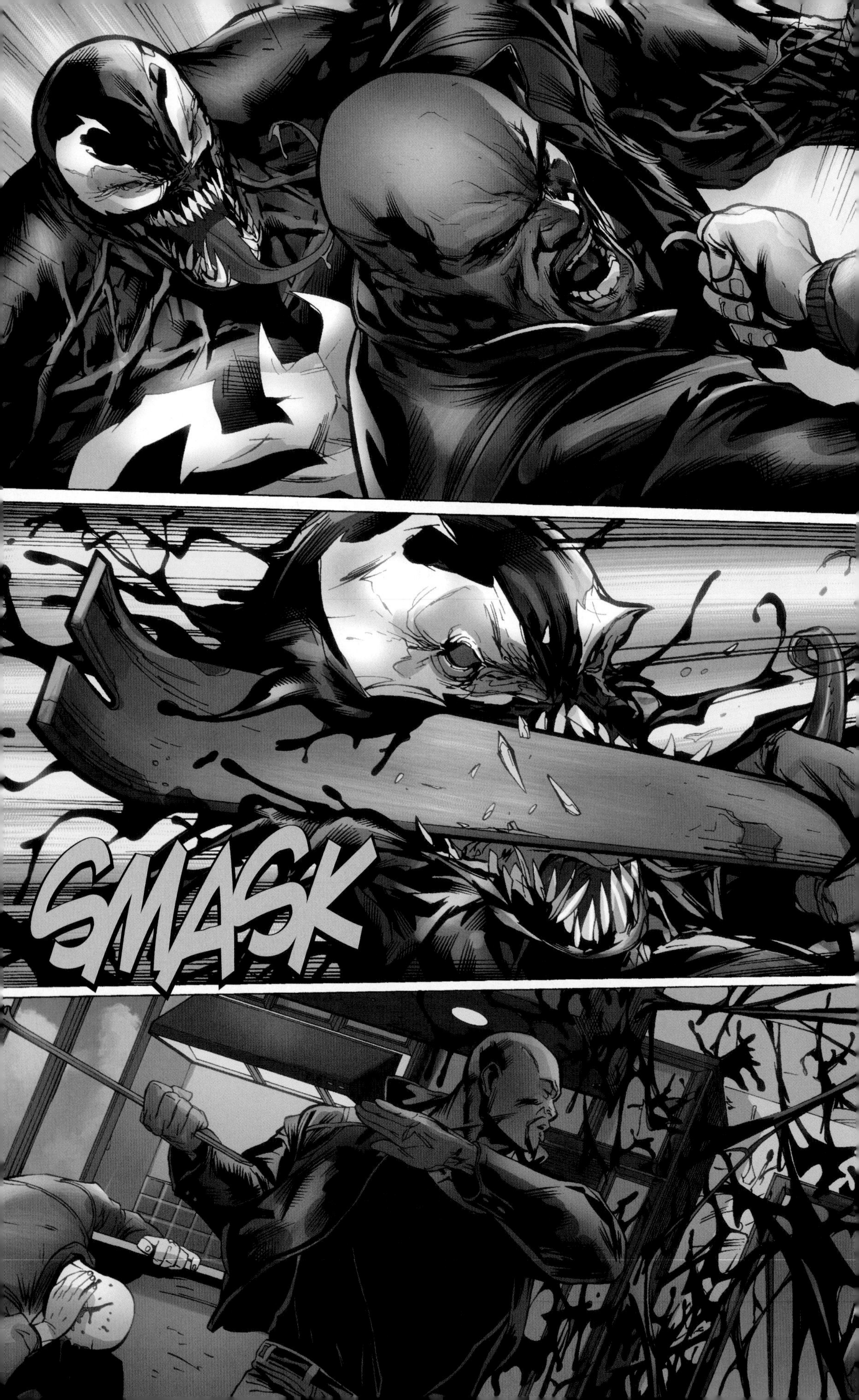
SMASK

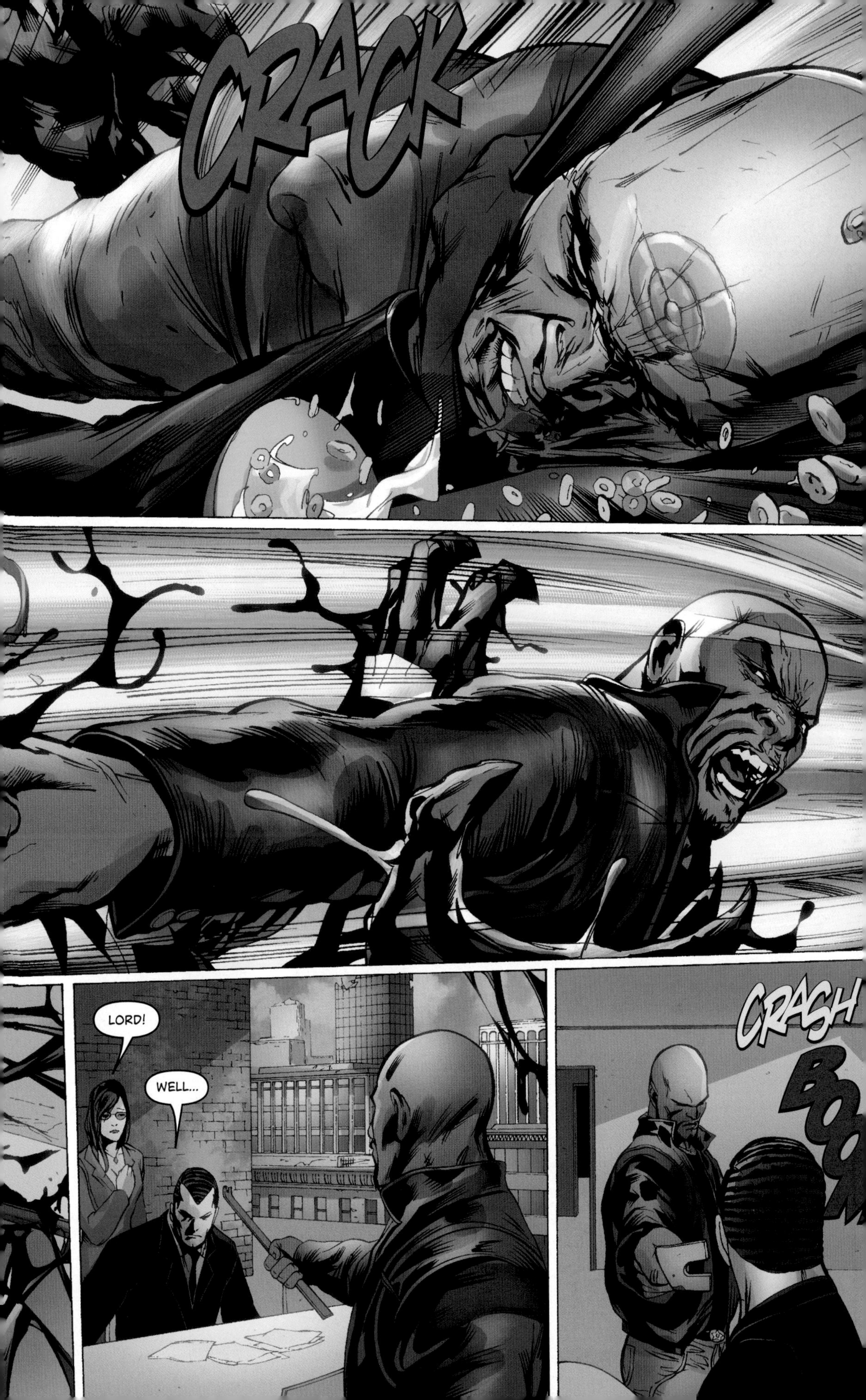
CRACK
LORD!
WELL...
CRASH

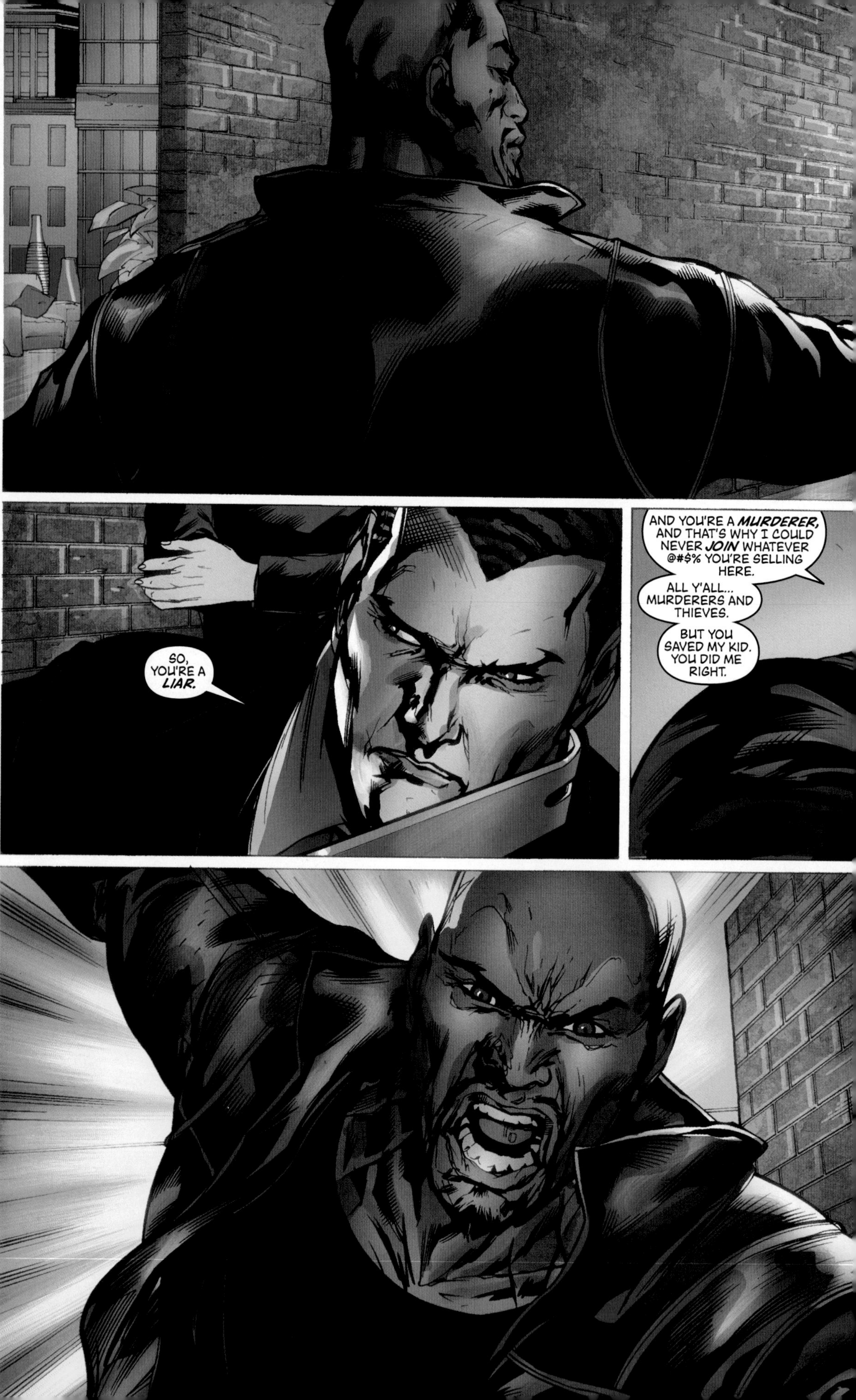
SO, YOU'RE A LIAR.
AND YOU'RE A MURDERER, AND THAT'S WHY I COULD NEVER JOIN WHATEVER @#$% YOU'RE SELLING HERE.
ALL Y'ALL... MURDERERS AND THIEVES.
BUT YOU SAVED MY KID. YOU DID ME RIGHT.

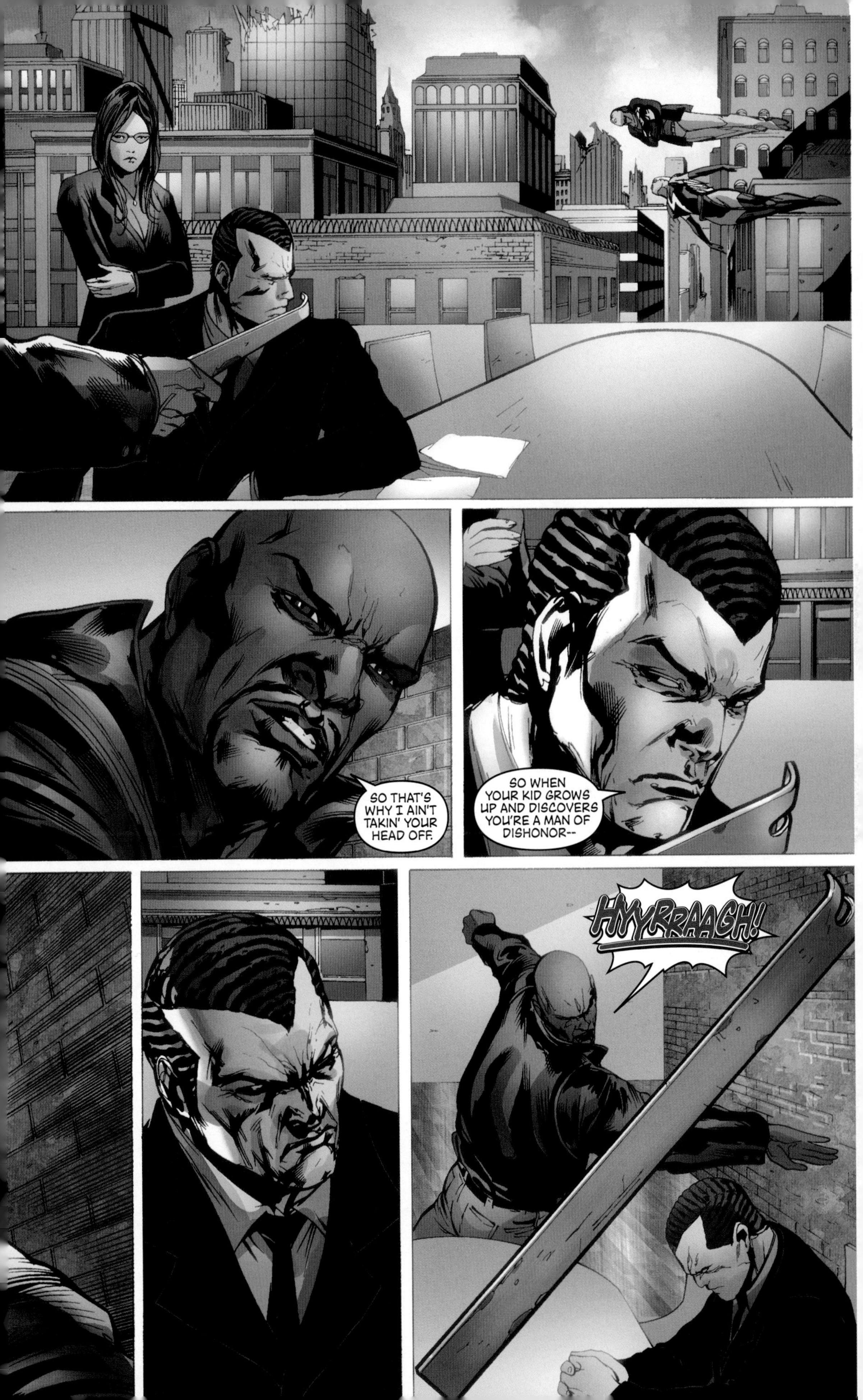
SO THAT'S WHY I AIN'T TAKIN' YOUR HEAD OFF.
SO WHEN YOUR KID GROWS UP AND DISCOVERS YOU'RE A MAN OF DISHONOR--
HYYRRAAGH!

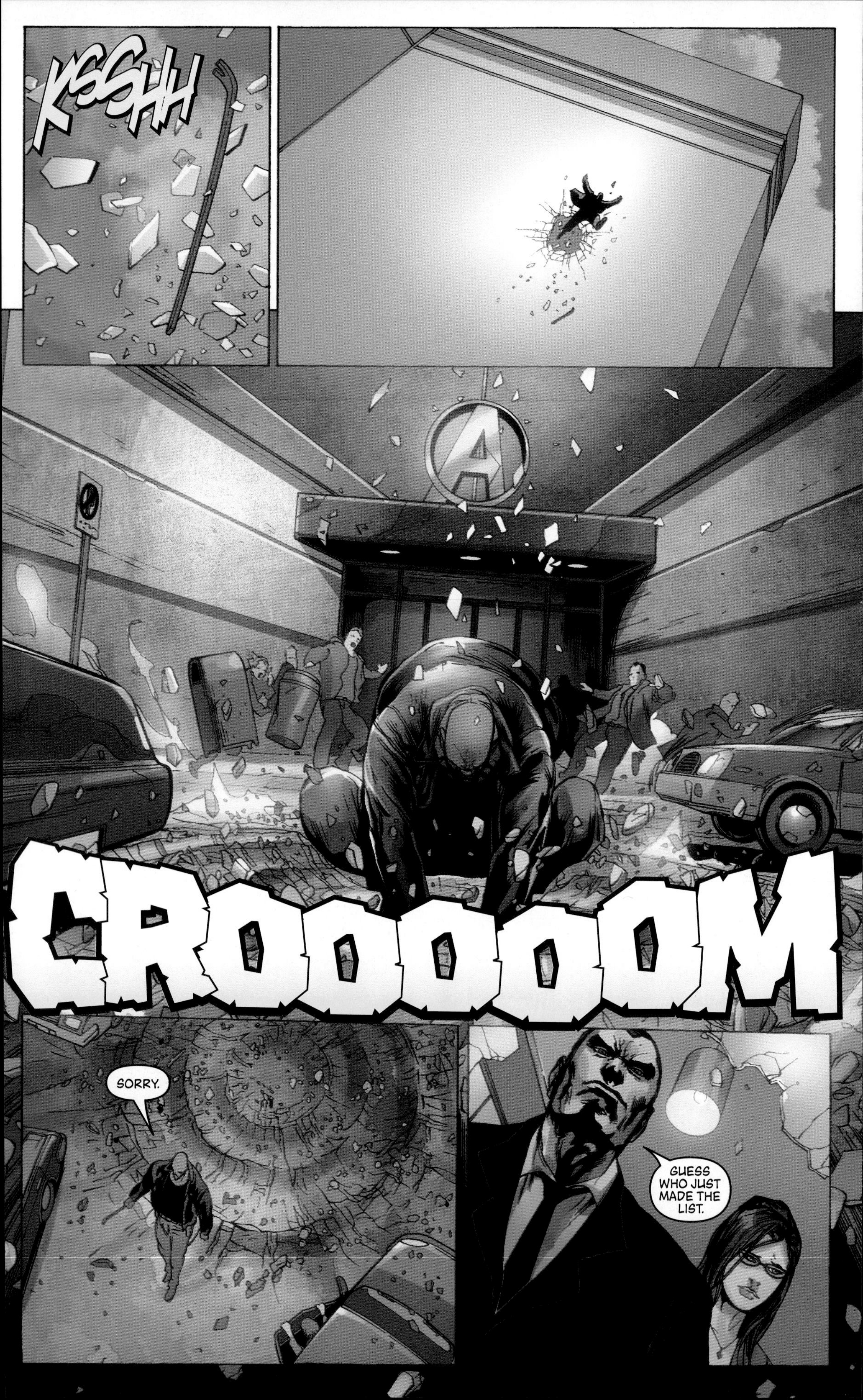
KSSHH
CROOOOOM
SORRY.
GUESS WHO JUST MADE THE LIST.

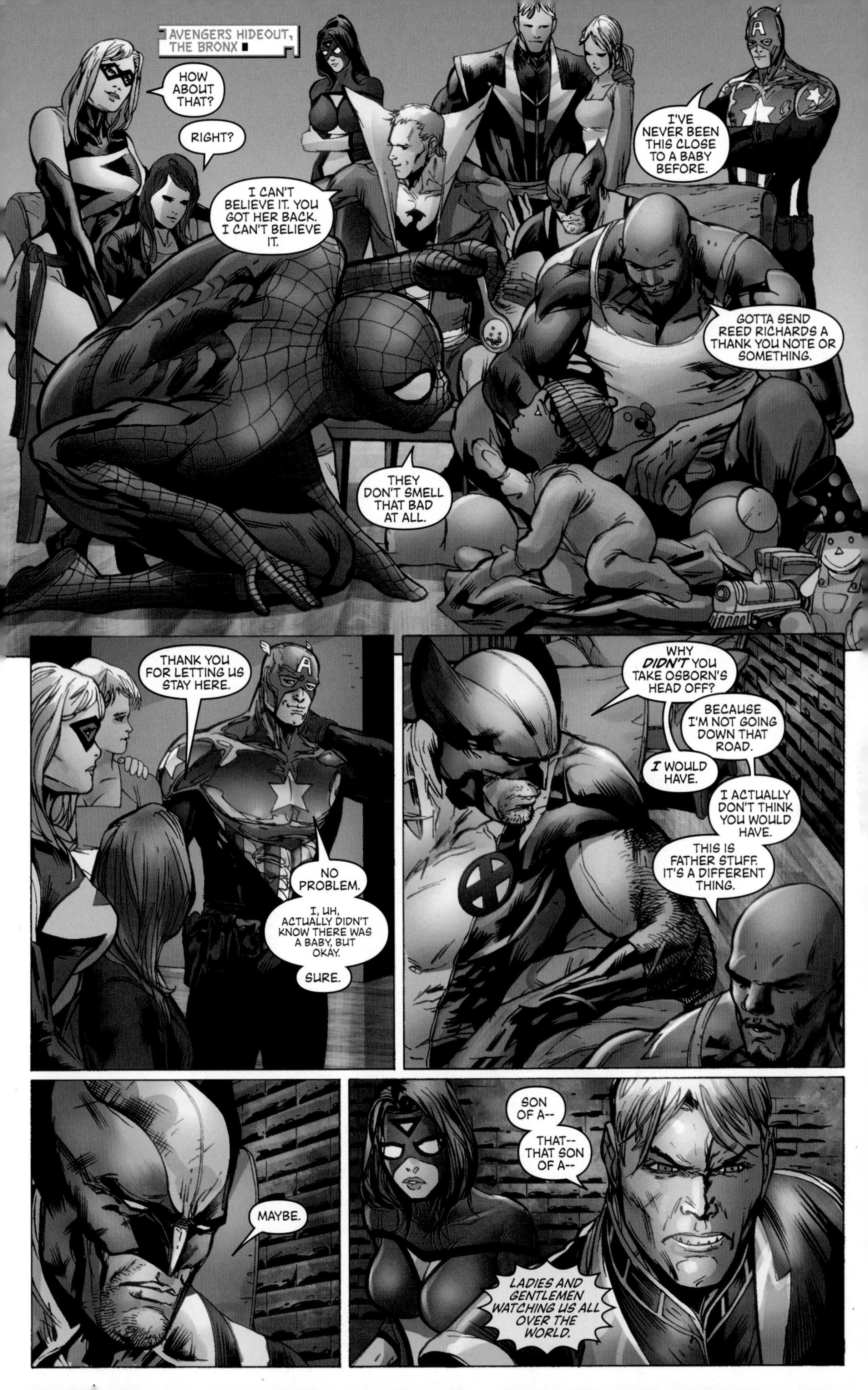
AVENGERS HIDEOUT, THE BRONX
HOW ABOUT THAT?
RIGHT?
I CAN'T BELIEVE IT. YOU GOT HER BACK. I CAN'T BELIEVE IT.
I'VE NEVER BEEN THIS CLOSE TO A BABY BEFORE.
GOTTA SEND REED RICHARDS A THANK YOU NOTE OR SOMETHING.
THEY DON'T SMELL THAT BAD AT ALL.
THANK YOU FOR LETTING US STAY HERE.
NO PROBLEM.
I, UH, ACTUALLY DIDN'T KNOW THERE WAS A BABY, BUT OKAY.
SURE.
WHY DIDN'T YOU TAKE OSBORN'S HEAD OFF?
BECAUSE I'M NOT GOING DOWN THAT ROAD.
I WOULD HAVE.
I ACTUALLY DON'T THINK YOU WOULD HAVE.
THIS IS FATHER STUFF. IT'S A DIFFERENT THING.
MAYBE.
SON OF A--
THAT-- THAT SON OF A--
LADIES AND GENTLEMEN WATCHING US ALL OVER THE WORLD.

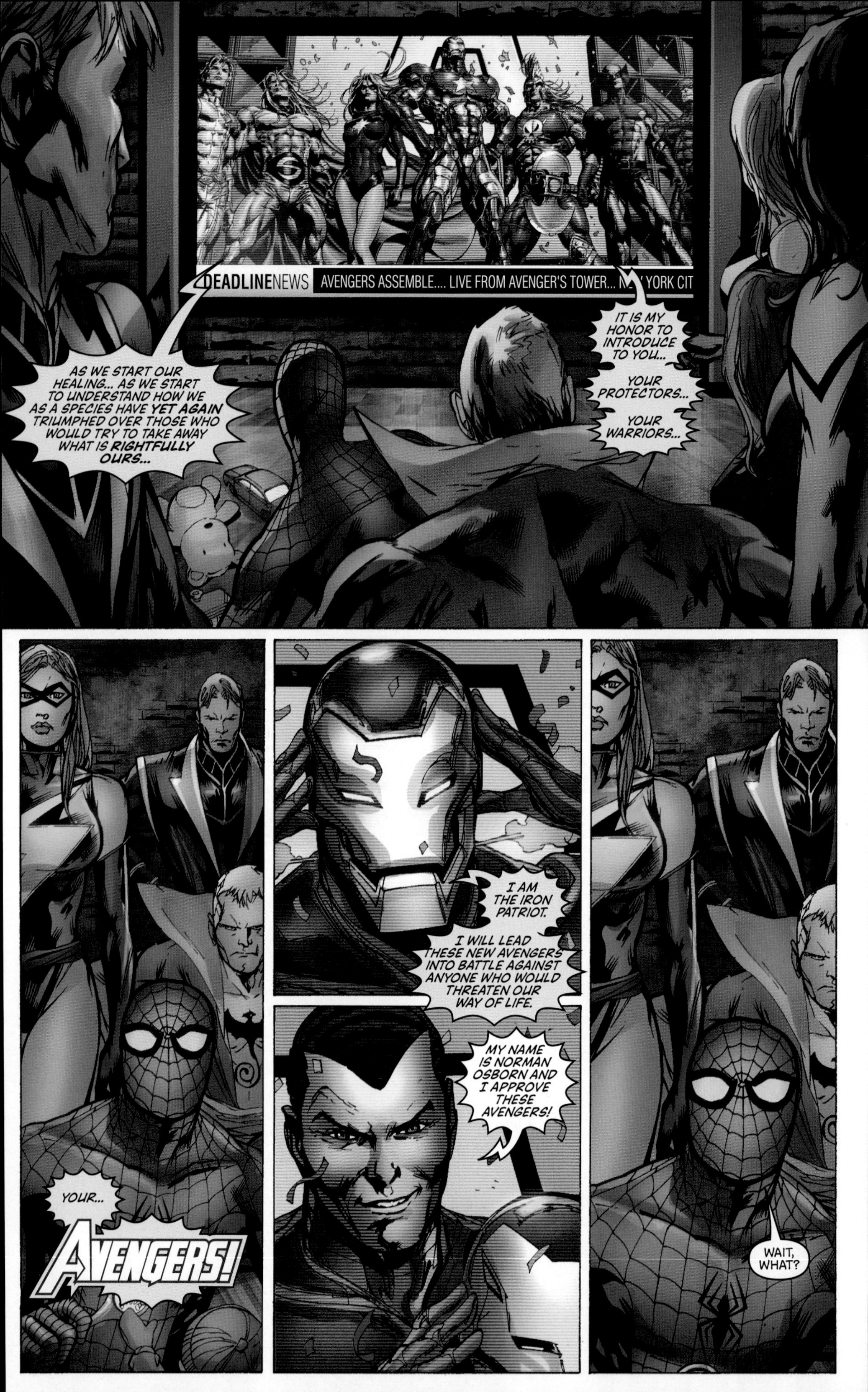
DEADLINENEWS AVENGERS ASSEMBLE.... LIVE FROM AVENGER'S TOWER... N' YORK CIT
AS WE START OUR HEALING... AS WE START TO UNDERSTAND HOW WE AS A SPECIES HAVE YET AGAIN TRIUMPHED OVER THOSE WHO WOULD TRY TO TAKE AWAY WHAT IS RIGHTFULLY OURS...
IT IS MY HONOR TO INTRODUCE TO YOU...
YOUR PROTECTORS...
YOUR WARRIORS...
YOUR...
AVENGERS!
I AM THE IRON PATRIOT.
I WILL LEAD THESE NEW AVENGERS INTO BATTLE AGAINST ANYONE WHO WOULD THREATEN OUR WAY OF LIFE.
MY NAME IS NORMAN OSBORN AND I APPROVE THESE AVENGERS!
WAIT, WHAT?

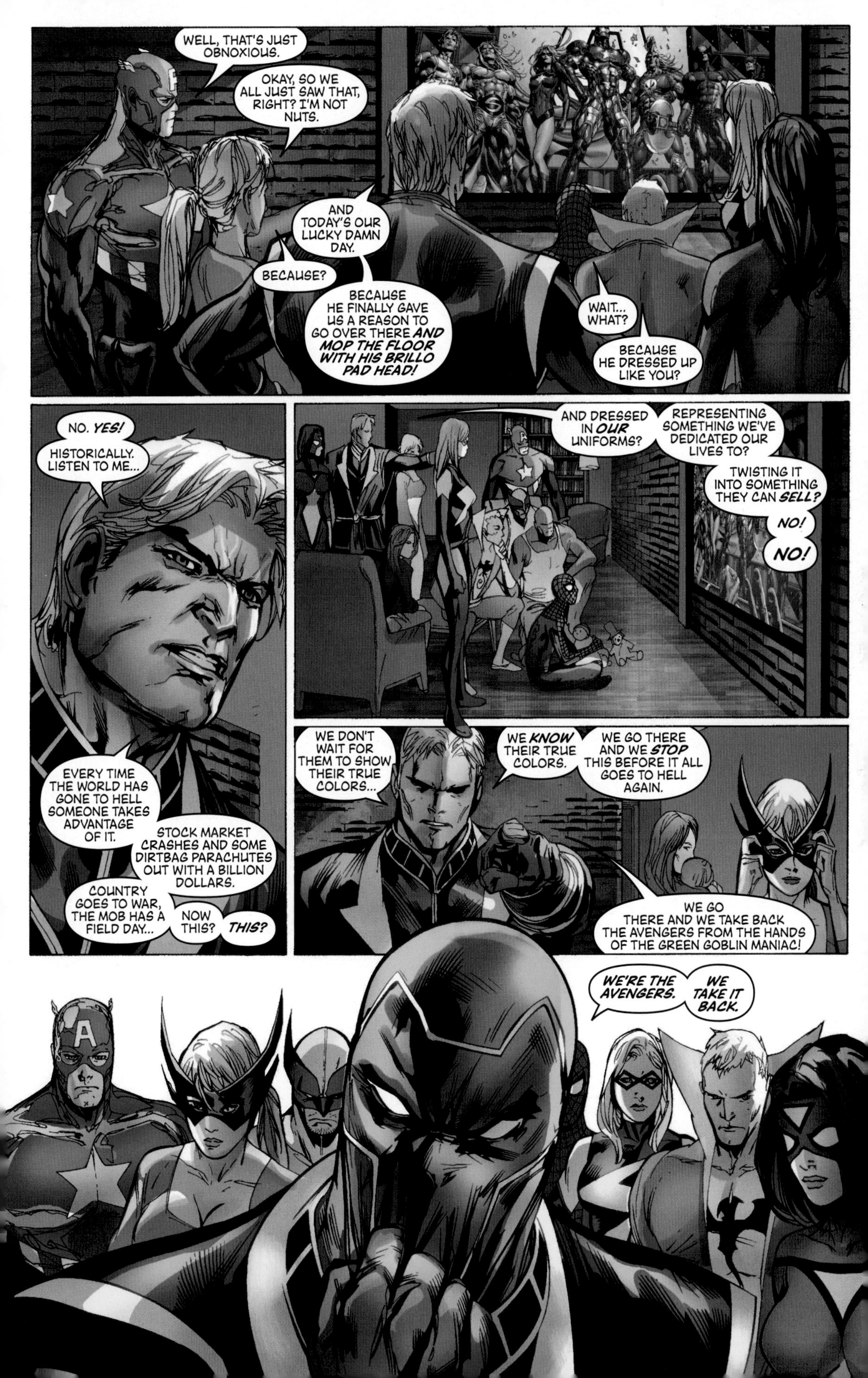

WELL, THAT'S JUST OBNOXIOUS.
OKAY, SO WE ALL JUST SAW THAT, RIGHT? I'M NOT NUTS.
AND TODAY'S OUR LUCKY DAMN DAY.
BECAUSE?
BECAUSE HE FINALLY GAVE US A REASON TO GO OVER THERE AND MOP THE FLOOR WITH HIS BRILLO PAD HEAD!
WAIT... WHAT?
BECAUSE HE DRESSED UP LIKE YOU?
NO. YES!
HISTORICALLY. LISTEN TO ME...
EVERY TIME THE WORLD HAS GONE TO HELL SOMEONE TAKES ADVANTAGE OF IT.
STOCK MARKET CRASHES AND SOME DIRTBAG PARACHUTES OUT WITH A BILLION DOLLARS.
COUNTRY GOES TO WAR, THE MOB HAS A FIELD DAY...
NOW THIS? THIS?
AND DRESSED IN OUR UNIFORMS?
REPRESENTING SOMETHING WE'VE DEDICATED OUR LIVES TO?
TWISTING IT INTO SOMETHING THEY CAN SELL?
NO!
NO!
WE DON'T WAIT FOR THEM TO SHOW THEIR TRUE COLORS...
WE KNOW THEIR TRUE COLORS.
WE GO THERE AND WE STOP THIS BEFORE IT ALL GOES TO HELL AGAIN.
WE GO THERE AND WE TAKE BACK THE AVENGERS FROM THE HANDS OF THE GREEN GOBLIN MANIAC!
WE'RE THE AVENGERS.
WE TAKE IT BACK.

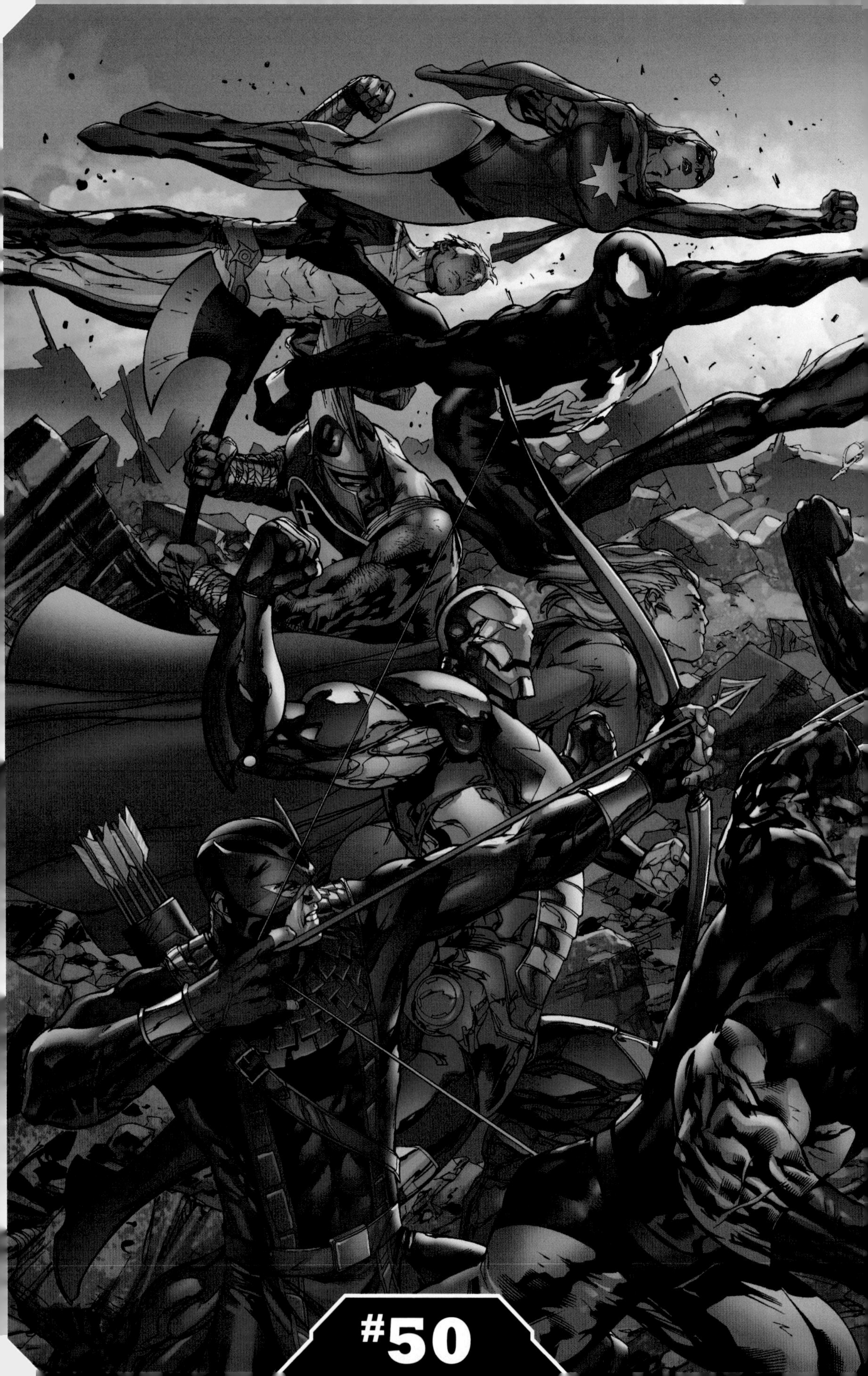
#50

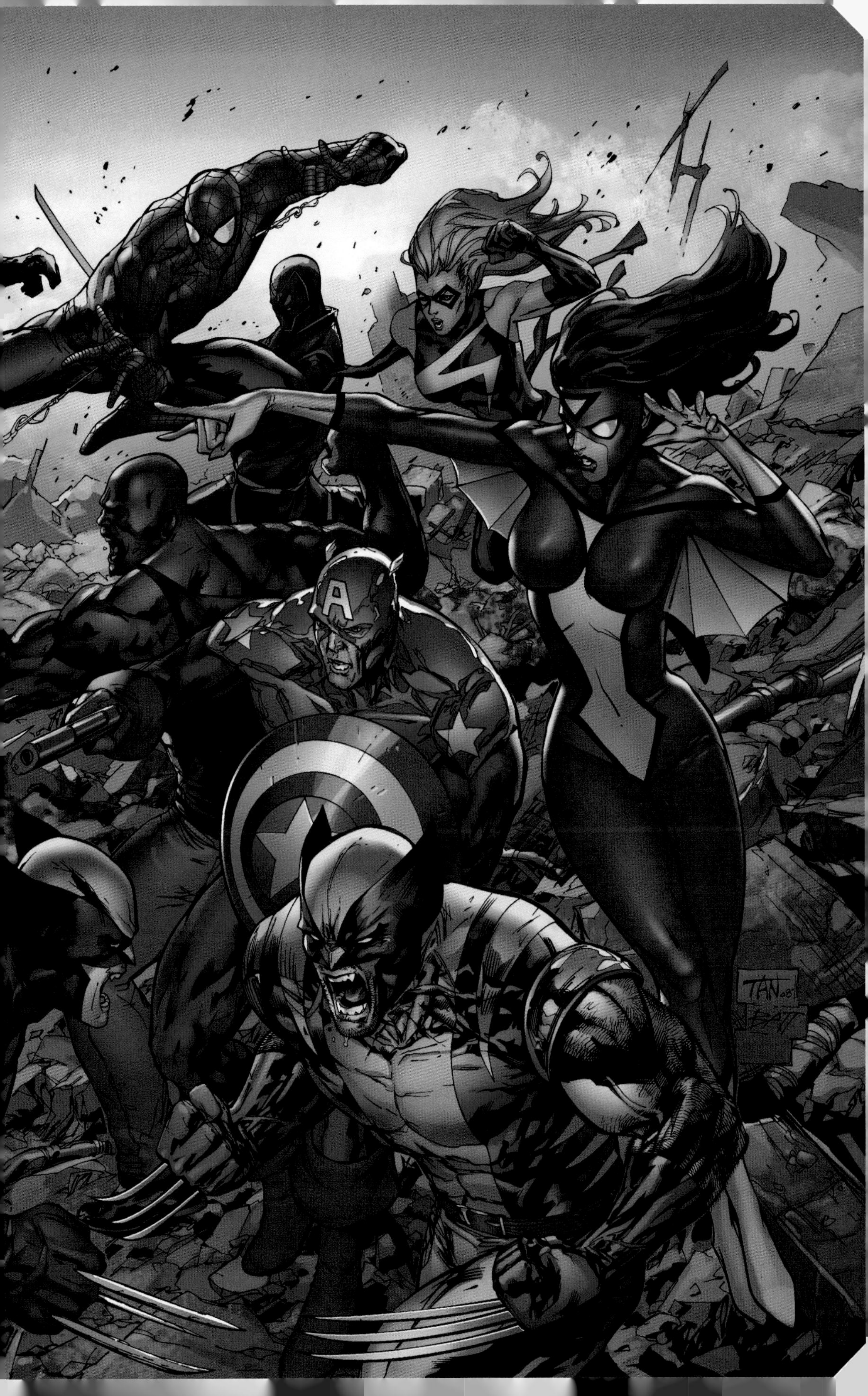

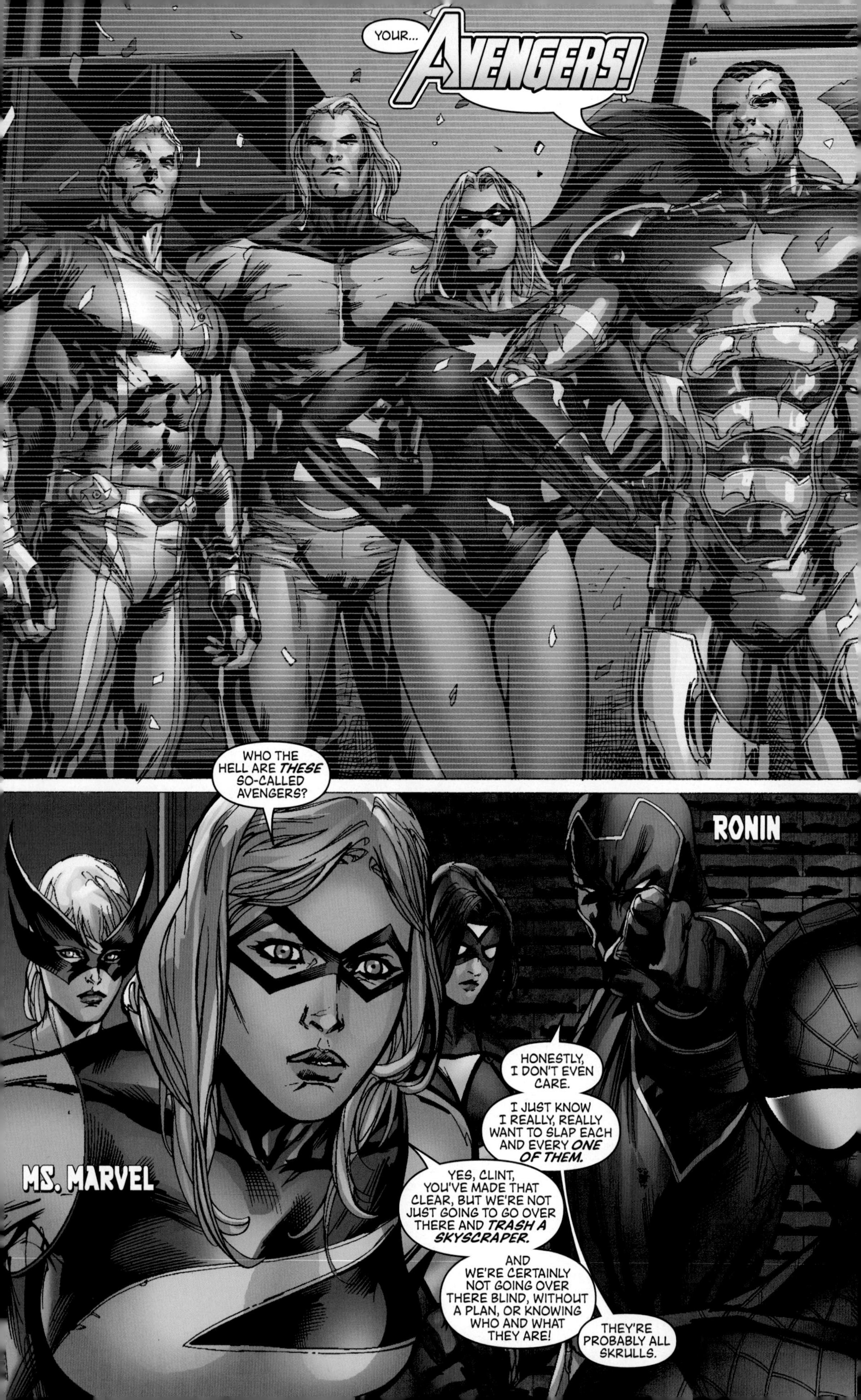
YOUR... AVENGERS!
WHO THE HELL ARE THESE SO-CALLED AVENGERS?
RONIN
HONESTLY, I DON'T EVEN CARE.
I JUST KNOW I REALLY, REALLY WANT TO SLAP EACH AND EVERY ONE OF THEM.
MS. MARVEL
YES, CLINT, YOU'VE MADE THAT CLEAR, BUT WE'RE NOT JUST GOING TO GO OVER THERE AND TRASH A SKYSCRAPER.
AND WE'RE CERTAINLY NOT GOING OVER THERE BLIND, WITHOUT A PLAN, OR KNOWING WHO AND WHAT THEY ARE!
THEY'RE PROBABLY ALL SKRULLS.

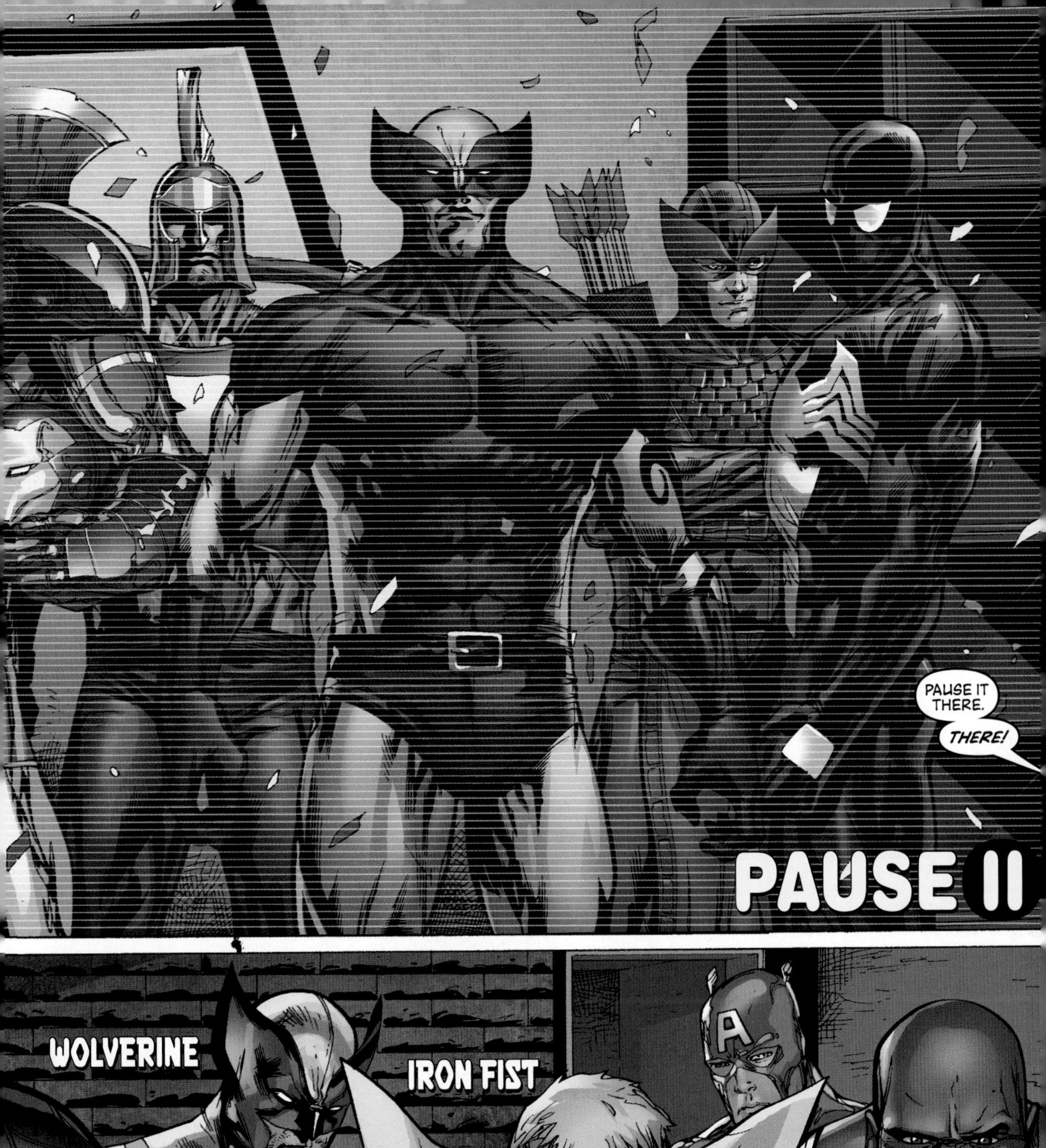
PAUSE IT THERE. *THERE!*
PAUSE II

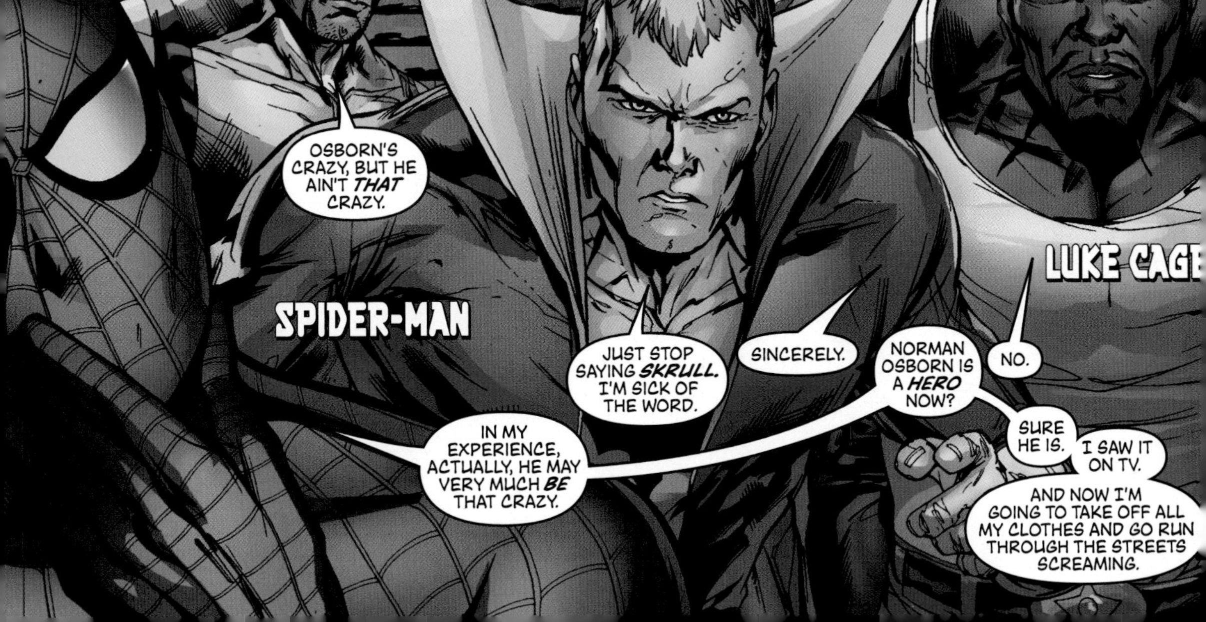
WOLVERINE
IRON FIST
SPIDER-MAN
LUKE CAGE
OSBORN'S CRAZY, BUT HE AIN'T *THAT* CRAZY.
JUST STOP SAYING *SKRULL.* I'M SICK OF THE WORD.
SINCERELY.
NORMAN OSBORN IS A *HERO* NOW?
NO.
IN MY EXPERIENCE, ACTUALLY, HE MAY VERY MUCH *BE* THAT CRAZY.
SURE HE IS.
I SAW IT ON TV.
AND NOW I'M GOING TO TAKE OFF ALL MY CLOTHES AND GO RUN THROUGH THE STREETS SCREAMING.

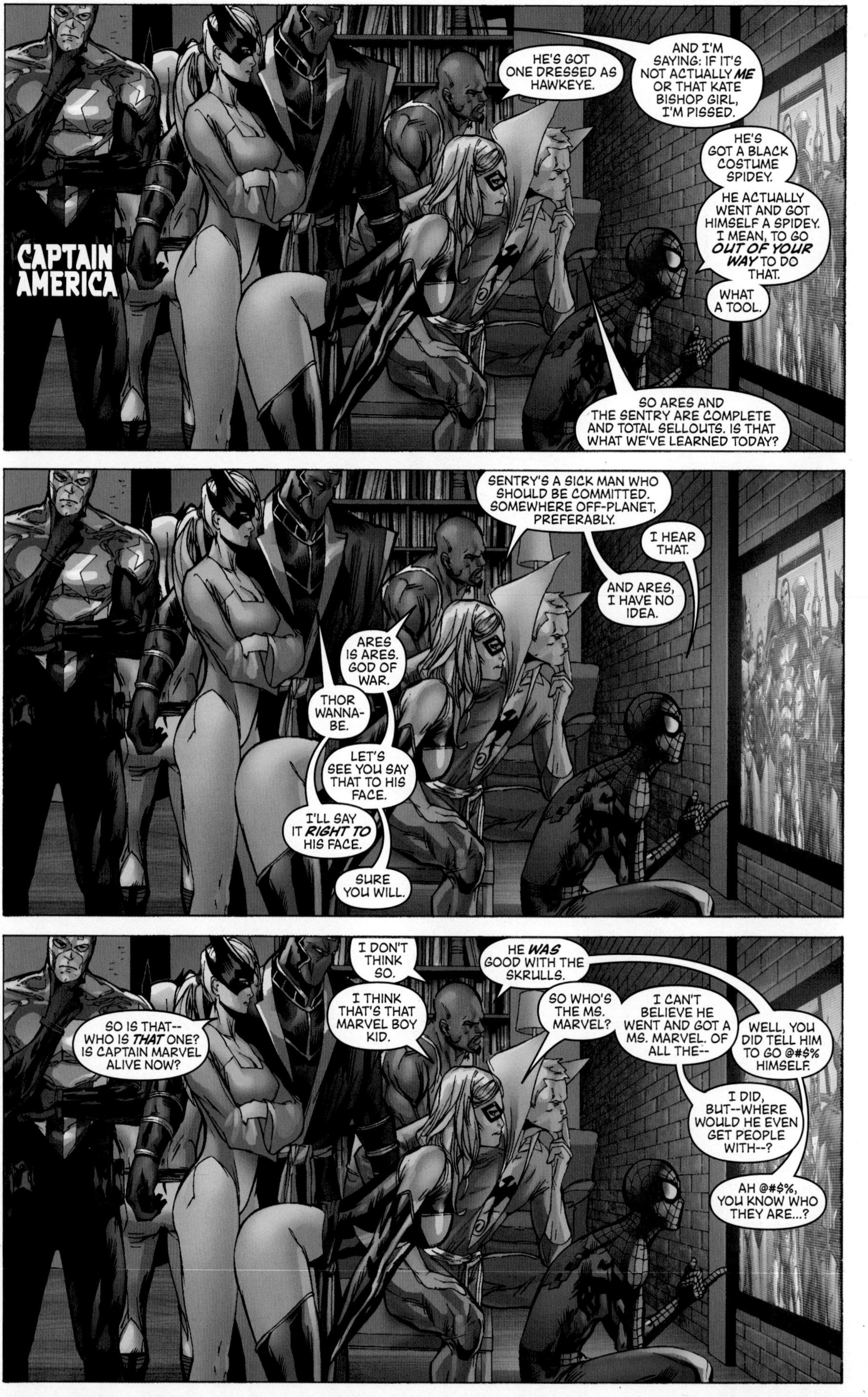
CAPTAIN AMERICA
HE'S GOT ONE DRESSED AS HAWKEYE.
AND I'M SAYING: IF IT'S NOT ACTUALLY ME OR THAT KATE BISHOP GIRL, I'M PISSED.
HE'S GOT A BLACK COSTUME SPIDEY.
HE ACTUALLY WENT AND GOT HIMSELF A SPIDEY. I MEAN, TO GO OUT OF YOUR WAY TO DO THAT.
WHAT A TOOL.
SO ARES AND THE SENTRY ARE COMPLETE AND TOTAL SELLOUTS. IS THAT WHAT WE'VE LEARNED TODAY?
SENTRY'S A SICK MAN WHO SHOULD BE COMMITTED. SOMEWHERE OFF-PLANET, PREFERABLY.
I HEAR THAT.
AND ARES, I HAVE NO IDEA.
ARES IS ARES. GOD OF WAR.
THOR WANNA-BE.
LET'S SEE YOU SAY THAT TO HIS FACE.
I'LL SAY IT RIGHT TO HIS FACE.
SURE YOU WILL.
SO IS THAT-- WHO IS THAT ONE? IS CAPTAIN MARVEL ALIVE NOW?
I DON'T THINK SO.
I THINK THAT'S THAT MARVEL BOY KID.
HE WAS GOOD WITH THE SKRULLS.
SO WHO'S THE MS. MARVEL?
I CAN'T BELIEVE HE WENT AND GOT A MS. MARVEL. OF ALL THE--
WELL, YOU DID TELL HIM TO GO @#$% HIMSELF.
I DID, BUT--WHERE WOULD HE EVEN GET PEOPLE WITH--?
AH @#$%, YOU KNOW WHO THEY ARE...?

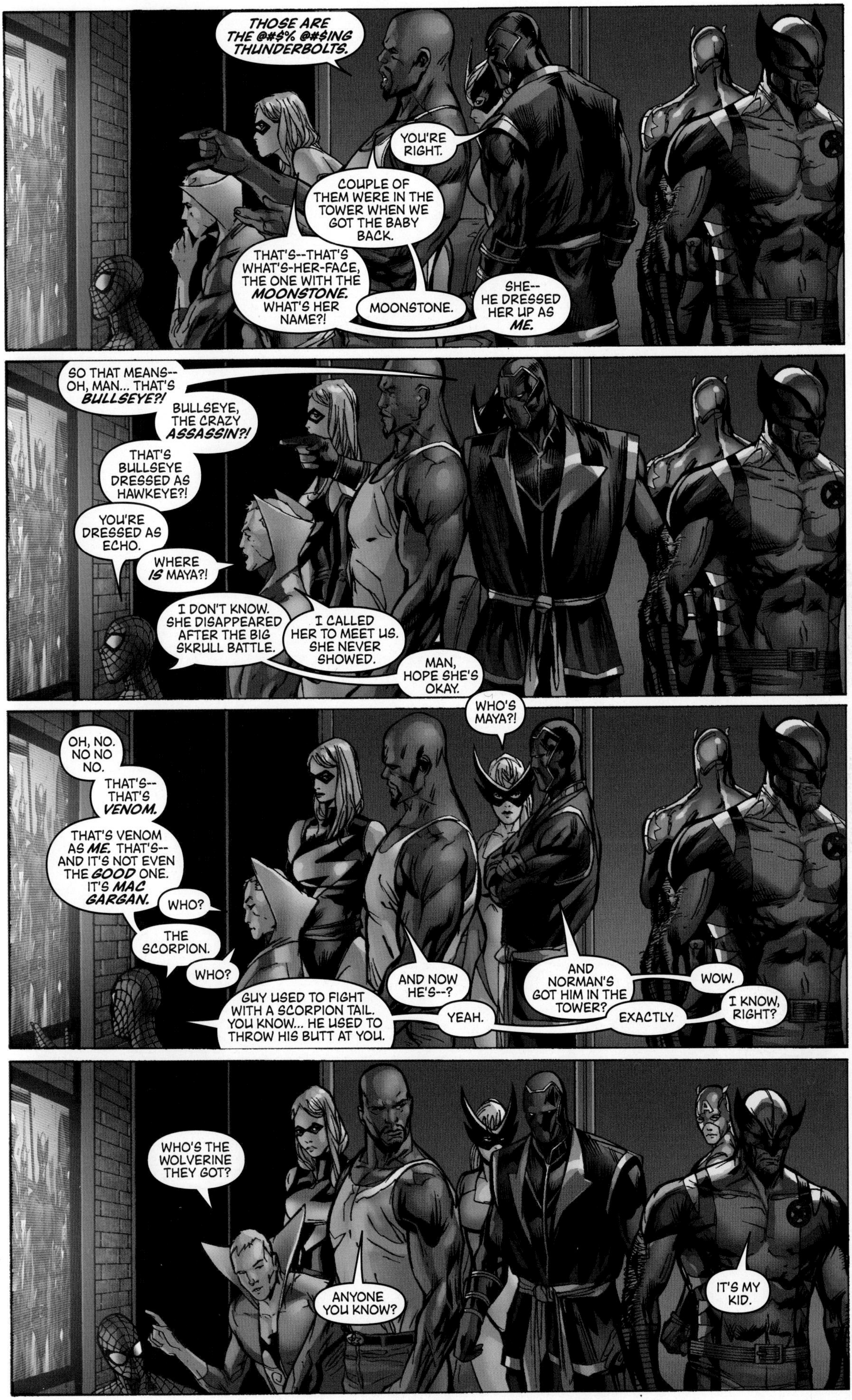
THOSE ARE THE @#$% @#$ING THUNDERBOLTS.
YOU'RE RIGHT.
COUPLE OF THEM WERE IN THE TOWER WHEN WE GOT THE BABY BACK.
THAT'S--THAT'S WHAT'S-HER-FACE, THE ONE WITH THE MOONSTONE. WHAT'S HER NAME?!
MOONSTONE.
SHE-- HE DRESSED HER UP AS ME.
SO THAT MEANS-- OH, MAN... THAT'S BULLSEYE?!
BULLSEYE, THE CRAZY ASSASSIN?!
THAT'S BULLSEYE DRESSED AS HAWKEYE?!
YOU'RE DRESSED AS ECHO.
WHERE IS MAYA?!
I DON'T KNOW. SHE DISAPPEARED AFTER THE BIG SKRULL BATTLE.
I CALLED HER TO MEET US. SHE NEVER SHOWED.
MAN, HOPE SHE'S OKAY.
WHO'S MAYA?!
OH, NO. NO NO NO.
THAT'S-- THAT'S VENOM.
THAT'S VENOM AS ME. THAT'S-- AND IT'S NOT EVEN THE GOOD ONE. IT'S MAC GARGAN.
WHO?
THE SCORPION.
WHO?
GUY USED TO FIGHT WITH A SCORPION TAIL. YOU KNOW... HE USED TO THROW HIS BUTT AT YOU.
AND NOW HE'S--?
YEAH.
AND NORMAN'S GOT HIM IN THE TOWER?
EXACTLY.
WOW.
I KNOW, RIGHT?
WHO'S THE WOLVERINE THEY GOT?
ANYONE YOU KNOW?
IT'S MY KID.

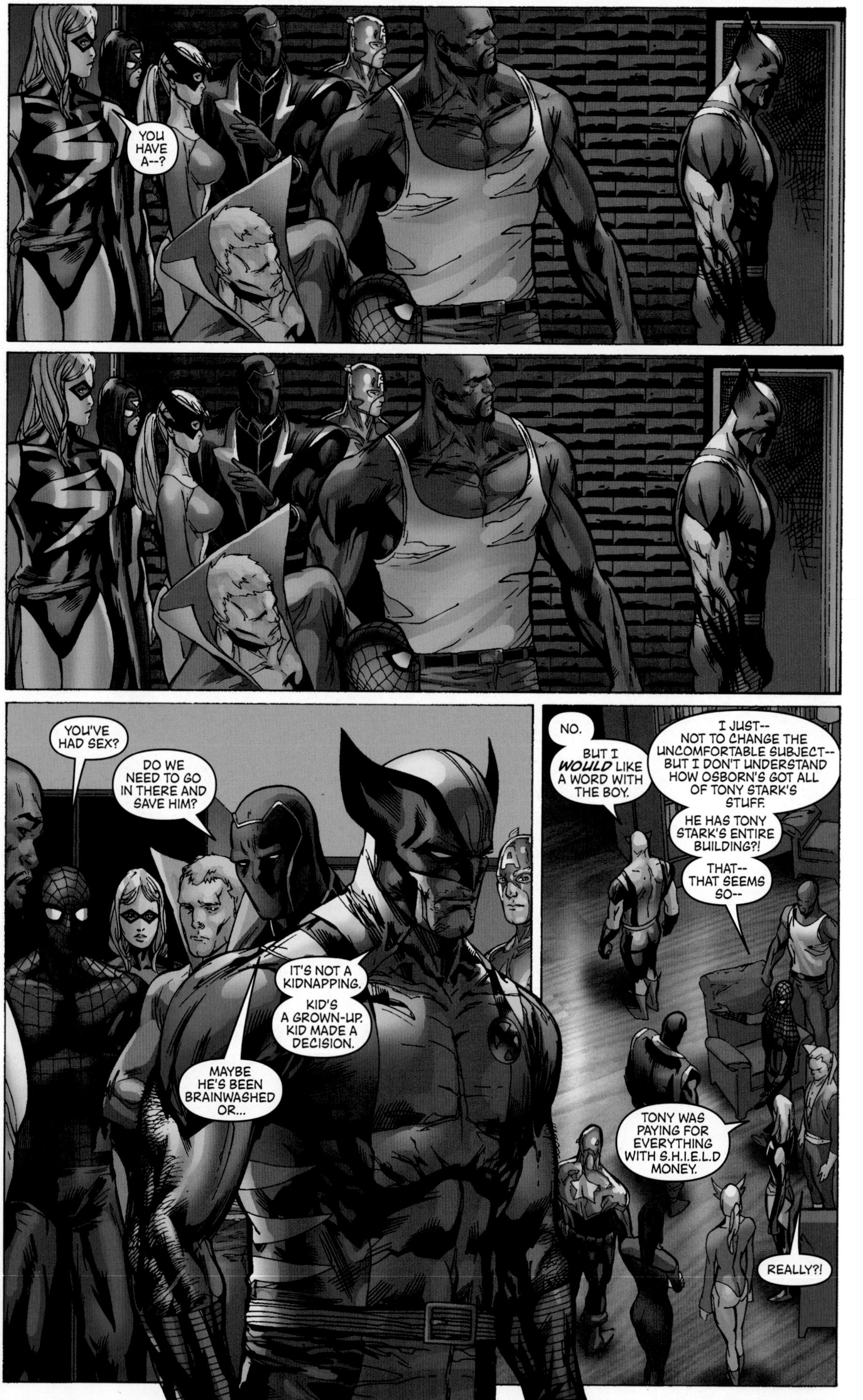
YOU HAVE A--?
YOU'VE HAD SEX?
DO WE NEED TO GO IN THERE AND SAVE HIM?
IT'S NOT A KIDNAPPING.
KID'S A GROWN-UP. KID MADE A DECISION.
MAYBE HE'S BEEN BRAINWASHED OR...
NO.
BUT I WOULD LIKE A WORD WITH THE BOY.
I JUST-- NOT TO CHANGE THE UNCOMFORTABLE SUBJECT-- BUT I DON'T UNDERSTAND HOW OSBORN'S GOT ALL OF TONY STARK'S STUFF.
HE HAS TONY STARK'S ENTIRE BUILDING?!
THAT-- THAT SEEMS SO--
TONY WAS PAYING FOR EVERYTHING WITH S.H.I.E.L.D MONEY.
REALLY?!

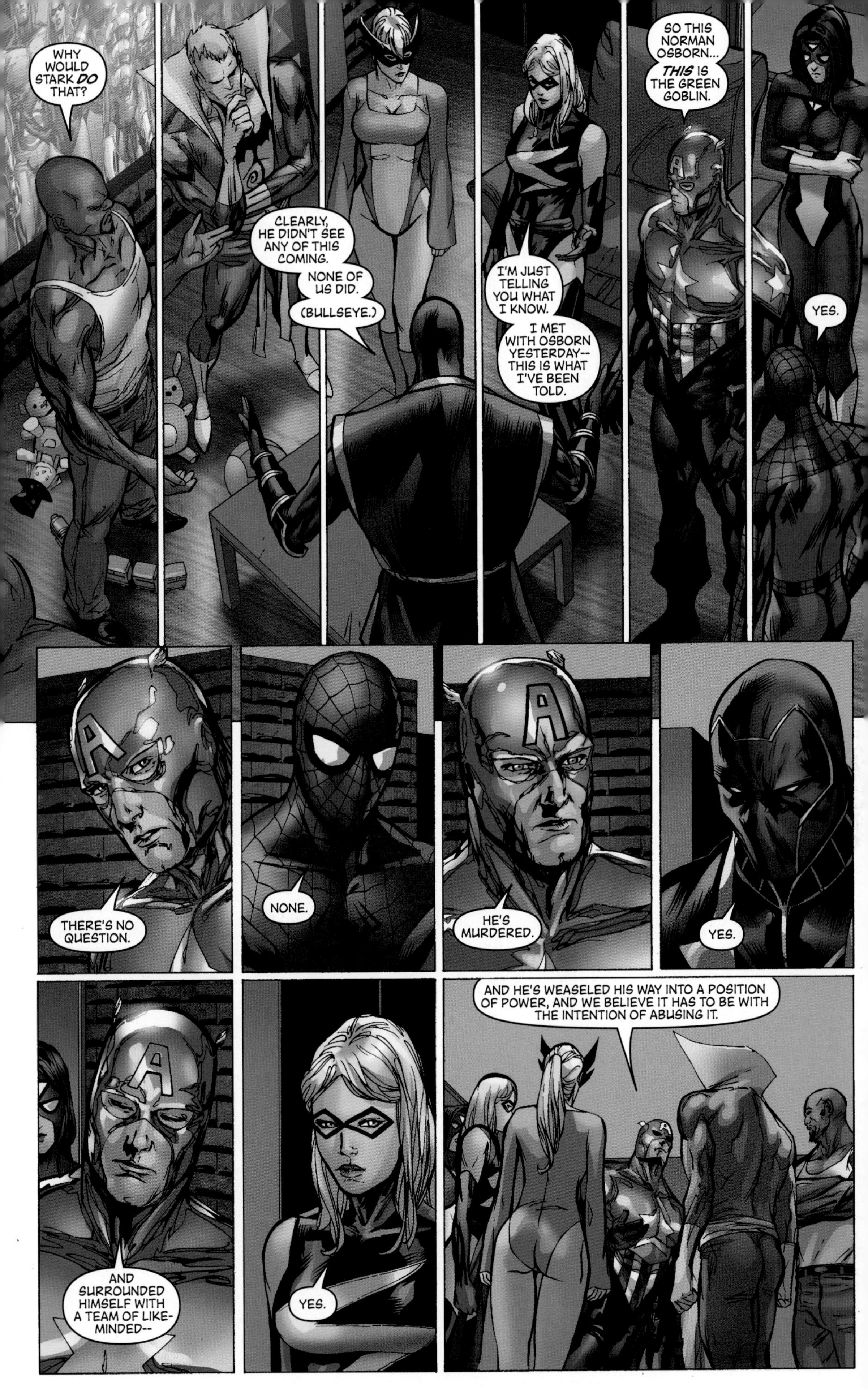
WHY WOULD STARK DO THAT?
CLEARLY, HE DIDN'T SEE ANY OF THIS COMING.
NONE OF US DID.
(BULLSEYE.)
I'M JUST TELLING YOU WHAT I KNOW.
I MET WITH OSBORN YESTERDAY-- THIS IS WHAT I'VE BEEN TOLD.
SO THIS NORMAN OSBORN... THIS IS THE GREEN GOBLIN.
YES.
THERE'S NO QUESTION.
NONE.
HE'S MURDERED.
YES.
AND SURROUNDED HIMSELF WITH A TEAM OF LIKE-MINDED--
YES.
AND HE'S WEASELED HIS WAY INTO A POSITION OF POWER, AND WE BELIEVE IT HAS TO BE WITH THE INTENTION OF ABUSING IT.

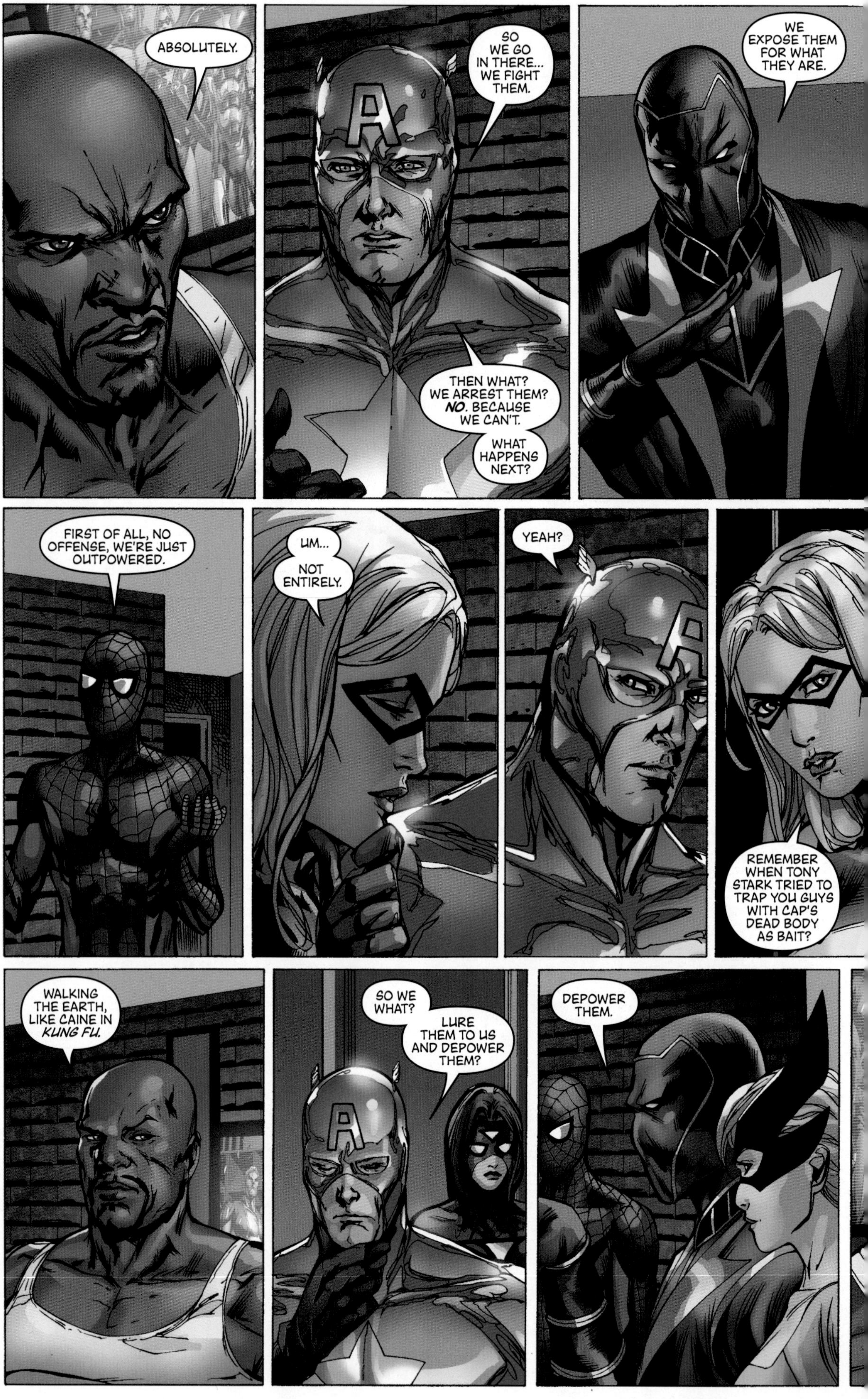
ABSOLUTELY.
SO WE GO IN THERE... WE FIGHT THEM.
THEN WHAT? WE ARREST THEM? *NO*. BECAUSE WE CAN'T.
WHAT HAPPENS NEXT?
WE EXPOSE THEM FOR WHAT THEY ARE.
FIRST OF ALL, NO OFFENSE, WE'RE JUST OUTPOWERED.
UM...
NOT ENTIRELY.
YEAH?
REMEMBER WHEN TONY STARK TRIED TO TRAP YOU GUYS WITH CAP'S DEAD BODY AS BAIT?
WALKING THE EARTH, LIKE CAINE IN *KUNG FU*.
SO WE WHAT?
LURE THEM TO US AND DEPOWER THEM?
DEPOWER THEM.

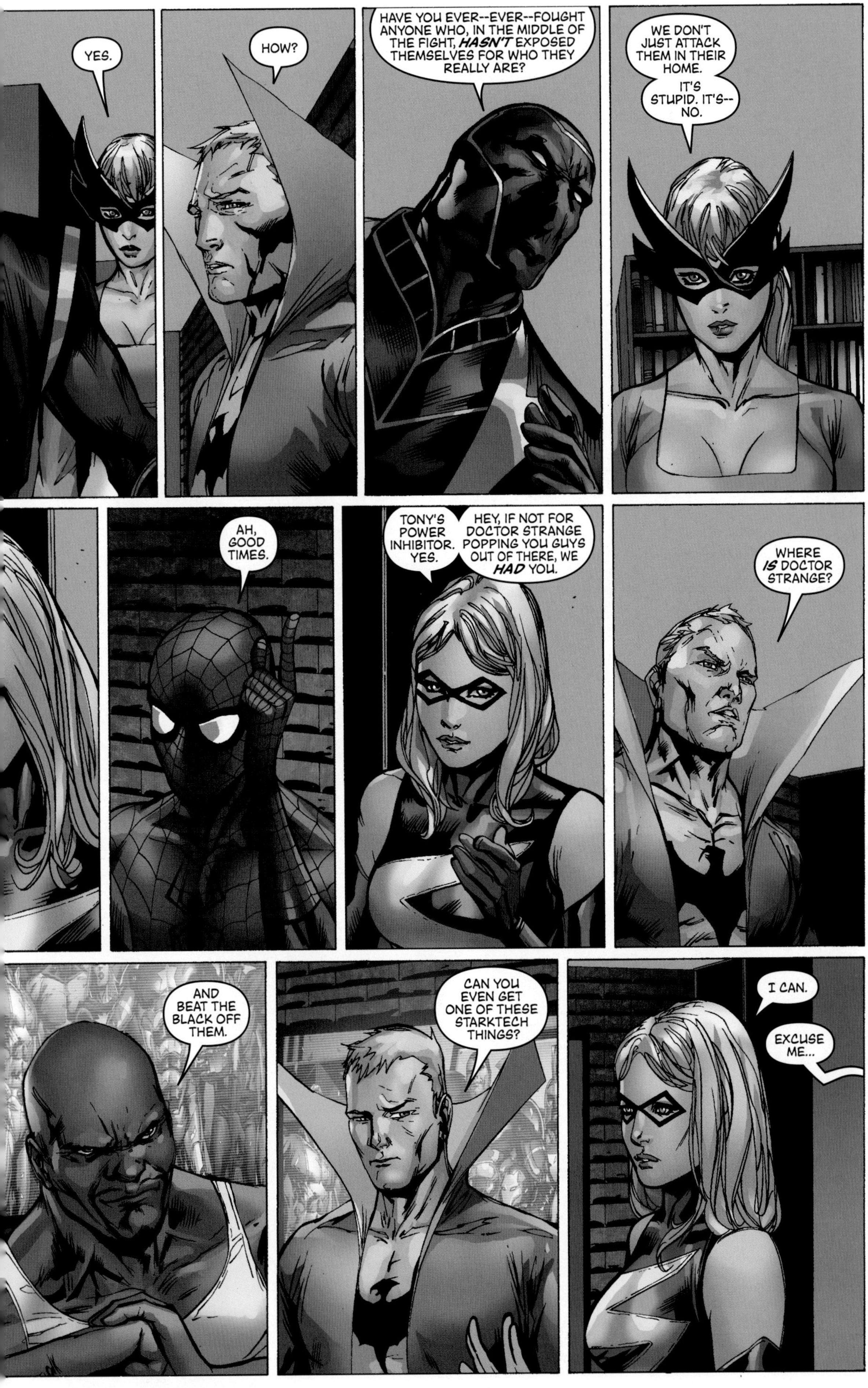
YES.
HOW?
HAVE YOU EVER--EVER--FOUGHT ANYONE WHO, IN THE MIDDLE OF THE FIGHT, ***HASN'T*** EXPOSED THEMSELVES FOR WHO THEY REALLY ARE?
WE DON'T JUST ATTACK THEM IN THEIR HOME.
IT'S STUPID. IT'S-- NO.
AH, GOOD TIMES.
TONY'S POWER INHIBITOR. YES.
HEY, IF NOT FOR DOCTOR STRANGE POPPING YOU GUYS OUT OF THERE, WE ***HAD*** YOU.
WHERE ***IS*** DOCTOR STRANGE?
AND BEAT THE BLACK OFF THEM.
CAN YOU EVEN GET ONE OF THESE STARKTECH THINGS?
I CAN.
EXCUSE ME...

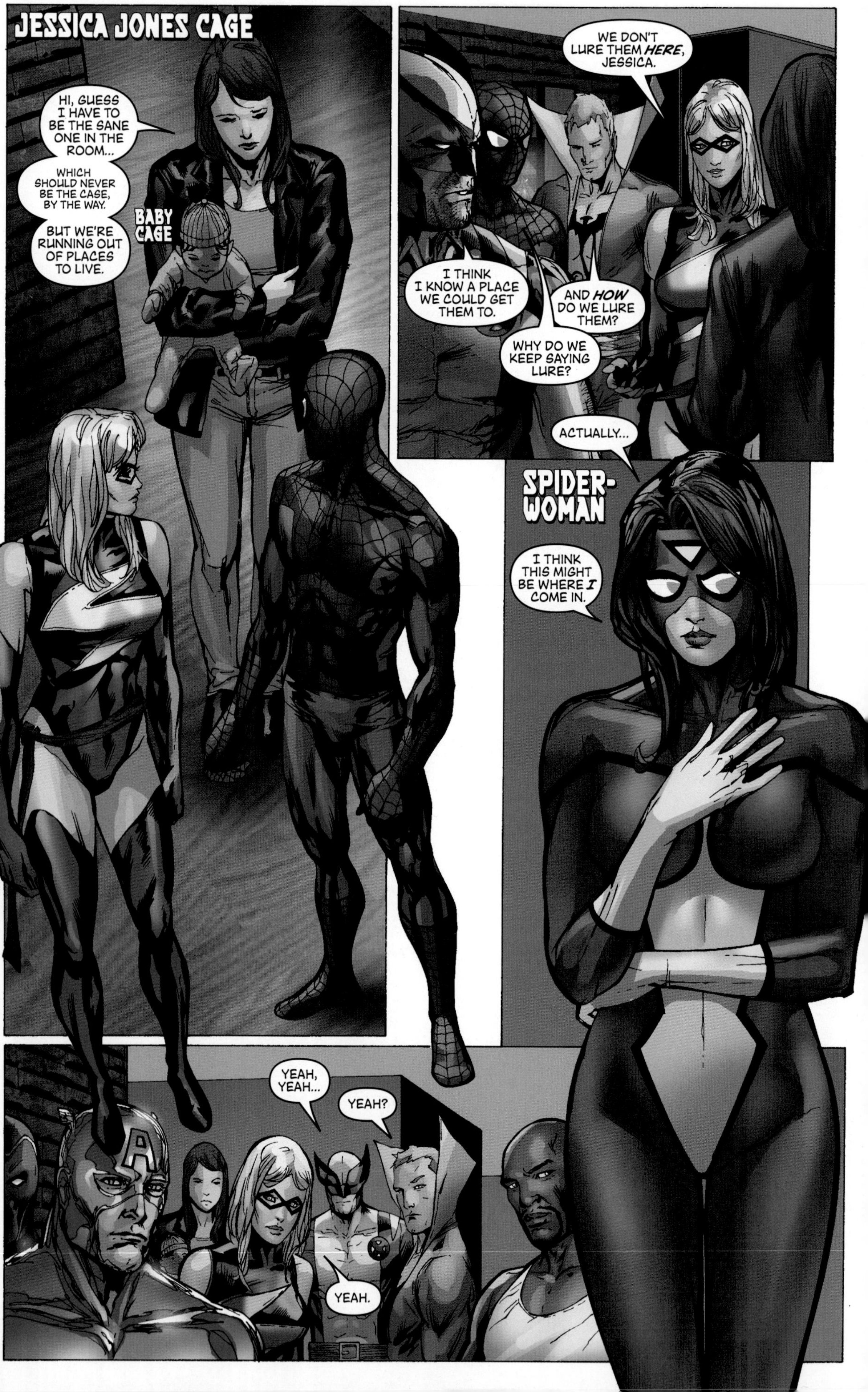
JESSICA JONES CAGE
HI, GUESS I HAVE TO BE THE SANE ONE IN THE ROOM...
WHICH SHOULD NEVER BE THE CASE, BY THE WAY.
BUT WE'RE RUNNING OUT OF PLACES TO LIVE.
BABY CAGE
WE DON'T LURE THEM HERE, JESSICA.
I THINK I KNOW A PLACE WE COULD GET THEM TO.
AND HOW DO WE LURE THEM?
WHY DO WE KEEP SAYING LURE?
ACTUALLY...
SPIDER-WOMAN
I THINK THIS MIGHT BE WHERE I COME IN.
YEAH, YEAH...
YEAH?
YEAH.

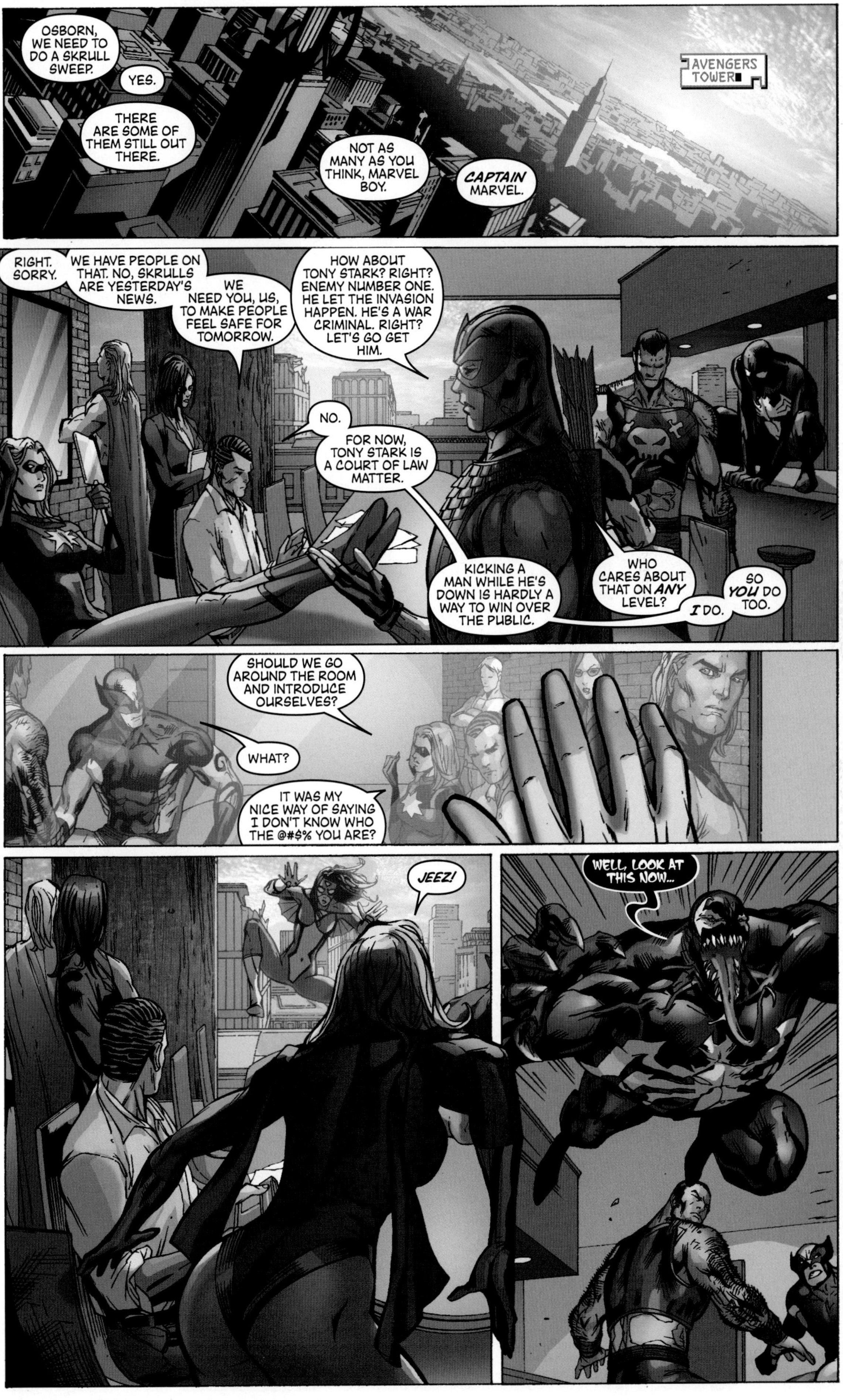

AVENGERS TOWER
OSBORN, WE NEED TO DO A SKRULL SWEEP.
YES.
THERE ARE SOME OF THEM STILL OUT THERE.
NOT AS MANY AS YOU THINK, MARVEL BOY.
CAPTAIN MARVEL.
RIGHT. SORRY.
WE HAVE PEOPLE ON THAT. NO, SKRULLS ARE YESTERDAY'S NEWS.
WE NEED YOU, US, TO MAKE PEOPLE FEEL SAFE FOR TOMORROW.
HOW ABOUT TONY STARK? RIGHT? ENEMY NUMBER ONE. HE LET THE INVASION HAPPEN. HE'S A WAR CRIMINAL. RIGHT? LET'S GO GET HIM.
NO.
FOR NOW, TONY STARK IS A COURT OF LAW MATTER.
KICKING A MAN WHILE HE'S DOWN IS HARDLY A WAY TO WIN OVER THE PUBLIC.
WHO CARES ABOUT THAT ON ANY LEVEL?
I DO.
SO YOU DO TOO.
SHOULD WE GO AROUND THE ROOM AND INTRODUCE OURSELVES?
WHAT?
IT WAS MY NICE WAY OF SAYING I DON'T KNOW WHO THE @#$% YOU ARE?
JEEZ!
WELL, LOOK AT THIS NOW...

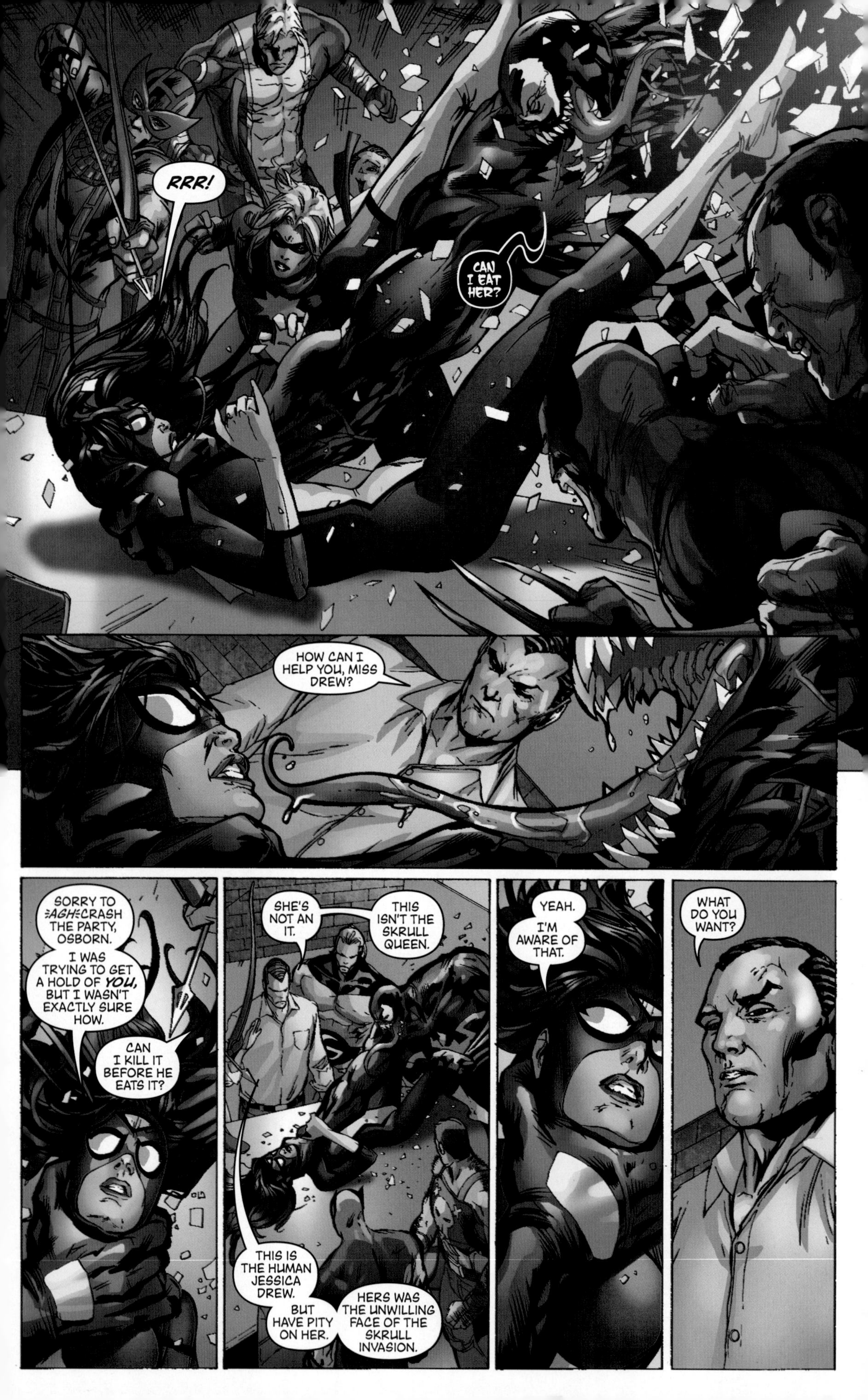
RRR!
CAN I EAT HER?
HOW CAN I HELP YOU, MISS DREW?
SORRY TO *AGH* CRASH THE PARTY, OSBORN.
I WAS TRYING TO GET A HOLD OF *YOU,* BUT I WASN'T EXACTLY SURE HOW.
CAN I KILL IT BEFORE HE EATS IT?
SHE'S NOT AN IT.
THIS ISN'T THE SKRULL QUEEN.
THIS IS THE HUMAN JESSICA DREW.
BUT HAVE PITY ON HER.
HERS WAS THE UNWILLING FACE OF THE SKRULL INVASION.
YEAH. I'M AWARE OF THAT.
WHAT DO YOU WANT?

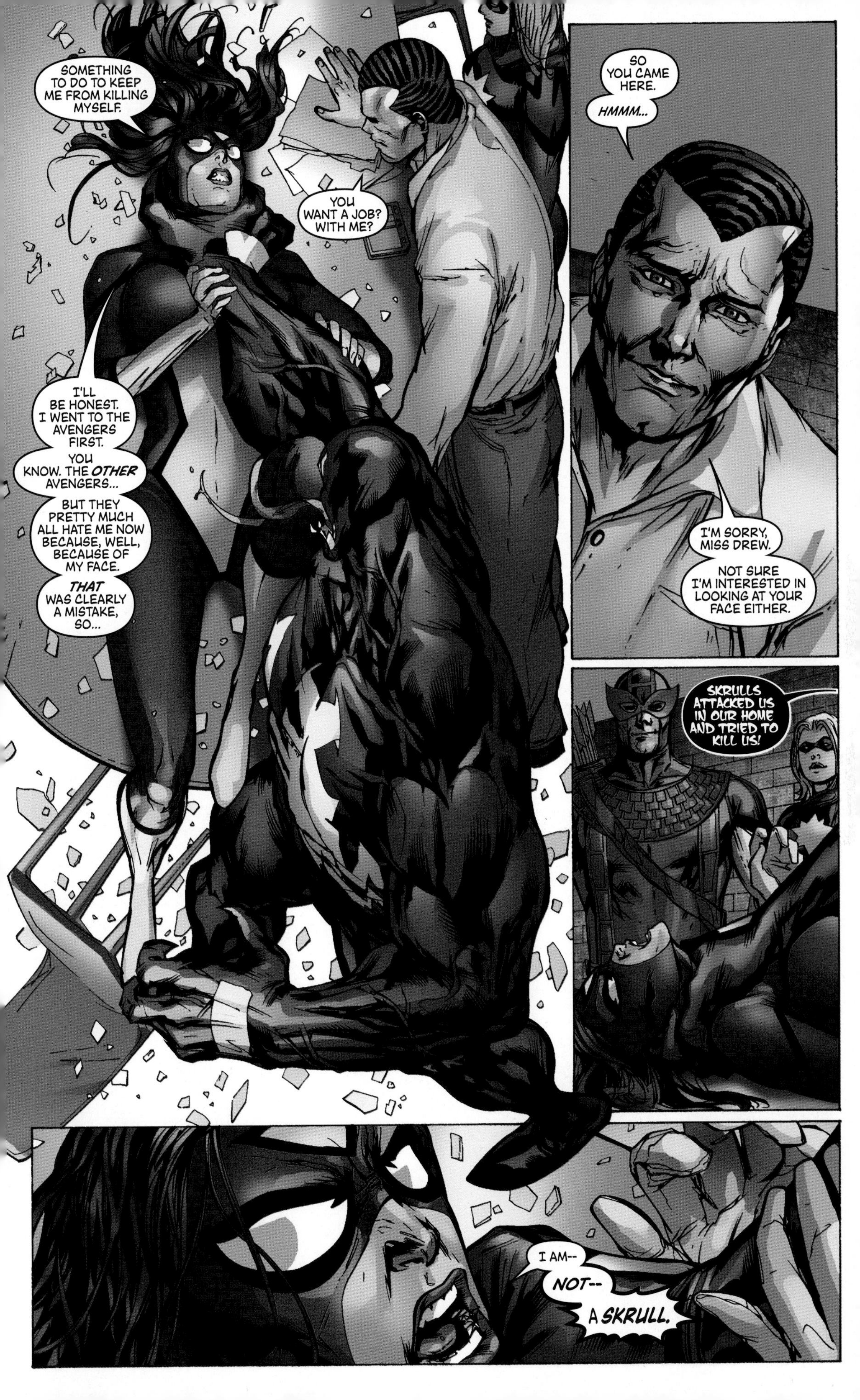
SOMETHING TO DO TO KEEP ME FROM KILLING MYSELF.
YOU WANT A JOB? WITH ME?
I'LL BE HONEST. I WENT TO THE AVENGERS FIRST.
YOU KNOW. THE OTHER AVENGERS...
BUT THEY PRETTY MUCH ALL HATE ME NOW BECAUSE, WELL, BECAUSE OF MY FACE.
THAT WAS CLEARLY A MISTAKE, SO...
SO YOU CAME HERE.
HMMM...
I'M SORRY, MISS DREW.
NOT SURE I'M INTERESTED IN LOOKING AT YOUR FACE EITHER.
SKRULLS ATTACKED US IN OUR HOME AND TRIED TO KILL US!
I AM--
NOT--
A SKRULL.

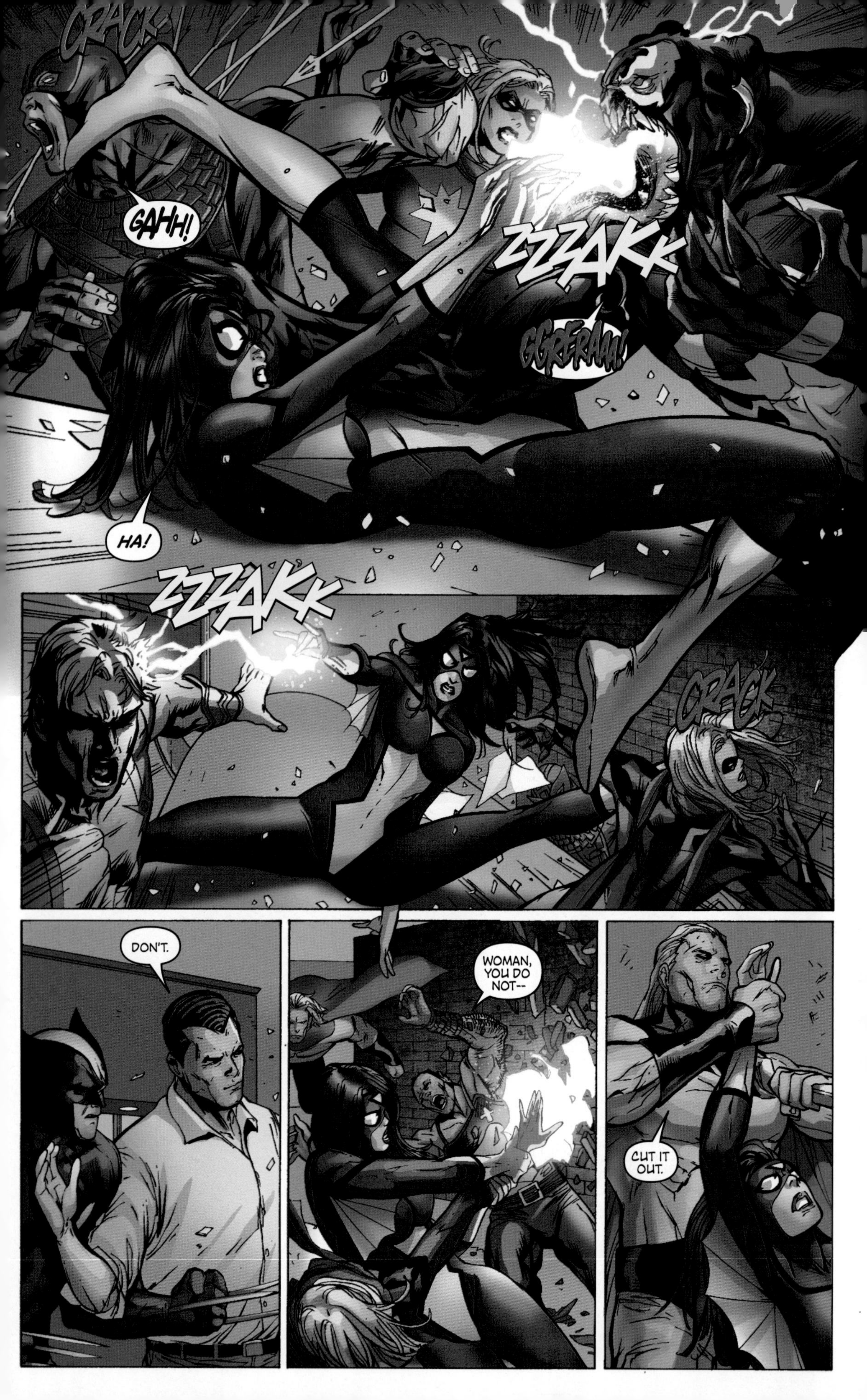
CRACK
GAHH!
ZZZAKK
GGRERAAA!
HA!
ZZZAKK
CRACK
DON'T.
WOMAN, YOU DO NOT--
CUT IT OUT.

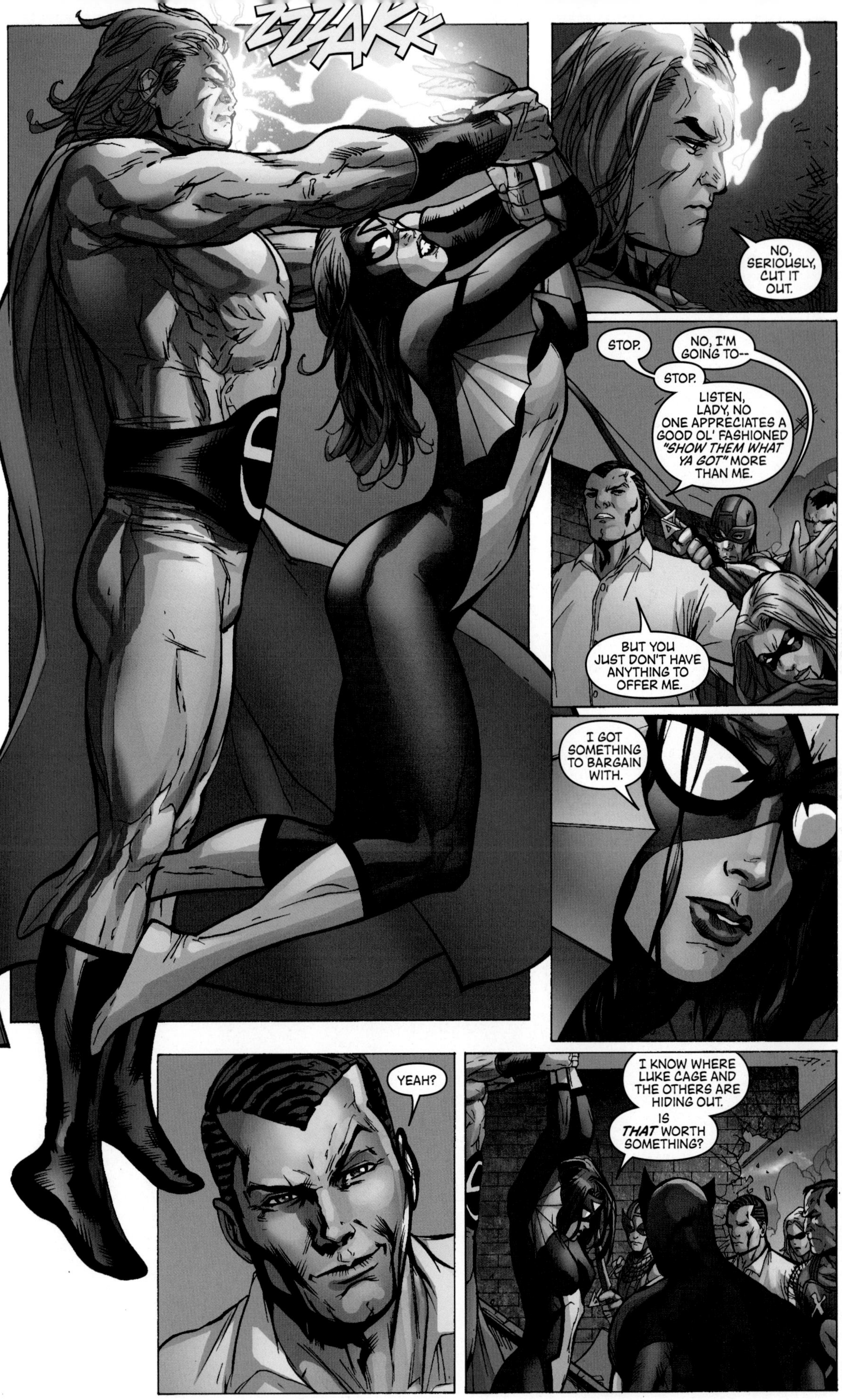
ZZZAKK
NO, SERIOUSLY, CUT IT OUT.
STOP.
NO, I'M GOING TO--
STOP.
LISTEN, LADY, NO ONE APPRECIATES A GOOD OL' FASHIONED *"SHOW THEM WHAT YA GOT"* MORE THAN ME.
BUT YOU JUST DON'T HAVE ANYTHING TO OFFER ME.
I GOT SOMETHING TO BARGAIN WITH.
YEAH?
I KNOW WHERE LUKE CAGE AND THE OTHERS ARE HIDING OUT.
IS ***THAT*** WORTH SOMETHING?

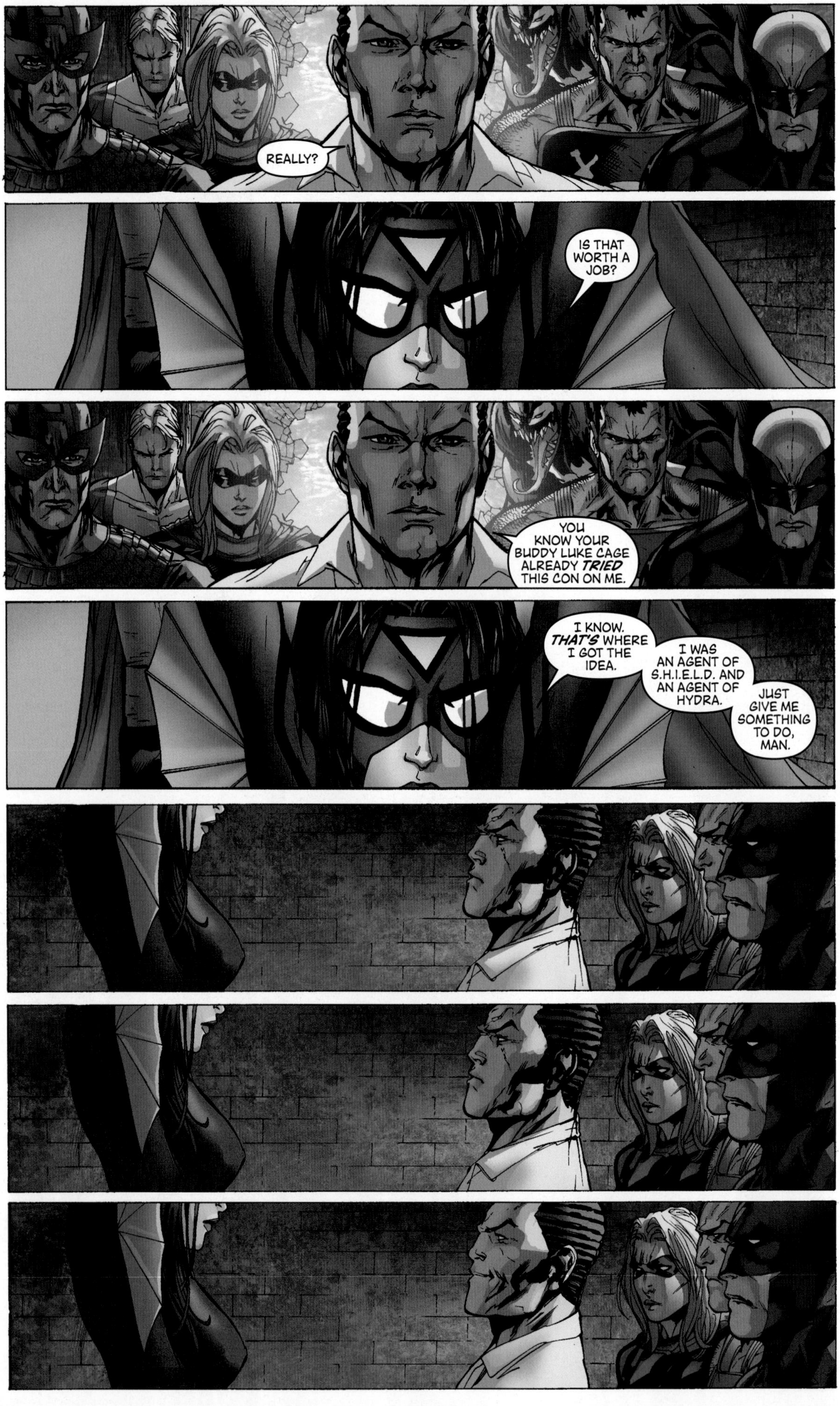
REALLY?
IS THAT WORTH A JOB?
YOU KNOW YOUR BUDDY LUKE CAGE ALREADY *TRIED* THIS CON ON ME.
I KNOW. *THAT'S* WHERE I GOT THE IDEA.
I WAS AN AGENT OF S.H.I.E.L.D. AND AN AGENT OF HYDRA.
JUST GIVE ME SOMETHING TO DO, MAN.

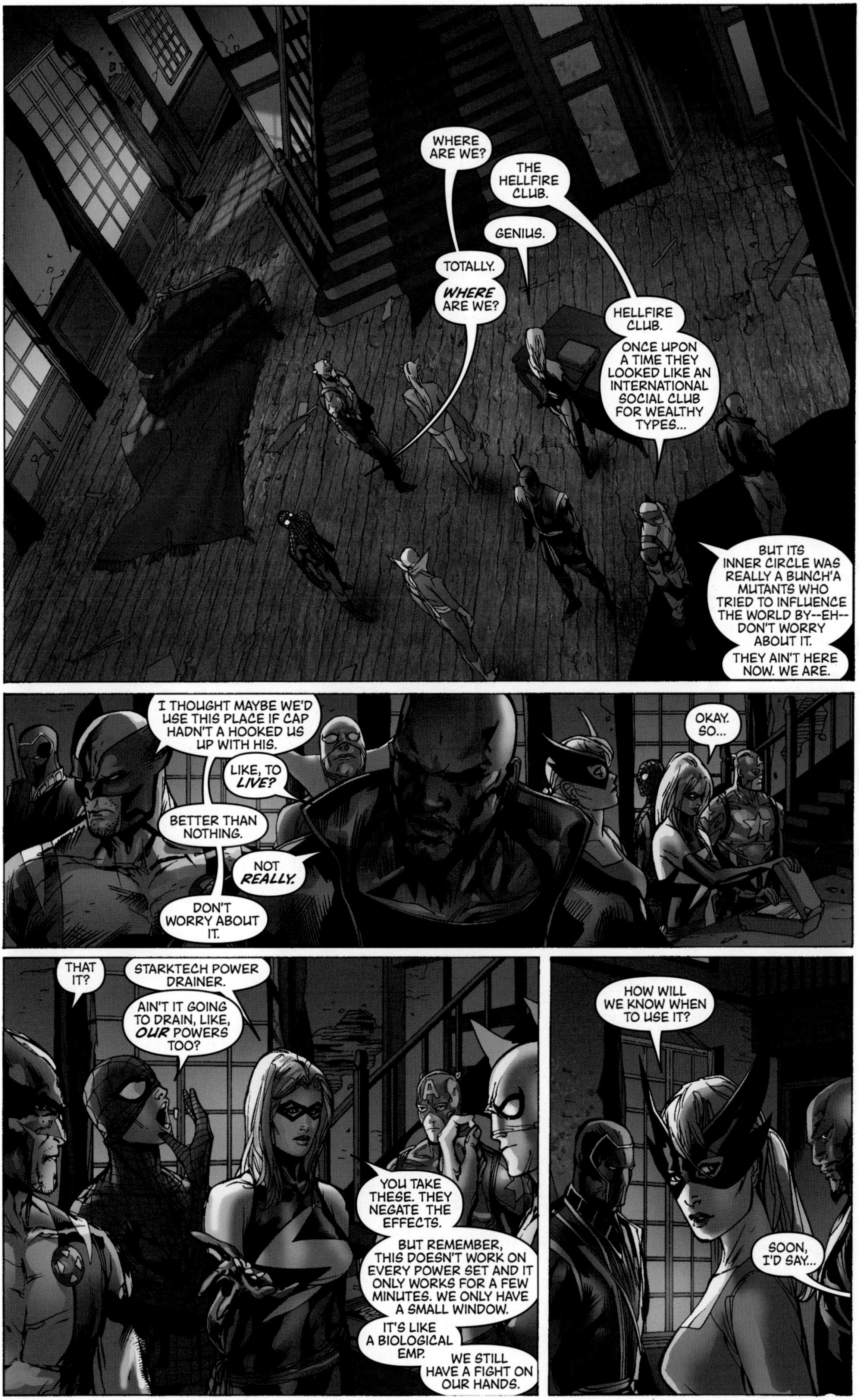

WHERE ARE WE?
THE HELLFIRE CLUB.
GENIUS.
TOTALLY. *WHERE* ARE WE?
HELLFIRE CLUB.
ONCE UPON A TIME THEY LOOKED LIKE AN INTERNATIONAL SOCIAL CLUB FOR WEALTHY TYPES...
BUT ITS INNER CIRCLE WAS REALLY A BUNCH'A MUTANTS WHO TRIED TO INFLUENCE THE WORLD BY--EH-- DON'T WORRY ABOUT IT.
THEY AIN'T HERE NOW. WE ARE.
I THOUGHT MAYBE WE'D USE THIS PLACE IF CAP HADN'T A HOOKED US UP WITH HIS.
LIKE, TO *LIVE?*
BETTER THAN NOTHING.
NOT *REALLY.*
DON'T WORRY ABOUT IT.
OKAY. SO...
THAT IT?
STARKTECH POWER DRAINER.
AIN'T IT GOING TO DRAIN, LIKE, *OUR* POWERS TOO?
YOU TAKE THESE. THEY NEGATE THE EFFECTS.
BUT REMEMBER, THIS DOESN'T WORK ON EVERY POWER SET AND IT ONLY WORKS FOR A FEW MINUTES. WE ONLY HAVE A SMALL WINDOW.
IT'S LIKE A BIOLOGICAL EMP.
WE STILL HAVE A FIGHT ON OUR HANDS.
HOW WILL WE KNOW WHEN TO USE IT?
SOON, I'D SAY...

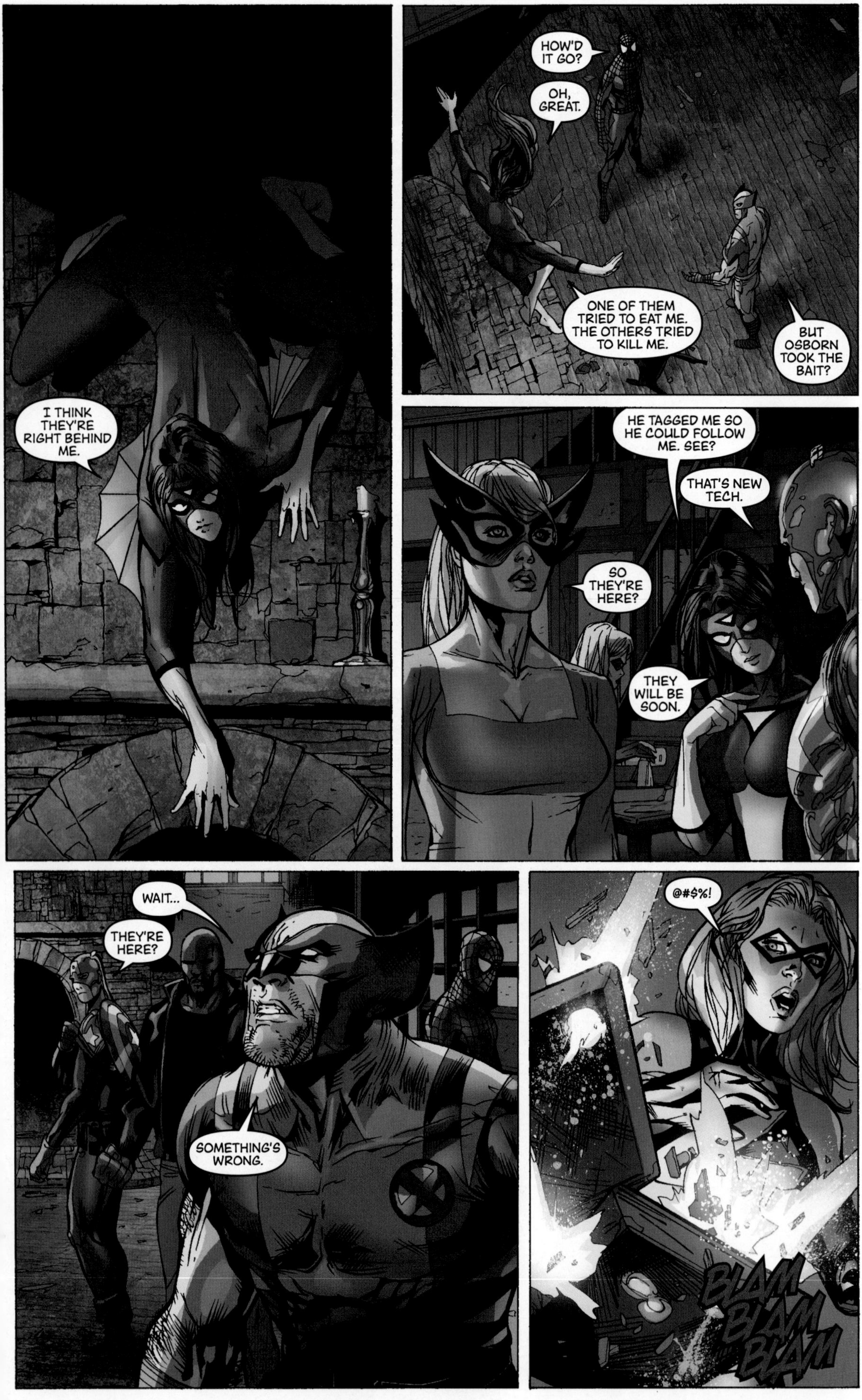
I THINK THEY'RE RIGHT BEHIND ME.
HOW'D IT GO?
OH, GREAT.
ONE OF THEM TRIED TO EAT ME. THE OTHERS TRIED TO KILL ME.
BUT OSBORN TOOK THE BAIT?
HE TAGGED ME SO HE COULD FOLLOW ME. SEE?
THAT'S NEW TECH.
SO THEY'RE HERE?
THEY WILL BE SOON.
WAIT...
THEY'RE HERE?
SOMETHING'S WRONG.
@#$%!
BLAM BLAM BLAM

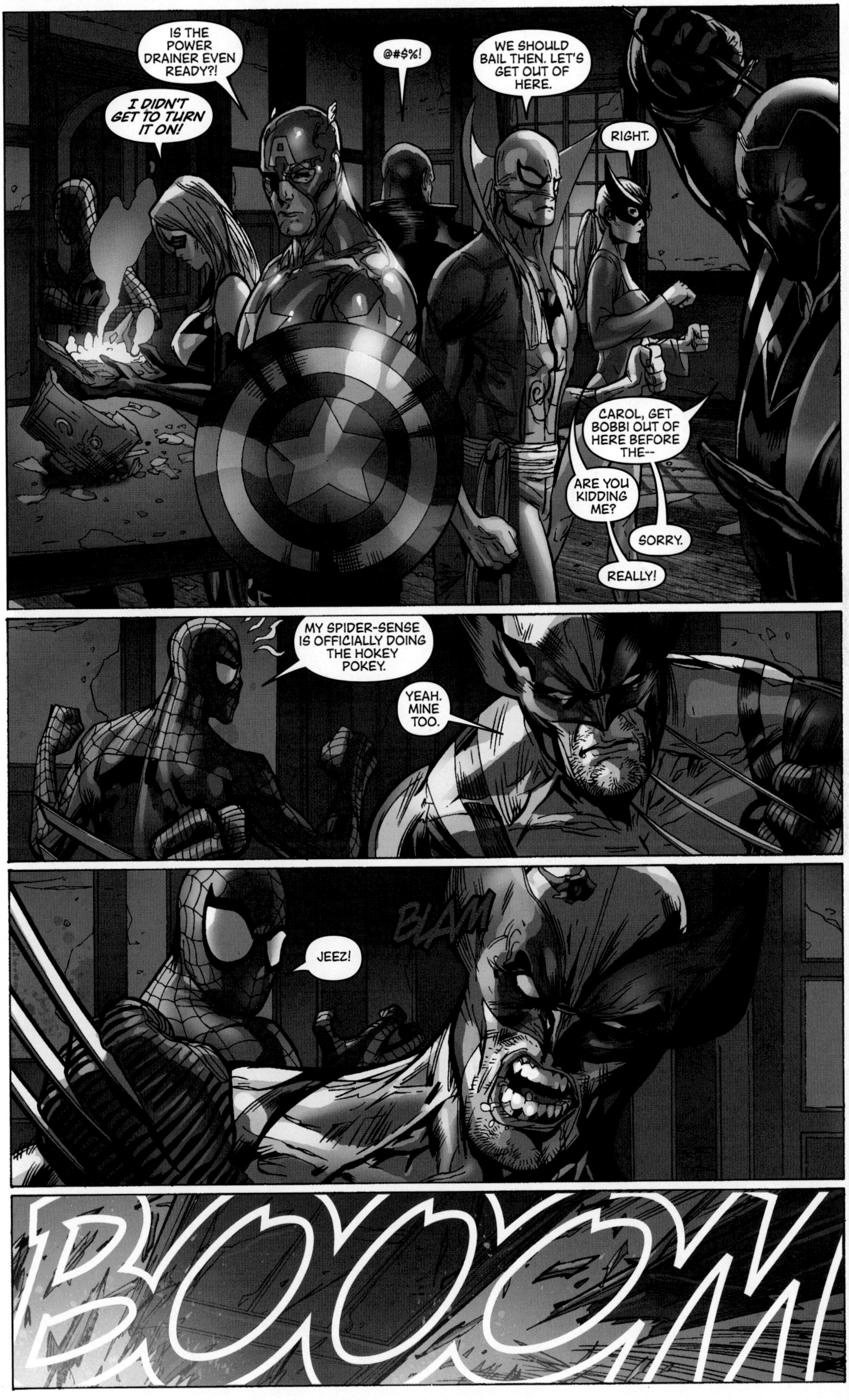
IS THE POWER DRAINER EVEN READY?!
I DIDN'T GET TO TURN IT ON!
@#$%!
WE SHOULD BAIL THEN. LET'S GET OUT OF HERE.
RIGHT.
CAROL, GET BOBBI OUT OF HERE BEFORE THE--
ARE YOU KIDDING ME?
SORRY.
REALLY!
MY SPIDER-SENSE IS OFFICIALLY DOING THE HOKEY POKEY.
YEAH. MINE TOO.
BLAM
JEEZ!
BOOOM

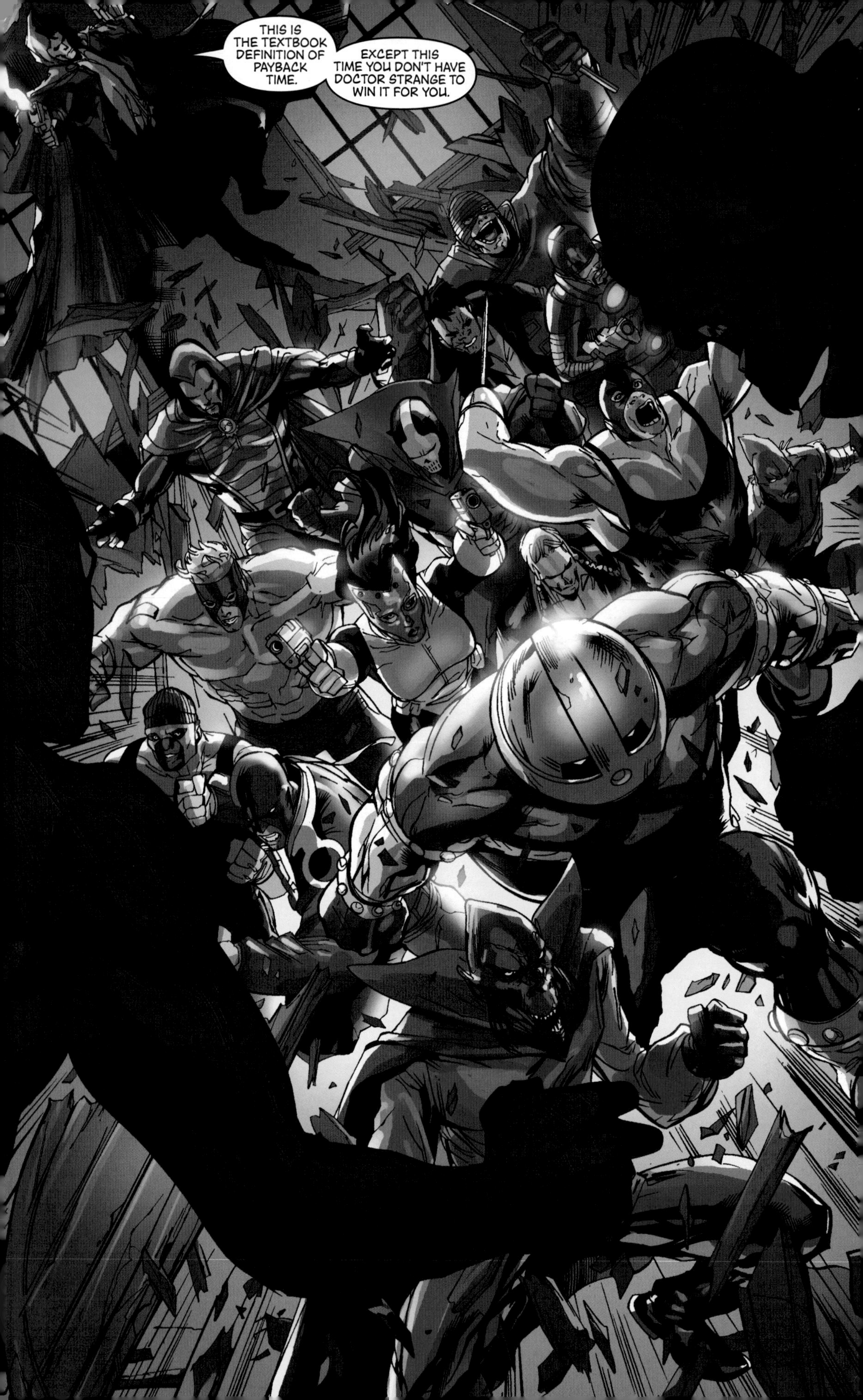
THIS IS THE TEXTBOOK DEFINITION OF PAYBACK TIME.
EXCEPT THIS TIME YOU DON'T HAVE DOCTOR STRANGE TO WIN IT FOR YOU.

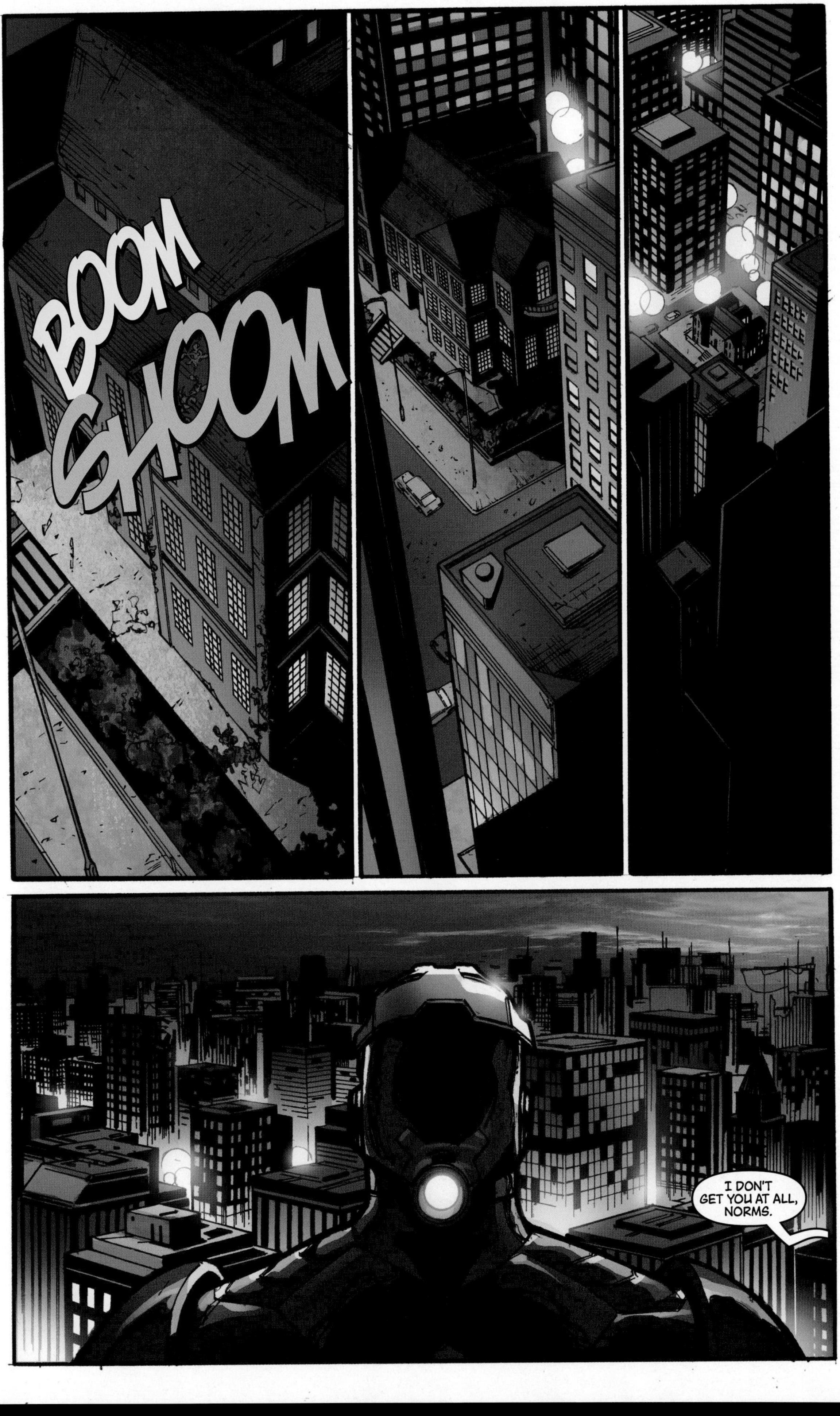
BOOM
SHOOM
I DON'T GET YOU AT ALL, NORMS.

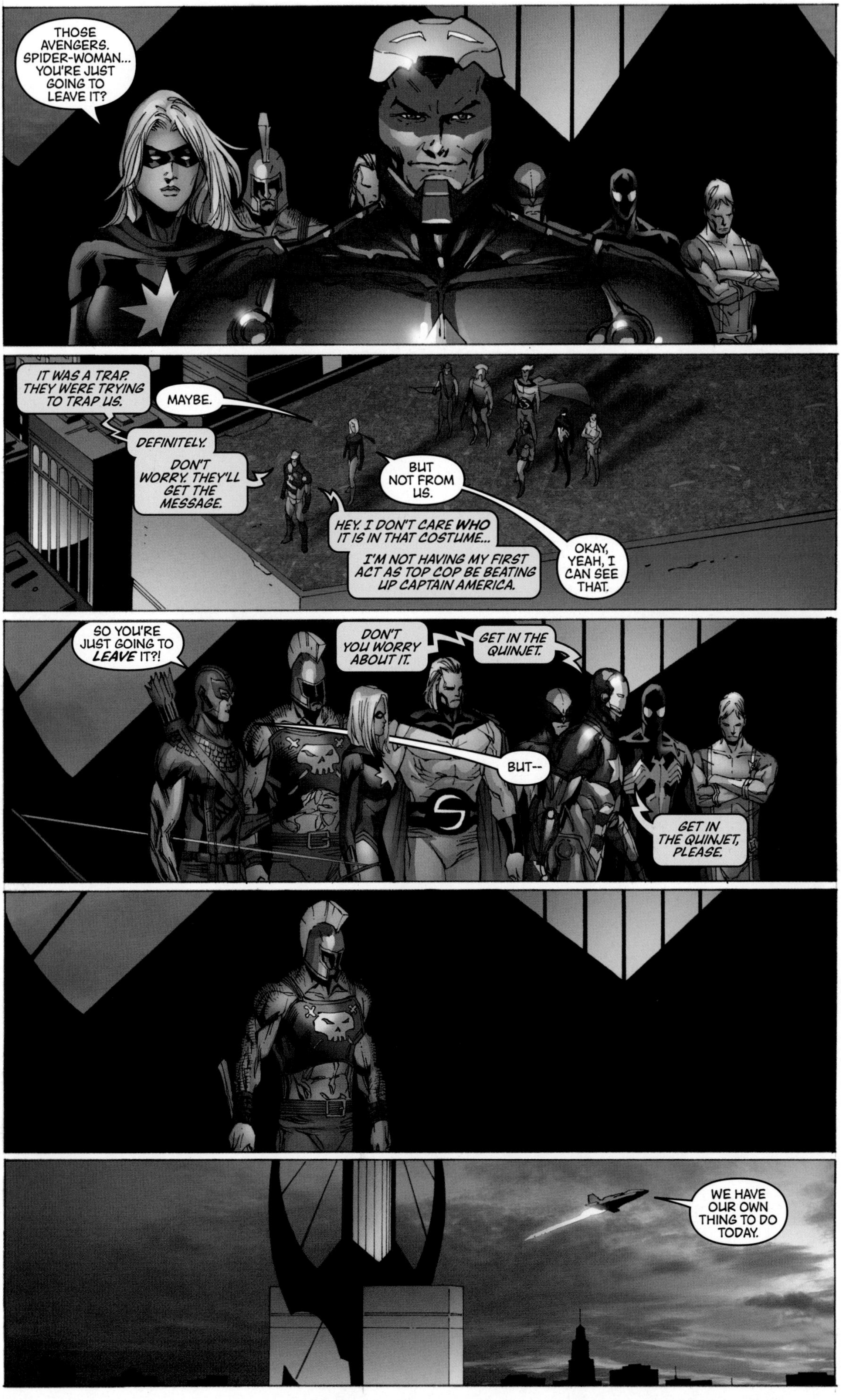
THOSE AVENGERS. SPIDER-WOMAN... YOU'RE JUST GOING TO LEAVE IT?
IT WAS A TRAP. THEY WERE TRYING TO TRAP US.
MAYBE.
DEFINITELY.
DON'T WORRY. THEY'LL GET THE MESSAGE.
BUT NOT FROM US.
HEY. I DON'T CARE WHO IT IS IN THAT COSTUME...
I'M NOT HAVING MY FIRST ACT AS TOP COP BE BEATING UP CAPTAIN AMERICA.
OKAY, YEAH, I CAN SEE THAT.
SO YOU'RE JUST GOING TO LEAVE IT?!
DON'T YOU WORRY ABOUT IT.
GET IN THE QUINJET.
BUT--
GET IN THE QUINJET, PLEASE.
WE HAVE OUR OWN THING TO DO TODAY.

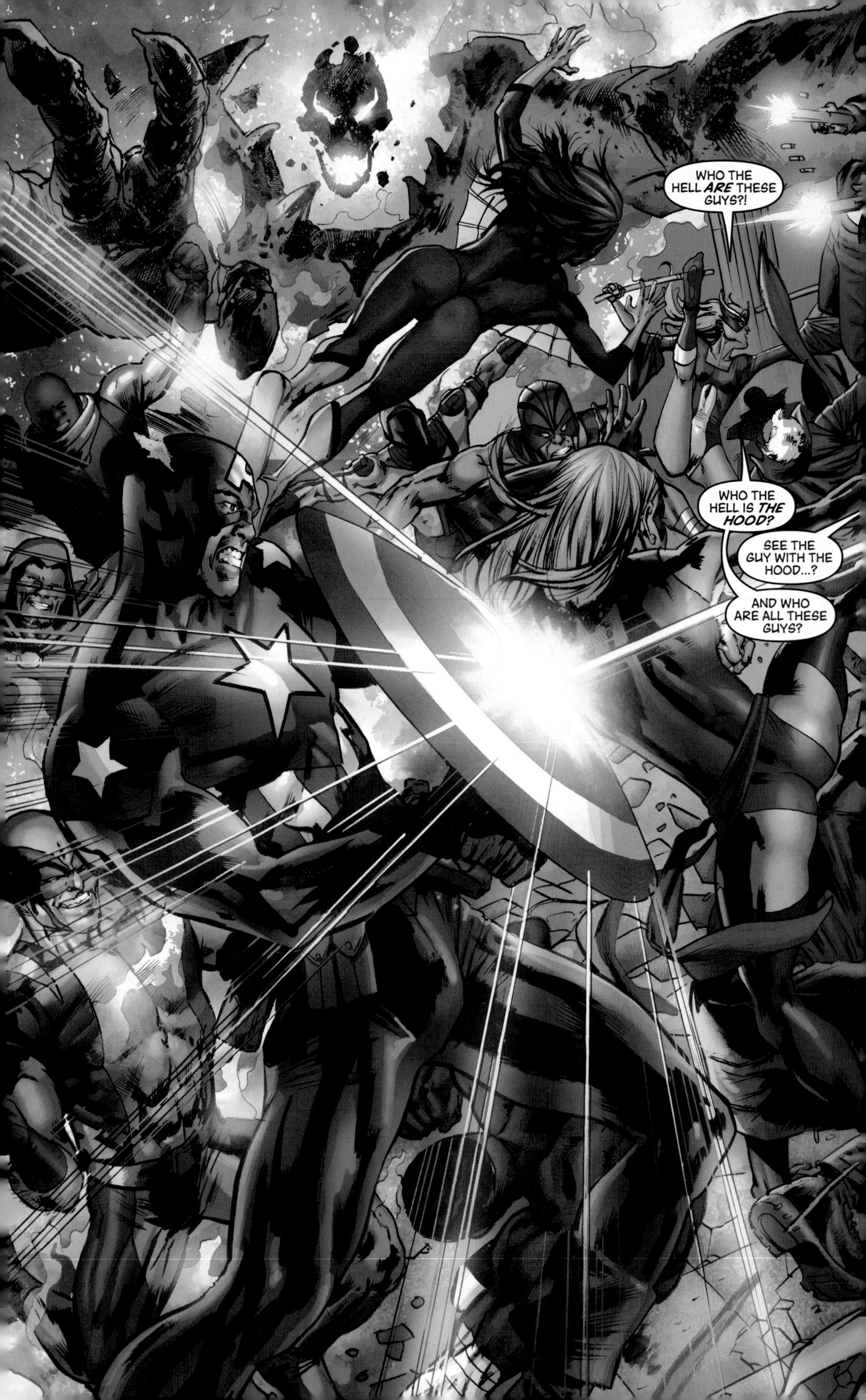
WHO THE HELL *ARE* THESE GUYS?!
WHO THE HELL IS *THE HOOD?*
SEE THE GUY WITH THE HOOD...?
AND WHO ARE ALL THESE GUYS?

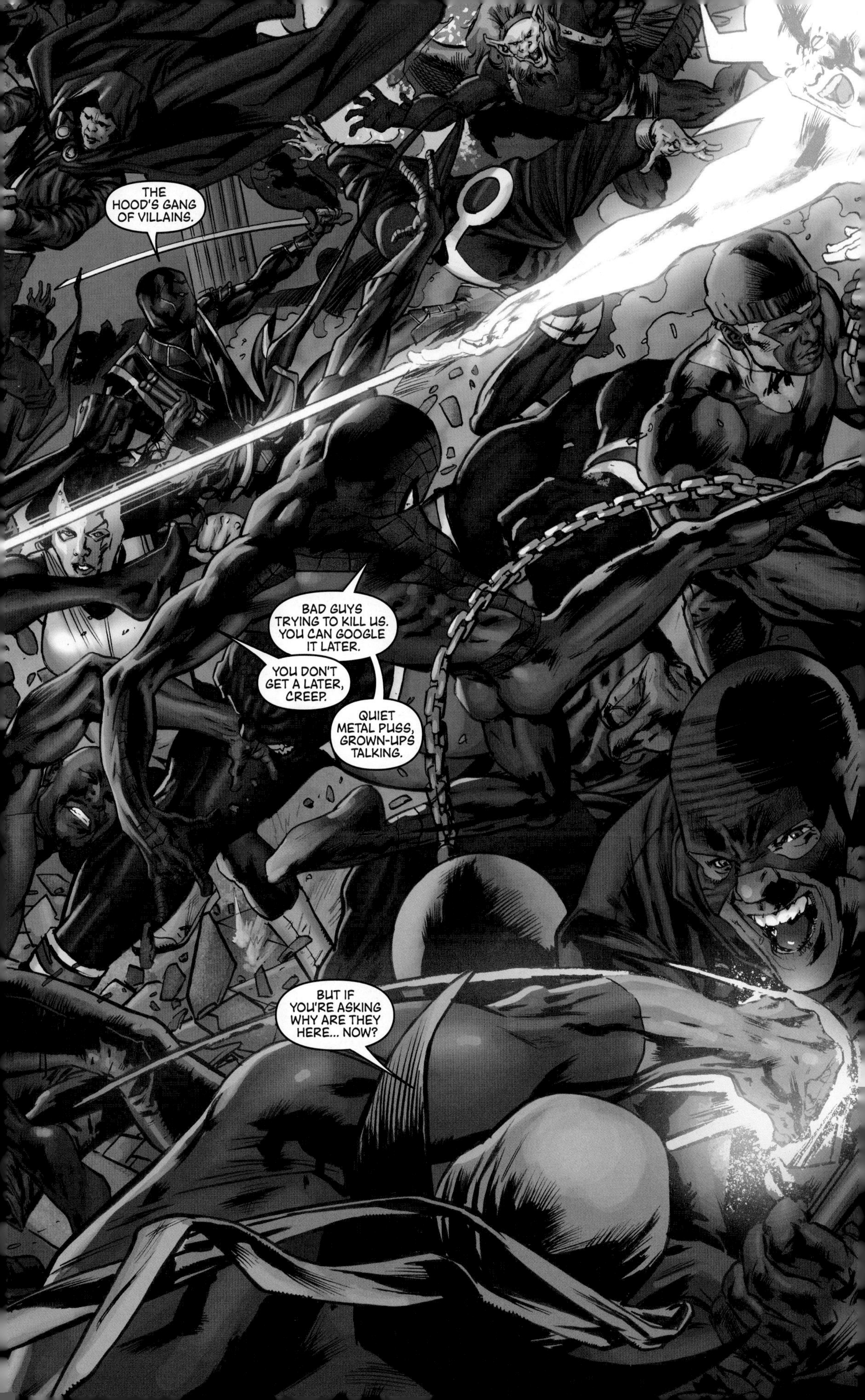
THE HOOD'S GANG OF VILLAINS.
BAD GUYS TRYING TO KILL US. YOU CAN GOOGLE IT LATER.
YOU DON'T GET A LATER, CREEP.
QUIET METAL PUSS, GROWN-UPS TALKING.
BUT IF YOU'RE ASKING WHY ARE THEY HERE... NOW?

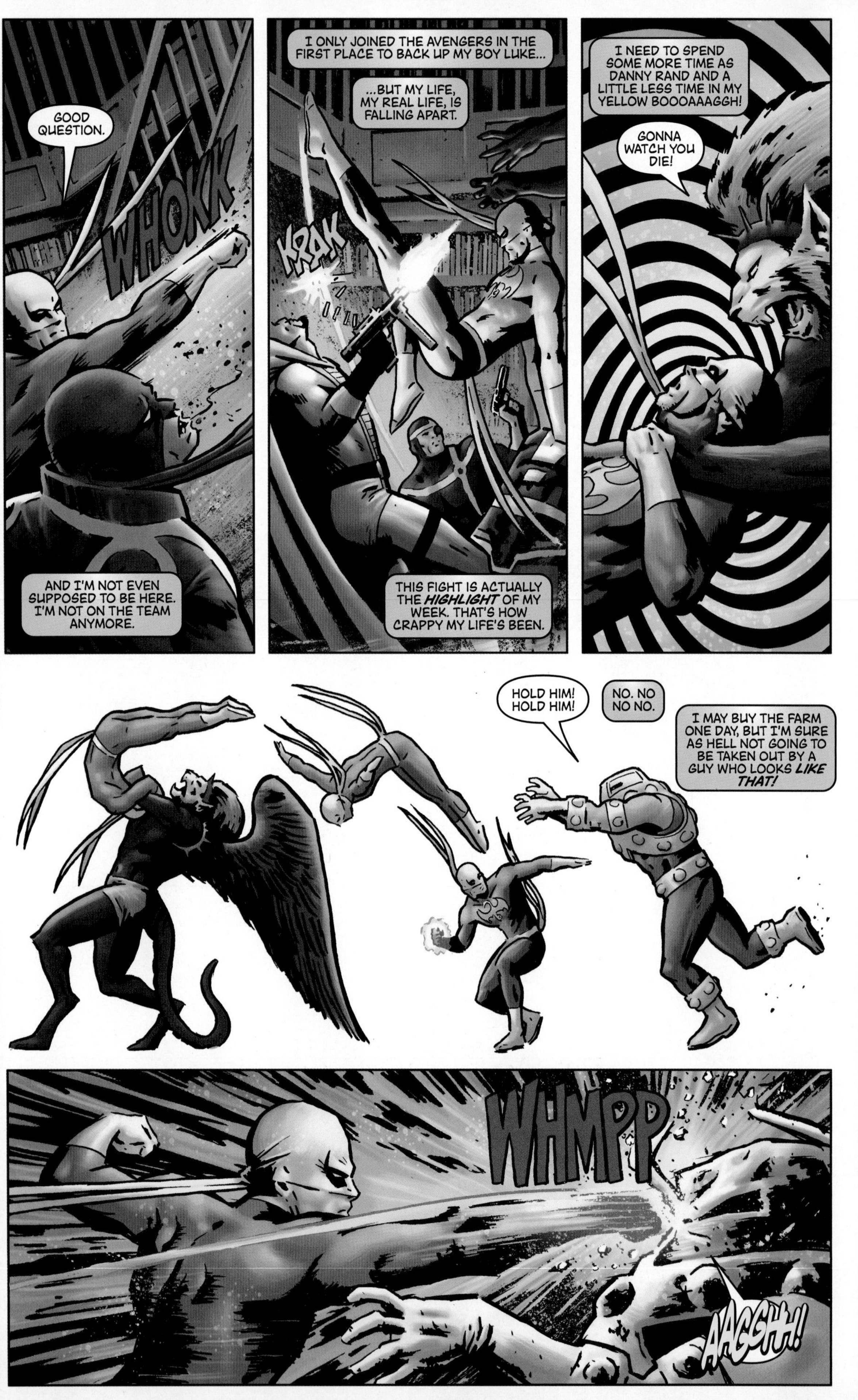
GOOD QUESTION.
WHOKK
AND I'M NOT EVEN SUPPOSED TO BE HERE. I'M NOT ON THE TEAM ANYMORE.
I ONLY JOINED THE AVENGERS IN THE FIRST PLACE TO BACK UP MY BOY LUKE...
...BUT MY LIFE, MY REAL LIFE, IS FALLING APART.
KRAK
THIS FIGHT IS ACTUALLY THE HIGHLIGHT OF MY WEEK. THAT'S HOW CRAPPY MY LIFE'S BEEN.
I NEED TO SPEND SOME MORE TIME AS DANNY RAND AND A LITTLE LESS TIME IN MY YELLOW BOOOAAAGGH!
GONNA WATCH YOU DIE!
HOLD HIM! HOLD HIM!
NO. NO NO NO.
I MAY BUY THE FARM ONE DAY, BUT I'M SURE AS HELL NOT GOING TO BE TAKEN OUT BY A GUY WHO LOOKS LIKE THAT!
WHMPP
AAGGHH!

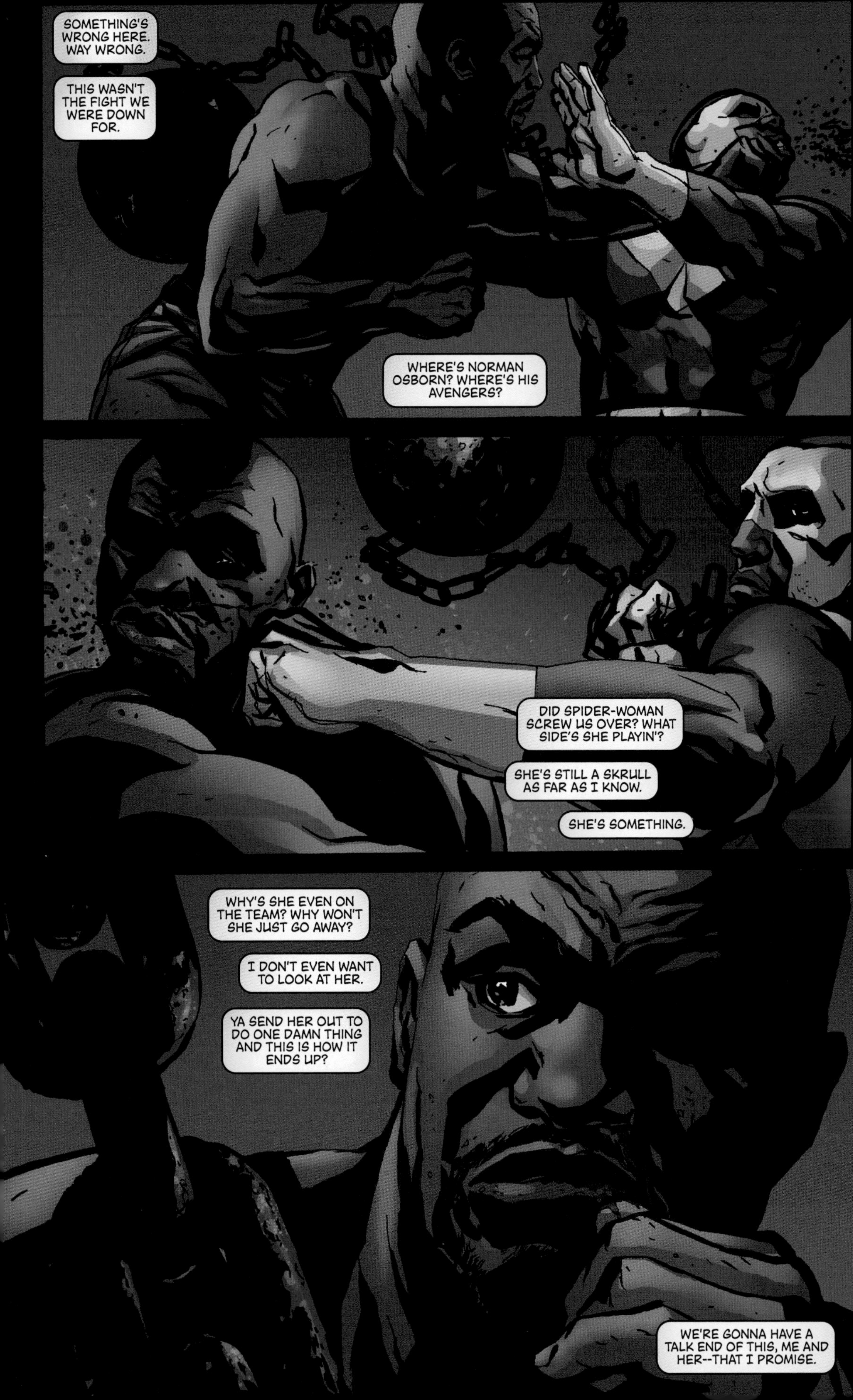
SOMETHING'S WRONG HERE. WAY WRONG.
THIS WASN'T THE FIGHT WE WERE DOWN FOR.
WHERE'S NORMAN OSBORN? WHERE'S HIS AVENGERS?
DID SPIDER-WOMAN SCREW US OVER? WHAT SIDE'S SHE PLAYIN'?
SHE'S STILL A SKRULL AS FAR AS I KNOW.
SHE'S SOMETHING.
WHY'S SHE EVEN ON THE TEAM? WHY WON'T SHE JUST GO AWAY?
I DON'T EVEN WANT TO LOOK AT HER.
YA SEND HER OUT TO DO ONE DAMN THING AND THIS IS HOW IT ENDS UP?
WE'RE GONNA HAVE A TALK END OF THIS, ME AND HER--THAT I PROMISE.

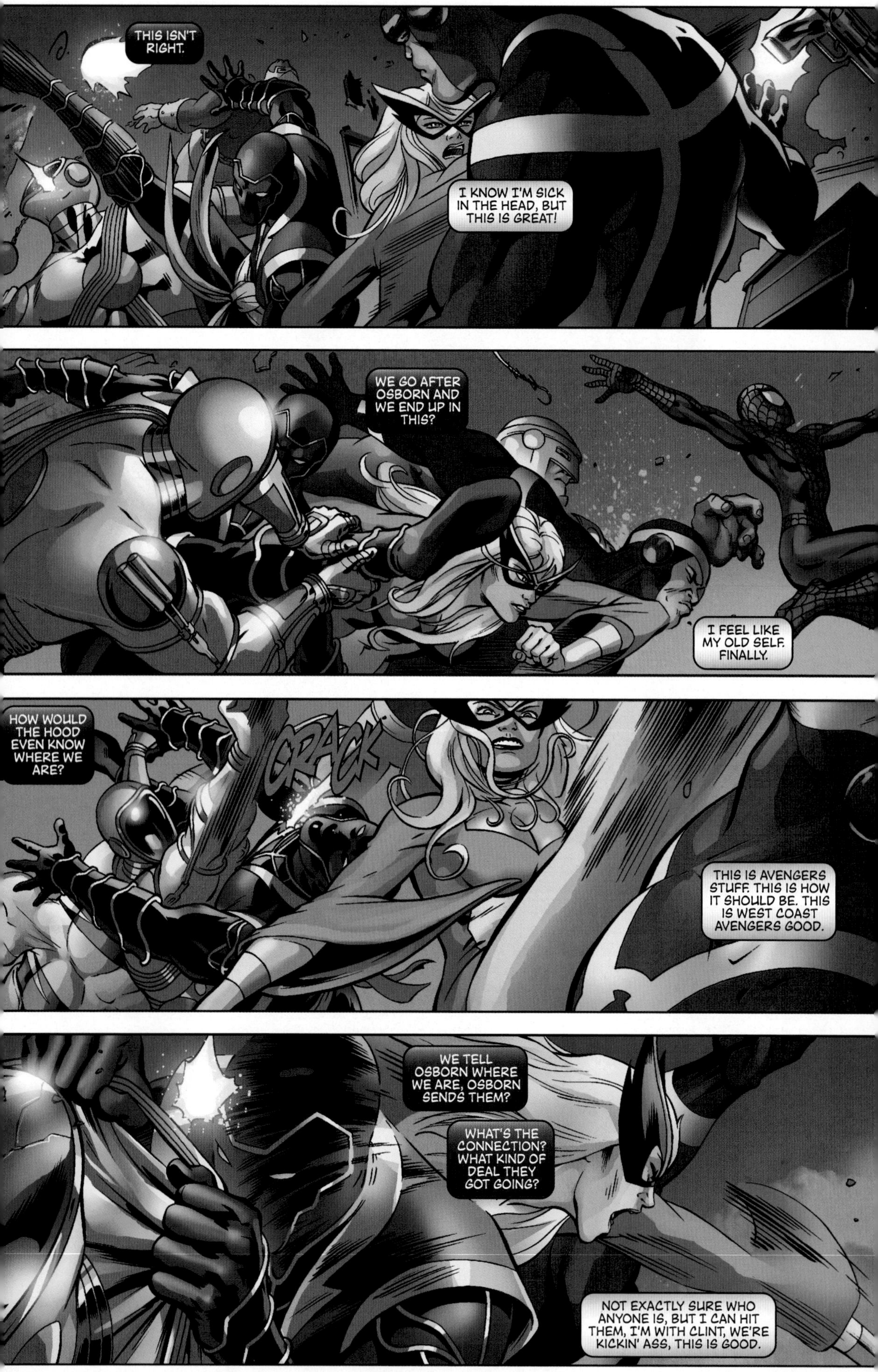
THIS ISN'T RIGHT.
I KNOW I'M SICK IN THE HEAD, BUT THIS IS GREAT!
WE GO AFTER OSBORN AND WE END UP IN THIS?
I FEEL LIKE MY OLD SELF. FINALLY.
HOW WOULD THE HOOD EVEN KNOW WHERE WE ARE?
CRACK
THIS IS AVENGERS STUFF. THIS IS HOW IT SHOULD BE. THIS IS WEST COAST AVENGERS GOOD.
WE TELL OSBORN WHERE WE ARE, OSBORN SENDS THEM?
WHAT'S THE CONNECTION? WHAT KIND OF DEAL THEY GOT GOING?
NOT EXACTLY SURE WHO ANYONE IS, BUT I CAN HIT THEM, I'M WITH CLINT, WE'RE KICKIN' ASS, THIS IS GOOD.

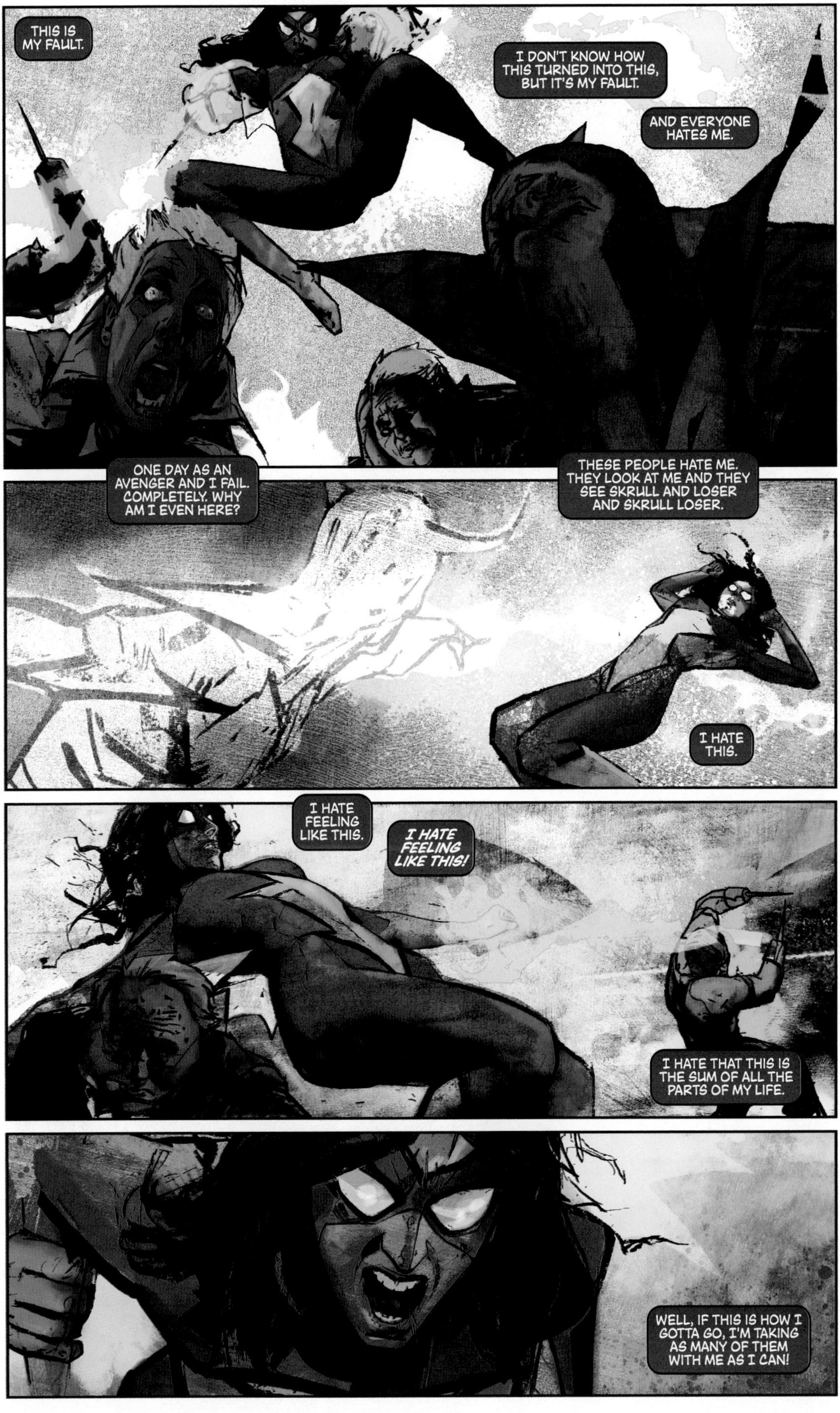

THIS IS MY FAULT.
I DON'T KNOW HOW THIS TURNED INTO THIS, BUT IT'S MY FAULT.
AND EVERYONE HATES ME.
ONE DAY AS AN AVENGER AND I FAIL. COMPLETELY. WHY AM I EVEN HERE?
THESE PEOPLE HATE ME. THEY LOOK AT ME AND THEY SEE SKRULL AND LOSER AND SKRULL LOSER.
I HATE THIS.
I HATE FEELING LIKE THIS.
I HATE FEELING LIKE THIS!
I HATE THAT THIS IS THE SUM OF ALL THE PARTS OF MY LIFE.
WELL, IF THIS IS HOW I GOTTA GO, I'M TAKING AS MANY OF THEM WITH ME AS I CAN!

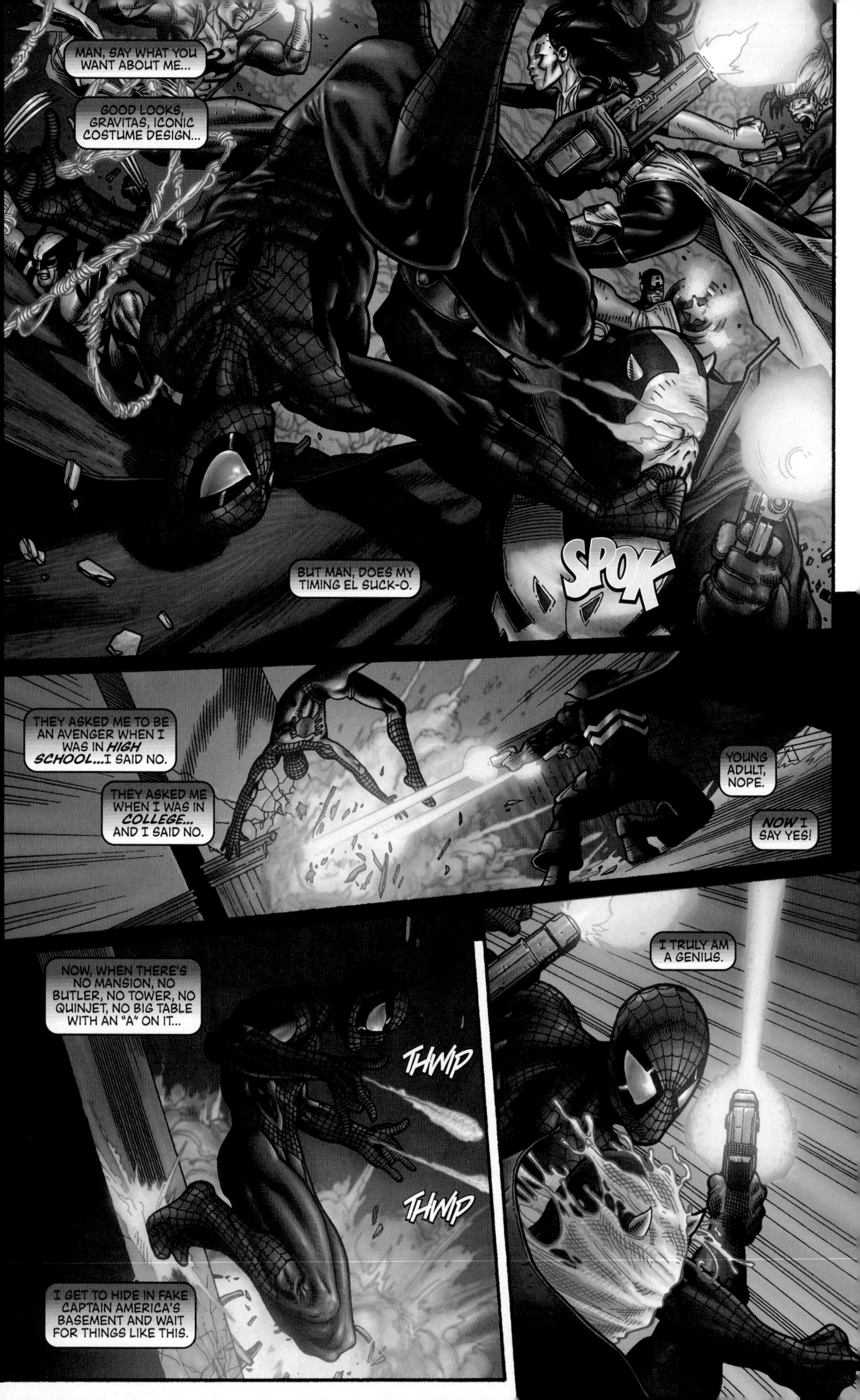
MAN, SAY WHAT YOU WANT ABOUT ME...
GOOD LOOKS, GRAVITAS, ICONIC COSTUME DESIGN...
BUT MAN, DOES MY TIMING EL SUCK-O.
SPOK
THEY ASKED ME TO BE AN AVENGER WHEN I WAS IN *HIGH SCHOOL*...I SAID NO.
THEY ASKED ME WHEN I WAS IN *COLLEGE*... AND I SAID NO.
YOUNG ADULT, NOPE.
NOW I SAY YES!
NOW, WHEN THERE'S NO MANSION, NO BUTLER, NO TOWER, NO QUINJET, NO BIG TABLE WITH AN "A" ON IT...
THWIP
THWIP
I GET TO HIDE IN FAKE CAPTAIN AMERICA'S BASEMENT AND WAIT FOR THINGS LIKE THIS.
I TRULY AM A GENIUS.

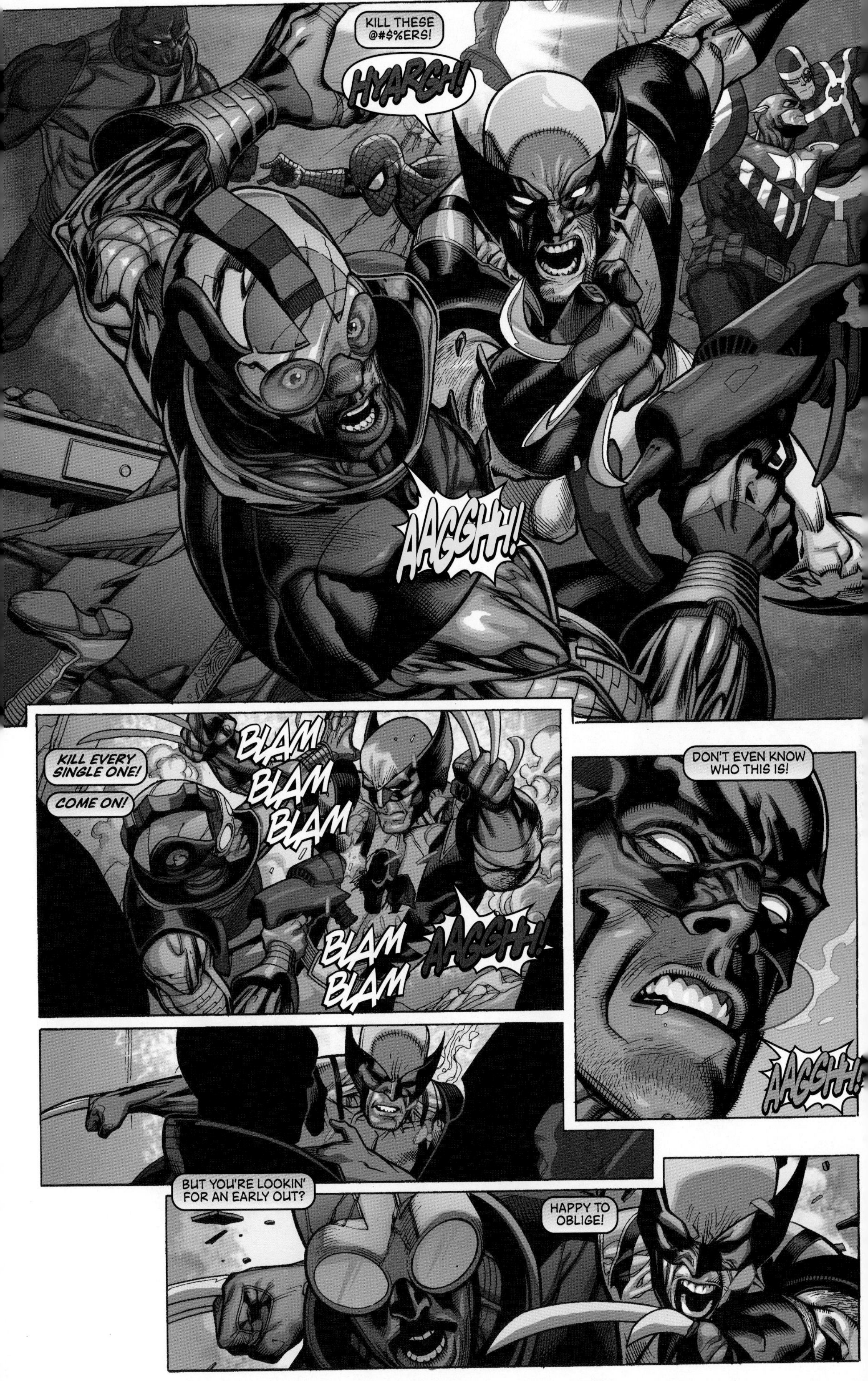
KILL THESE @#$%ERS!
HYARGH!
AAGGHH!
KILL EVERY SINGLE ONE!
COME ON!
BLAM
BLAM
BLAM
BLAM
BLAM
AAGGHH!
DON'T EVEN KNOW WHO THIS IS!
AAGGHH!
BUT YOU'RE LOOKIN' FOR AN EARLY OUT?
HAPPY TO OBLIGE!

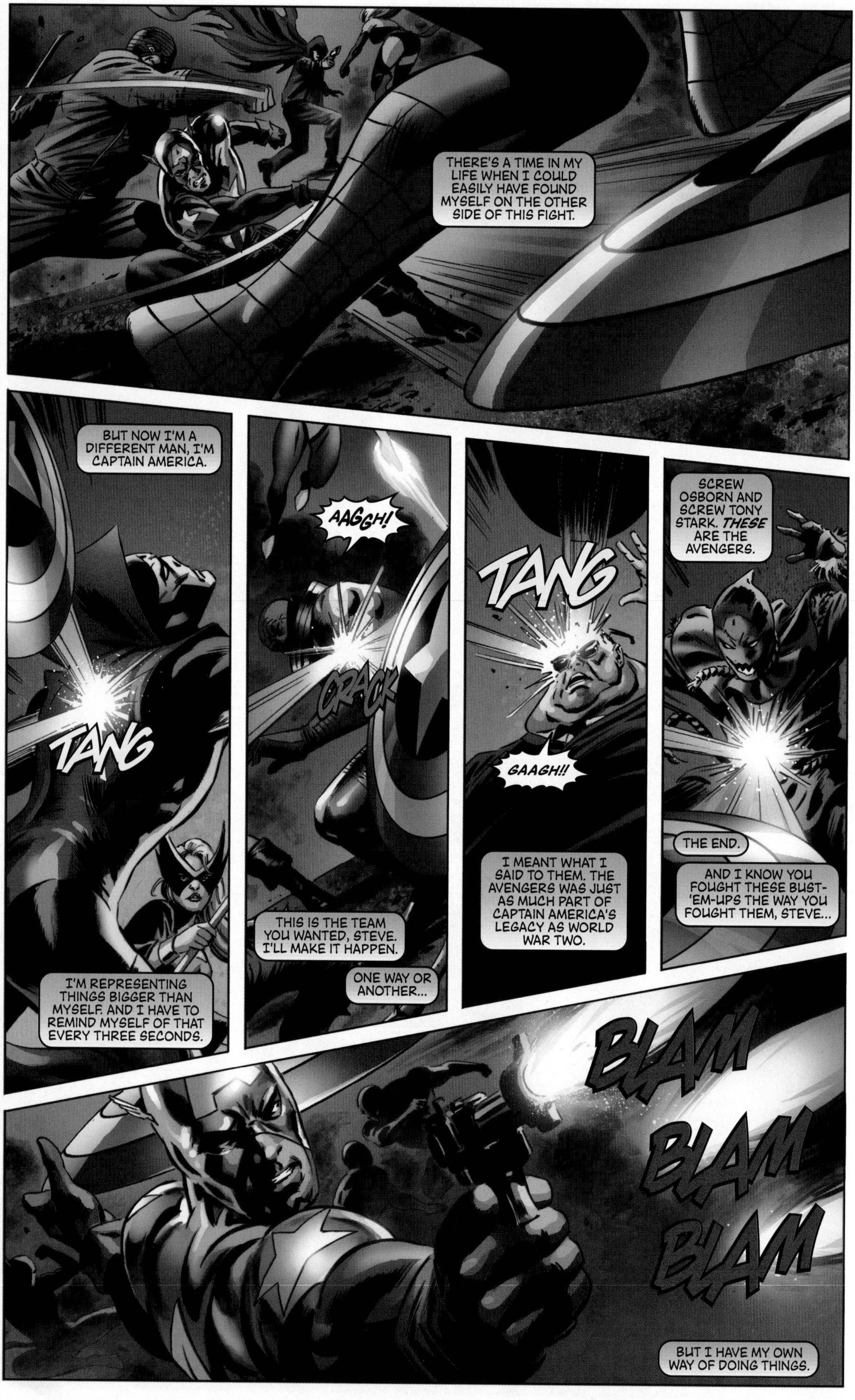
THERE'S A TIME IN MY LIFE WHEN I COULD EASILY HAVE FOUND MYSELF ON THE OTHER SIDE OF THIS FIGHT.
BUT NOW I'M A DIFFERENT MAN, I'M CAPTAIN AMERICA.
TANG
I'M REPRESENTING THINGS BIGGER THAN MYSELF. AND I HAVE TO REMIND MYSELF OF THAT EVERY THREE SECONDS.
AAGGH!
CRACK
THIS IS THE TEAM YOU WANTED, STEVE. I'LL MAKE IT HAPPEN.
ONE WAY OR ANOTHER...
TANG
GAAGH!!
I MEANT WHAT I SAID TO THEM. THE AVENGERS WAS JUST AS MUCH PART OF CAPTAIN AMERICA'S LEGACY AS WORLD WAR TWO.
SCREW OSBORN AND SCREW TONY STARK. *THESE* ARE THE AVENGERS.
THE END.
AND I KNOW YOU FOUGHT THESE BUST-'EM-UPS THE WAY YOU FOUGHT THEM, STEVE...
BLAM
BLAM
BLAM
BUT I HAVE MY OWN WAY OF DOING THINGS.

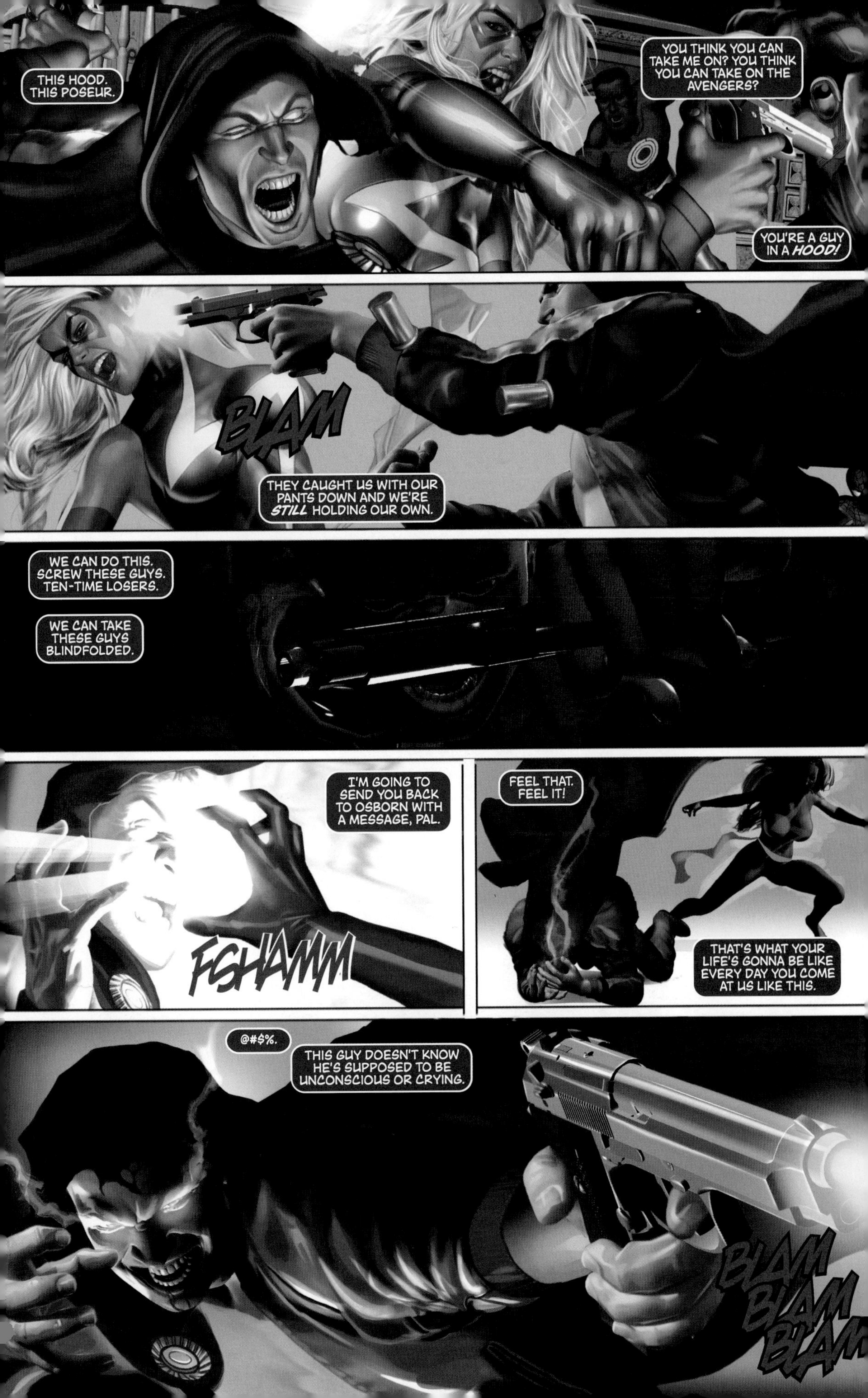
THIS HOOD. THIS POSEUR.
YOU THINK YOU CAN TAKE ME ON? YOU THINK YOU CAN TAKE ON THE AVENGERS?
YOU'RE A GUY IN A HOOD!
BLAM
THEY CAUGHT US WITH OUR PANTS DOWN AND WE'RE STILL HOLDING OUR OWN.
WE CAN DO THIS. SCREW THESE GUYS. TEN-TIME LOSERS.
WE CAN TAKE THESE GUYS BLINDFOLDED.
I'M GOING TO SEND YOU BACK TO OSBORN WITH A MESSAGE, PAL.
FSHAMM
FEEL THAT. FEEL IT!
THAT'S WHAT YOUR LIFE'S GONNA BE LIKE EVERY DAY YOU COME AT US LIKE THIS.
@#$%.
THIS GUY DOESN'T KNOW HE'S SUPPOSED TO BE UNCONSCIOUS OR CRYING.
BLAM
BLAM
BLAM

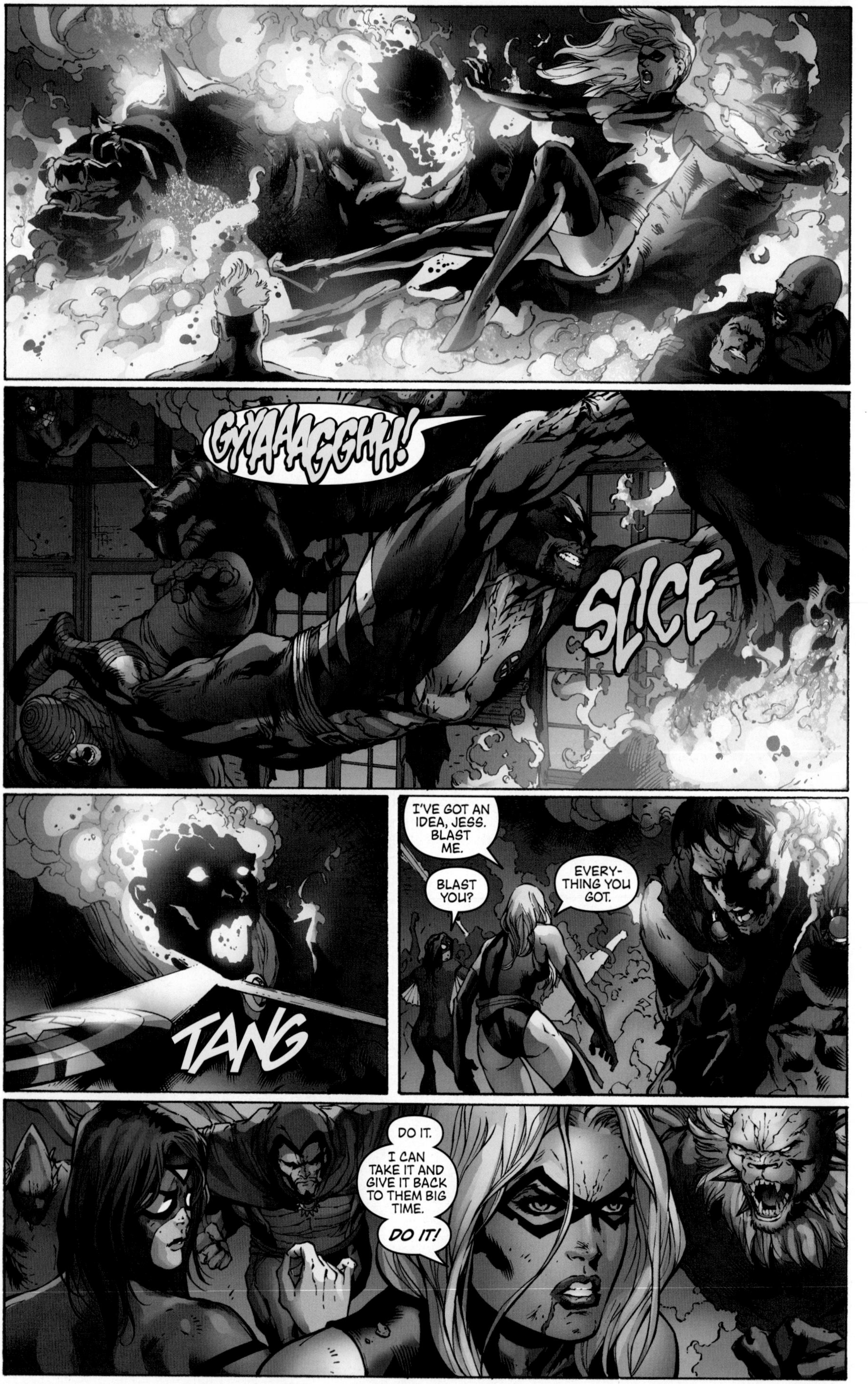
GYAAAGGHH!
SLICE
TANG
I'VE GOT AN IDEA, JESS. BLAST ME.
BLAST YOU?
EVERY-THING YOU GOT.
DO IT.
I CAN TAKE IT AND GIVE IT BACK TO THEM BIG TIME.
DO IT!

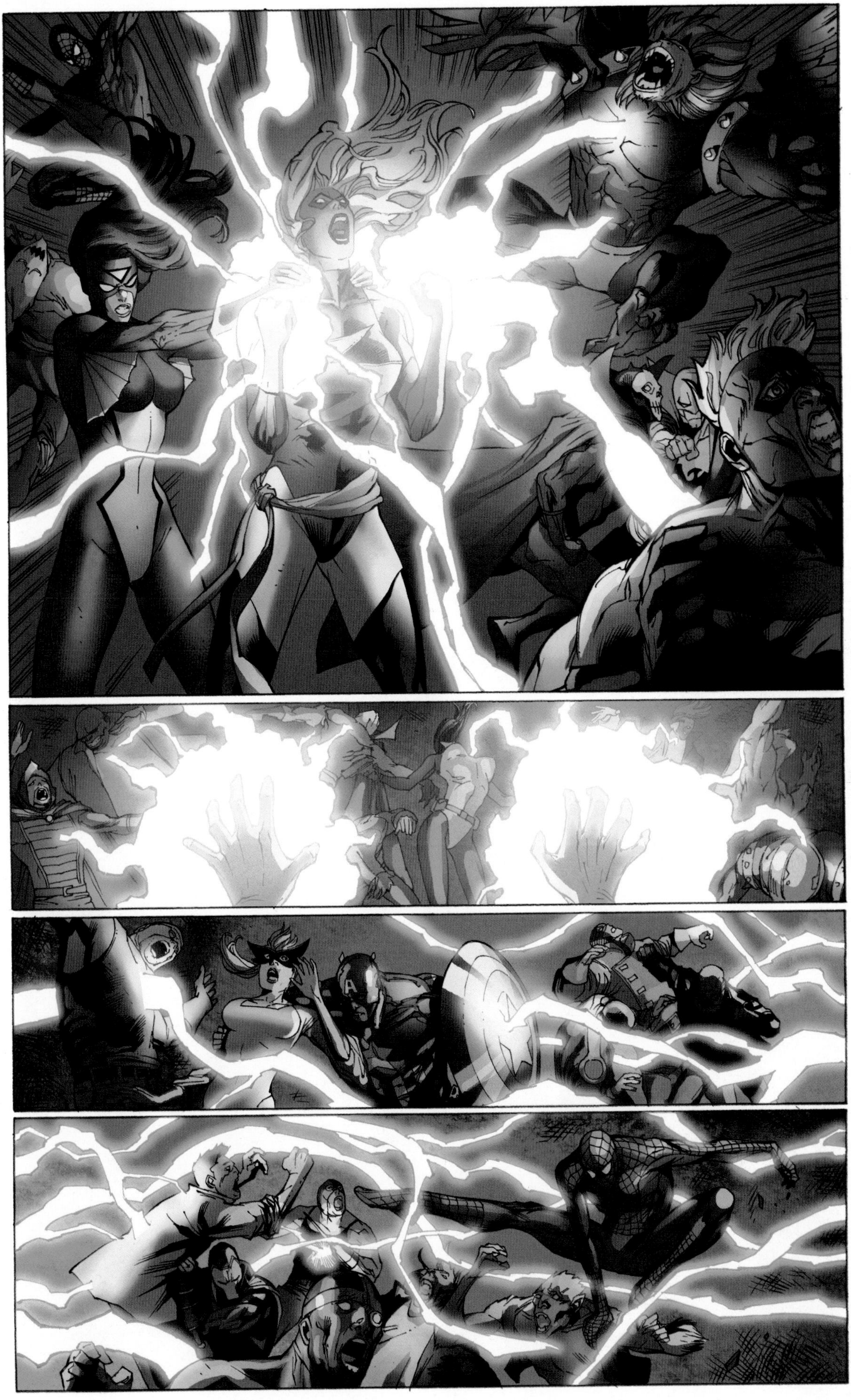

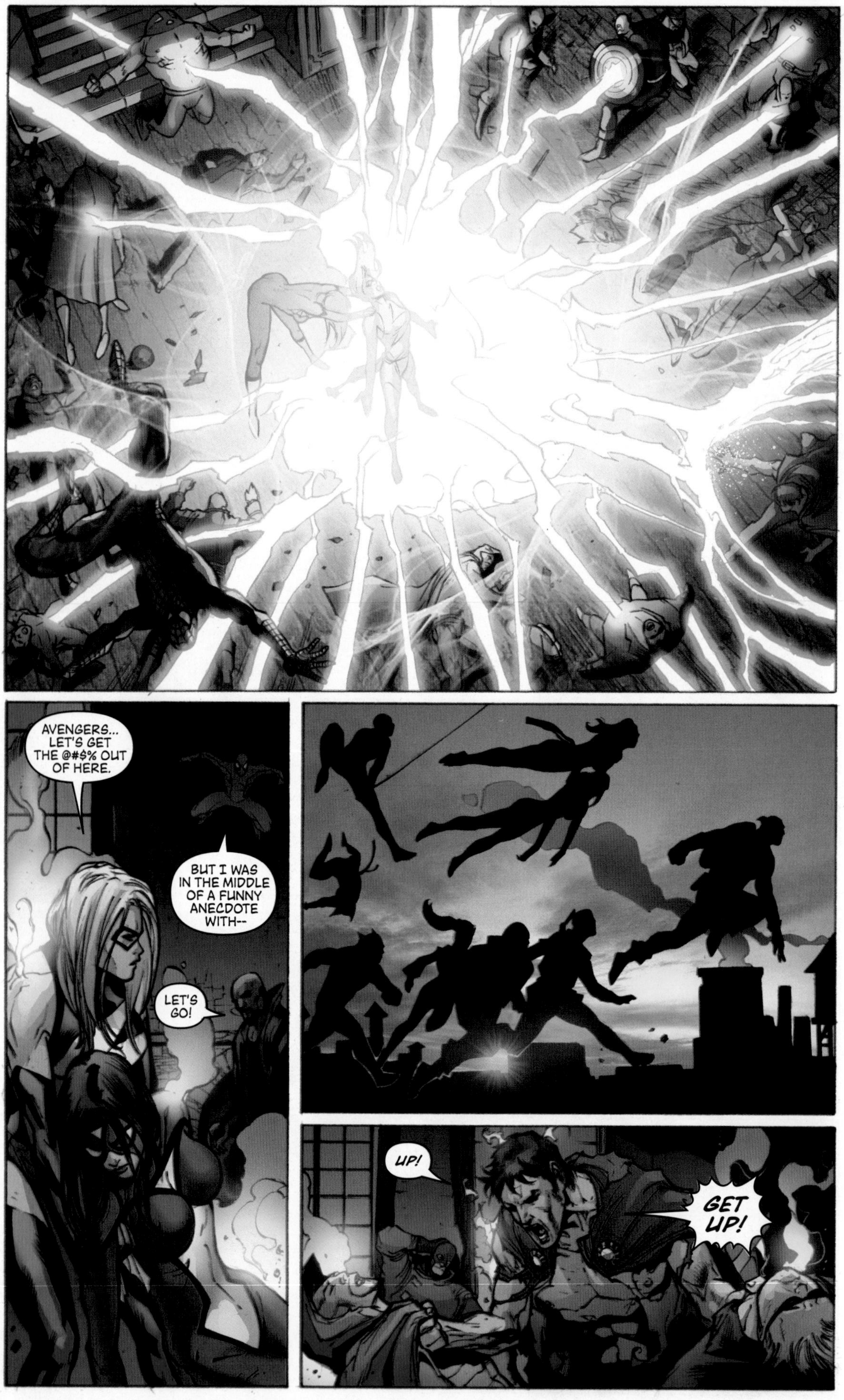
AVENGERS... LET'S GET THE @#$% OUT OF HERE.
BUT I WAS IN THE MIDDLE OF A FUNNY ANECDOTE WITH--
LET'S GO!
UP!
GET UP!

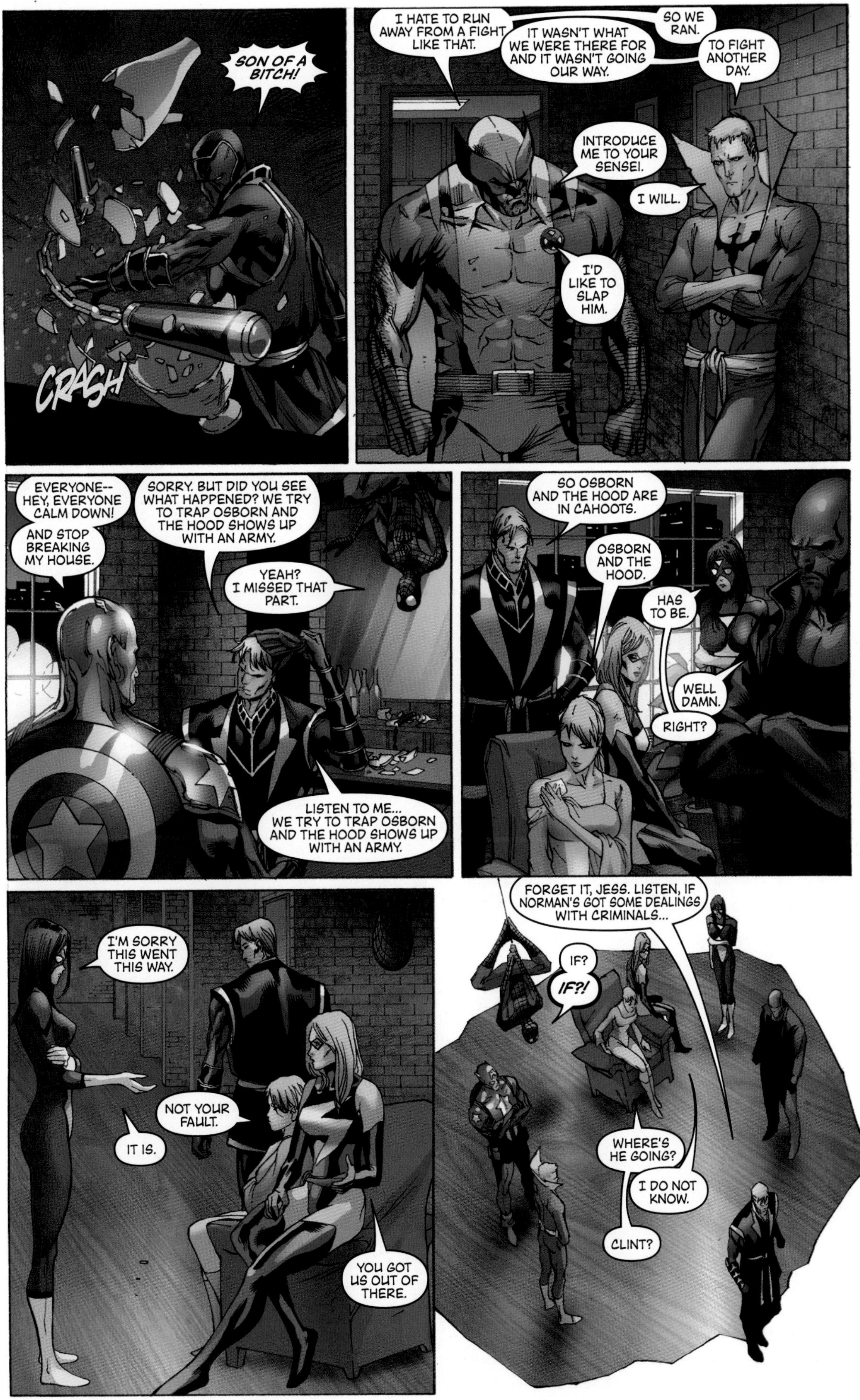
SON OF A BITCH!
CRASH
I HATE TO RUN AWAY FROM A FIGHT LIKE THAT.
SO WE RAN.
IT WASN'T WHAT WE WERE THERE FOR AND IT WASN'T GOING OUR WAY.
TO FIGHT ANOTHER DAY.
INTRODUCE ME TO YOUR SENSEI.
I WILL.
I'D LIKE TO SLAP HIM.
EVERYONE-- HEY, EVERYONE CALM DOWN!
AND STOP BREAKING MY HOUSE.
SORRY. BUT DID YOU SEE WHAT HAPPENED? WE TRY TO TRAP OSBORN AND THE HOOD SHOWS UP WITH AN ARMY.
YEAH? I MISSED THAT PART.
LISTEN TO ME... WE TRY TO TRAP OSBORN AND THE HOOD SHOWS UP WITH AN ARMY.
SO OSBORN AND THE HOOD ARE IN CAHOOTS.
OSBORN AND THE HOOD.
HAS TO BE.
WELL DAMN.
RIGHT?
I'M SORRY THIS WENT THIS WAY.
NOT YOUR FAULT.
IT IS.
YOU GOT US OUT OF THERE.
FORGET IT, JESS. LISTEN, IF NORMAN'S GOT SOME DEALINGS WITH CRIMINALS...
IF?
IF?!
WHERE'S HE GOING?
I DO NOT KNOW.
CLINT?

WE INTERRUPT THIS BROADCAST TO BRING YOU THE FOLLOWING NEWS EXCLUSIVE.

BREAKING NEWS

A STORY LITERALLY DROPPED IN OUR LAPS TONIGHT.

IN OUR STUDIO, LIVE, IS A MAN OF NOTORIOUS LEGEND AND... HE HAS SOMETHING HE WANTS TO SAY.

SO WE'RE GOING TO LET HIM... WELCOME.

DEADLINENEWS ANNIE DEACONS, CORRESPONDENT

YES, HI. THANK YOU.

MY NAME IS CLINT BARTON.

I USED TO BE KNOWN AS THE AVENGER HAWKEYE, I WAS GOLIATH FOR A WHILE AS WELL... NOW I GO BY RONIN.

I AM HERE TODAY TO SAY A FEW THINGS.

DEADLINENEWS CLINT BARTON, WORLD EXCLUSIVE

NORMAN OSBORN IS A CRIMINAL SOCIOPATH.

MOST PEOPLE DON'T EVEN KNOW OR SEEM TO HAVE FORGOTTEN, BUT HE USED TO BE THE MURDERER KNOWN AS THE GREEN GOBLIN.

HE WENT TO *JAIL* AND A *MENTAL INSTITUTION* BECAUSE OF THIS.

DEADLINENEWS HAWKEYE COMES CLEAN, WORLD EXCLUSIVE

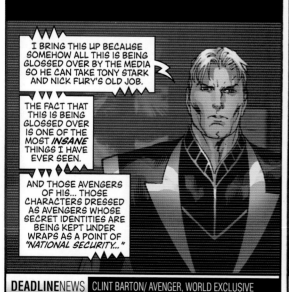

I BRING THIS UP BECAUSE SOMEHOW ALL THIS IS BEING GLOSSED OVER BY THE MEDIA SO HE CAN TAKE TONY STARK AND NICK FURY'S OLD JOB.

THE FACT THAT THIS IS BEING GLOSSED OVER IS ONE OF THE MOST *INSANE* THINGS I HAVE EVER SEEN.

AND THOSE AVENGERS OF HIS... THOSE CHARACTERS DRESSED AS AVENGERS WHOSE SECRET IDENTITIES ARE BEING KEPT UNDER WRAPS AS A POINT OF *"NATIONAL SECURITY..."*

DEADLINENEWS CLINT BARTON/ AVENGER, WORLD EXCLUSIVE

THOSE ARE CRIMINALS AS WELL. *FELONS.* KNOWN *ASSASSINS* AND *MURDERERS.*

THEY ARE NOT *AVENGERS.* THEY ARE NOT *HEROES.* THEY ARE GUNS FOR HIRE AND BAD ONES AT THAT.

DEADLINENEWS CLINT BARTON, WORLD EXCLUSIVE

AND THIS ISN'T ME HAVING A TANTRUM BECAUSE SOMEONE ELSE IS RUNNING AROUND DRESSED IN MY OLD COSTUME.

I'M A GROWN MAN-- I CAN HANDLE THAT.

I CAME HERE BECAUSE TONIGHT, ME AND MY TEAM, THE *REAL* AVENGERS...

DEADLINENEWS WORLD EXCLUSIVE, AVENGER CONTROVERSY

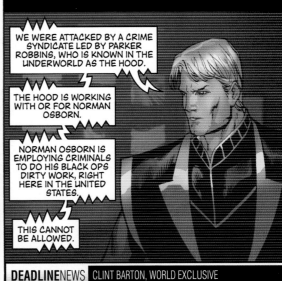

WE WERE ATTACKED BY A CRIME SYNDICATE LED BY PARKER ROBBINS, WHO IS KNOWN IN THE UNDERWORLD AS THE HOOD.

THE HOOD IS WORKING WITH OR FOR NORMAN OSBORN.

NORMAN OSBORN IS EMPLOYING CRIMINALS TO DO HIS BLACK OPS DIRTY WORK, RIGHT HERE IN THE UNITED STATES.

THIS CANNOT BE ALLOWED.

DEADLINENEWS CLINT BARTON, WORLD EXCLUSIVE

THIS NEEDS TO BE LOOKED INTO BY PEOPLE OF AUTHORITY. THIS NEEDS TO BE STOPPED.

I CAME HERE TONIGHT TO TELL PEOPLE THE TRUTH.

TO TELL PEOPLE WHAT IS GOING ON.

I CAME HERE TO TELL NORMAN OSBORN AND HIS GAGGLE OF CRIMINALS THAT WE'RE NOT AFRAID OF YOU.

AT ALL.

DEADLINENEWS CLINT BARTON, WORLD EXCLUSIVE

MY NAME IS CLINT BARTON AND I AM AN AVENGER.

I DON'T CARE WHO LIVES IN THAT BIG TOWER-- I'M AN AVENGER, AND MY TEAM OF AVENGERS IS GOING TO BE OUT THERE EVERY DAY.

FIGHTING FOR *YOU.* FIGHTING AGAINST *THIS.*

DEADLINENEWS CLINT BARTON, WORLD EXCLUSIVE

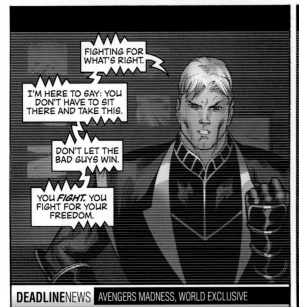

FIGHTING FOR WHAT'S RIGHT.

I'M HERE TO SAY: YOU DON'T HAVE TO SIT THERE AND TAKE THIS.

DON'T LET THE BAD GUYS WIN.

YOU *FIGHT.* YOU FIGHT FOR YOUR FREEDOM.

DEADLINENEWS AVENGERS MADNESS, WORLD EXCLUSIVE

AND I'LL BE RIGHT THERE FIGHTING ALONGSIDE YOU.

I PROMISE THAT.

THAT'S IT.

I'M DONE.

TO BE CONTINUED...

DEADLINENEWS RONIN/ AVENGER, WORLD EXCLUSIVE

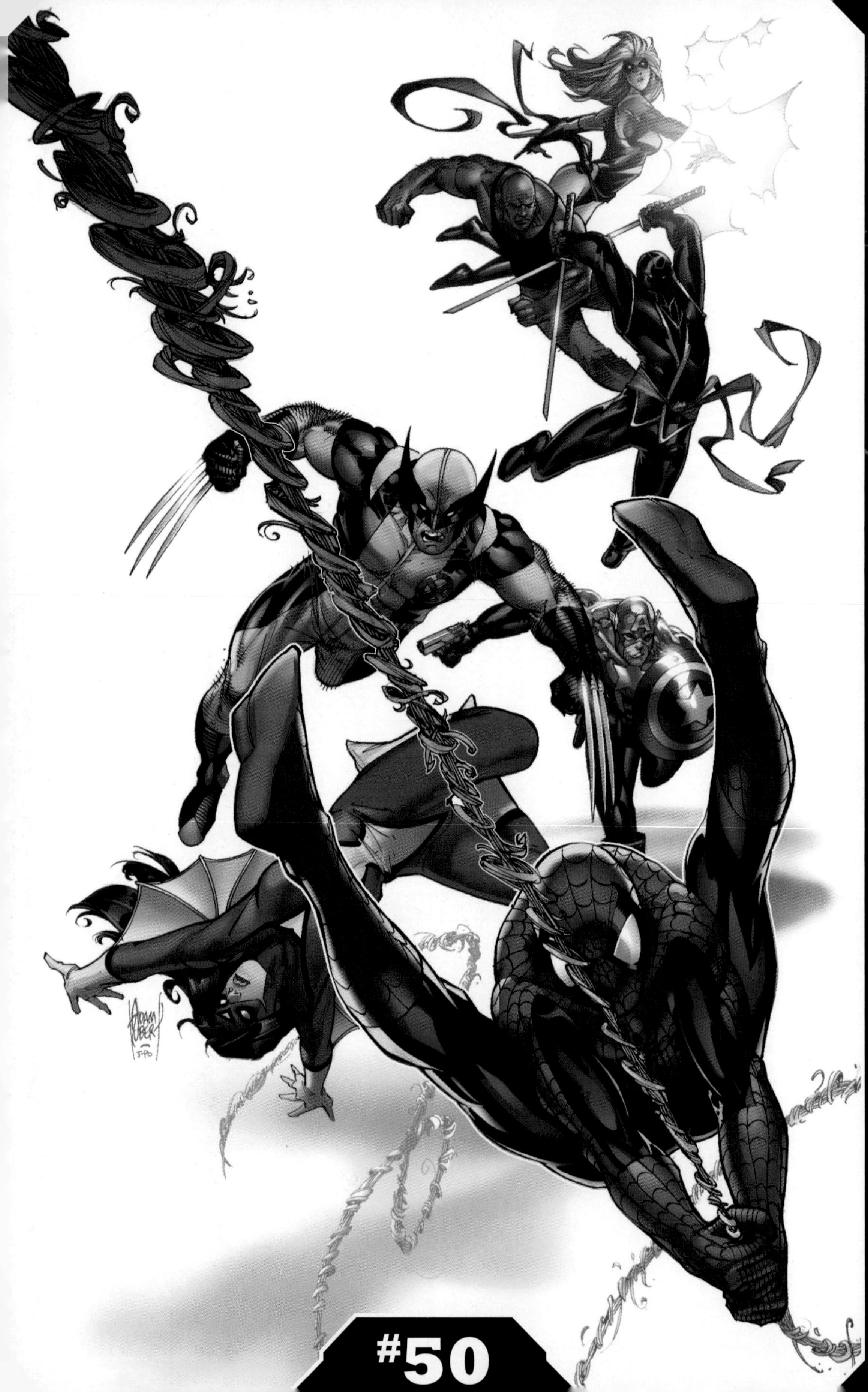
#50